CHEVROLET CORVETTE
Gold Portfolio
1953~1962

Compiled by
R.M. Clarke

ISBN 1 85520 0295

Distributed by
Brooklands Book Distribution Ltd.
'Holmerise', Seven Hills Road,
Cobham, Surrey, England
Printed in Hong Kong

BROOKLANDS BOOKS

BROOKLANDS ROAD TEST SERIES
AC Ace & Aceca 1953-1983
Alfa Romeo Alfasud 1972-1984
Alfa Romeo Alfetta Coupes GT, GTV, GTV6 1974-1987
Alfa Romeo Giulia Berlinas 1962-1976
Alfa Romeo Giulia Coupes 1963-1976
Alfa Romeo Spider 1966-1987
Allard Gold Portfolio 1937-1958
Alvis Gold Portfolio 1919-1969
American Motors Muscle Cars 1966-1970
Aston Martin Gold Portfolio 1972-1985
Austin Seven 1922-1982
Austin A30 & A35 1951-1962
Austin Healey 3000 1959-1967
Austin Healey 100 & 3000 Col No.1
Austin Healey 'Frogeye' Sprite Col No.1 1958-1961
Austin Healey Sprite 1958-1971
Avanti 1962-1983
BMW Six Cylinder Coupes 1969-1975
BMW 1600 Col. 1 1966-1981
BMW 2002 1968-1976
Bristol Cars Gold Portfolio 1946-1985
Buick Automobiles 1947-1960
Buick Muscle Cars 1965-1970
Buick Riviera 1963-1978
Cadillac Automobiles 1949-1959
Cadillac Automobiles 1960-1969
Cadillac Eldorado 1967-1978
High Performance Capris Gold Portfolio 1969-1987
Chevrolet Camaro & Z-28 1973-1981
High Performance Camaros 1982-1988
Chevrolet Camaro Col No.1 1967-1973
Camaro Muscle Cars 1966-1972
Chevrolet 1955-1957
Chevrolet Impala & SS 1958-1971
Chevrolet Muscle Cars 1966-1971
Chevelle and SS 1964-1972
Chevy EL Camino & SS 1959-1987
Chevy II Nova & SS 1962-1973
Chrysler 300 1955-1970
Citroen Traction Avant Gold Portfolio 1934-1957
Citroen DS & ID 1955-1975
Citroen 2CV 1949-1988
Shelby Cobra Gold Portfolio 1962-1969
Cobras & Replicas 1962-1983
Corvair 1959-1968
Chevrolet Corvette Gold Portfolio 1953 1962
Corvette Stingray Gold Portfolio 1963-1967
High Performance Corvettes 1983-1989
Datsun 240Z 1970-1973
Datsun 280Z & ZX 1975-1983
De Tomaso Collection No.1 1962-1981
Dodge Charger 1966-1974
Dodge Muscle Cars 1967-1970
Excalibur Collection No.1 1952-1981
Ferrari Cars 1946-1956
Ferrari Cars 1973-1977
Ferrari Dino 1965-1974
Ferrari Dino 308 1974-1979
Ferrari 308 & Mondial 1980-1984
Ferrair Collection No.1 1960-1970
Fiat-Bertone X1/9 1973-1988
Fiat Pininfarina 124 + 2000 Spider 1968-1985
Ford Automobiles 1949-1959
Ford GT40 Gold Portfolio 1964-1987
Ford Fairlane 1955-1970
Ford Falcon 1960-1970
High Perfomance Mustangs 1982-1988
Ford Cortina 1600E & GT 1967-1970
Ford RS Escorts 1968-1980
High Performance Escorts Mk1 1968-1974
High Performance Escorts Mk II 1975-1980
Honda CRX 1983-1987
Hudson & Railton 1936-1940
Jaguar Cars 1957-1961
Jaguar Cars 1961-1964
Jaguar Mk2 1959-1969
Jaguar E-Type Gold Portfolio 1961-1971
Jaguar E-Type 1966-1971
Jaguar E-Type V-12 1971-1975
Jaguar XKE Collection No.1 1961-1974
Jaguar XJ6 1968-1972
Jaguar XJ6 Series II 1973-1979
Jaguar XJ6 & XJ12 Series III 1979-1985
Jaguar XJ12 1972-1980
Jaguar XJS Gold Portfolio 1975-1988
Jaguar XK120.XK140.XK150 Gold Portfolio 1948-1960
Jeep CJ5 & CJ6 1960-1976
Jeep CJ5 & CJ7 1976-1986
Jensen Cars 1946-1967
Jensen Cars 1967-1979
Jensen Interceptor Gold Portfolio 1966-1986
Jensen Healey 1972-1976
Lamborghini Cars 1964-1970
Lamborghini Cars 1970-1975
Lamborghini Countach Col No.1 1971-1982
Lamborghini Countach & Urraco 1974-1980
Lamborghini Countach & Jalpa 1980-1985
Lancia Stratos 1972-1985
Land Rover 1948-1973 - A Collection
Land Rover Series II & IIa 1958-1971
Land Rover Series III 1971-1985
Land Rover 90 & 110 1983-1989
Lincoln Gold Portfolio 1949-1960
Lincoln Continental 1961-1969
Lotus and Caterham Seven Gold Portfolio 1957-1989
Lotus Elan Gold Portfolio 1962-1974
Lotus Elan Collection No.2 1963-1972
Lotus Elite 1957-1964
Lotus Elite & Eclat 1974-1982
Lotus Turbo Esprit 1980-1986
Lotus Europa 1966-1975
Lotus Europa Collection No.1 1966-1974
Lotus Seven Collection No.1 1957-1982
Marcos Cars 1960-1988
Maserati 1965-1970
Maserati 1970-1975
Mazda RX-7 Collection No.1 1978-1981
Mercedes 190 & 300SL 1954-1963

Mercedes 230/250/280SL 1963-1971
Mercedes Benz SLs & SLCs Gold Portfolio 1971-1989
Mercedes Benz Cars 1949-1954
Mercedes Benz Cars 1954-1957
Mercedes Benz Cars 1957-1961
Mercedes Benz Competition Cars 1950-1957
Mercury Muscle Cars 1966-1971
Metropolitan 1954-1962
MG TC 1945-1949
MG TD 1949-1953
MG TF 1953-1955
MG Cars 1959-1962
MGA Roadsters 1955-1962
MGA Collection No.1 1955-1982
MGB Roadsters 1962-1980
MGB GT 1965-1980
MG Midget 1961-1980
Mini Moke 1964-1989
Mini Muscle Cars 1961-1979
Mopar Muscle Cars 1964-1967
Mopar Muscle Cars 1968-1971
Morgan Three-Wheeler Gold Portfolio 1910-1952
Morgan Cars 1960-1970
Morgan Cars Gold Portfolio 1968-1989
Morris Minor Collection No.1
Mustang Muscle Cars 1967-1971
Oldsmobile Automobiles 1955-1963
Old's Cutlass & 4-4-2 1964-1972
Oldsmobile Muscle Cars 1964-1971
Oldsmobile Toronado 1966-1978
Opel GT 1968-1973
Packard Gold Portfolio 1946-1958
Pantera Gold Portfolio 1970-1989
Plymouth Barracuda 1964-1974
Plymoutn Muscle Cars 1966-1971
Pontiac Tempest & GTO 1961-1965
Pontiac GTO 1964-1970
Pontiac Firebird 1967-1973
Pontiac Firebird and Trans-Am 1973-1981
High Performance Firebirds 1982-1988
Pontiac Fiero 1984-1988
Pontiac Muscle Cars 1966-1972
Porsche 356 1952-1965
Porsche Cars in the 60's
Porsche Cars 1960-1964
Porsche Cars 1964-1968
Porsche Cars 1968-1972
Porsche Cars 1972-1975
Porsche Turbo Collection No.1 1975-1980
Porsche 911 1965-1969
Porsche 911 1970-1972
Porsche 911 1973-1977
Porsche 911 Carrera 1973-1977
Porsche 911 Turbo 1975-1984
Porsche 911 SC 1978-1983
Porsche 914 Gold Portfolio 1969-1976
Porsche 914 Collection No.1 1969-1983
Porsche 924 Gold Portfolio 1975-1988
Porsche 928 1977-1989
Porsche 944 1981-1985
Range Rover Gold Portfolio 1970-1988
Reliant Scimitar 1964-1986
Riley 11/2 & 21/2 Litre Gold Portfolio 1945-1955
Rolls Royce Silver Cloud 1955-1965
Rolls Royce Silver Shadow 1965-1981
Rover P4 1949-1959
Rover P4 1955-1964
Rover 3 & 3.5 Litre 1958-1973
Rover 2000 + 2200 1963-1977
Rover 3500 1968-1977
Rover 3500 & Vitesse 1976-1986
Saab Sonett Collection No.1 1966-1974
Saab Turbo 1976-1983
Shelby Mustang Muscle Cars 1965-1970
Stubebaker Gold Portfolio 1947-1966
Stubebaker Hawks & Larks 1956-1963
Sunbeam Tiger & Alpine Gold Portfolio 1959-1967
Thunderbird 1955-1957
Thunderbird 1958-1963
Thunderbird 1964-1976
Toyota MR2 1984-1988
Triumph 2000. 2.5. 2500 1963-1977
Triumph GT6 1966-1974
Triumph Spitfire 1962-1980
Triumph Spitfire Col No.1 1962-1982
Triumph Stag 1970-1980
Triumph Stag Collection No.1 1970-1984
Triumph TR2 & TR3 1952-60
Triumph TR4-TR5-TR250 1961-1968
Triumph TR6 1969-1976
Triumph TR6 Collection No.1 1969-1983
Triumph TR7 & TR8 1975-1982
Triumph Vitesse & Herald 1959-1971
TVR Gold Portfolio 1959-1988
Volkswagen Cars 1936-1956
VW Beetle Collection No.1 1970-1982
VW Golf GTi 1976-1986
VW Karmann Ghia 1955-1982
VW Kubelwagen 1940-1975
VW Scirocco 1974-1981
VW Bus. Camper. Van 1954-1967
VW Bus. Camper. Van 1968-1979
VW Bus. Camper. Van 1979-1989
Volvo 120 1956-1970
Volvo 1800 1960-1973

BROOKLANDS ROAD & TRACK SERIES
Road & Track on Alfa Romeo 1949-1963
Road & Track on Alfa Romeo 1964-1970
Road & Track on Alfa Romeo 1971-1976
Road & Track on Alfa Romeo 1977-1989
Road & Track on Aston Martin 1962-1984
Road & Track on Auburn Cord and Duesenburg 1952-1984
Road & Track on Audi & Auto Union 1952-1980
Road & Track on Audi 1980-1986
Road & Track on Austin Healey 1953-1970
Road & Track on BMW Cars 1966-1974
Road & Track on BMW Cars 1975-1978
Road & Track on BMW Cars 1979-1983

Road & Track on Cobra, Shelby & GT40 1962-1983
Road & Track on Corvette 1953-1967
Road & Track on Corvette 1968-1982
Road & Track on Corvette 1982-1986
Road & Track on Datsun Z 1970-1983
Road & Track on Ferrari 1950-1968
Road & Track on Ferrari 1968-1974
Road & Track on Ferrari 1975-1981
Road & Track on Ferrari 1981-1984
Road & Track on Fiat Sports Cars 1968-1987
Road & Track on Jaguar 1950-1960
Road & Track on Jaguar 1961-1968
Road & Track on Jaguar 1968-1974
Road & Track on Jaguar 1974-1982
Road & Track on Jaguar 1983-1989
Road & Track on Lamborghini 1964-1985
Road & Track on Lotus 1972-1981
Road & Track on Maserati 1952-1974
Road & Track on Maserati 1975-1983
Road & Track on Mazda RX7 1978-1986
Road & Track on Mercedes 1952-1962
Road & Track on Mercedes 1963-1970
Road & Track on Mercedes 1971-1979
Road & Track on Mercedes 1980-1987
Road & Track on MG Sports Cars 1949-1961
Road & Track on MG Sprots Cars 1962-1980
Road & Track on Mustang 1964-1977
Road & Track on Peugeot 1955-1986
Road & Track on Pontiac 1960-1983
Road & Track on Porsche 1961-1967
Road & Track on Porsche 1968-1971
Road & Track on Porsche 1972-1975
Road & Track on Porsche 1975-1978
Road & Track on Porsche 1979-1982
Road & Track on Porsche 1982-1985
Road & Track on Porsche 1985-1988
Road & Track on Rolls Royce & B'ley 1950-1965
Road & Track on Rolls Royce & B'ley 1966-1984
Road & Track on Saab 1955-1985
Road & Track on Toyota Sports & GT Cars 1966-1984
Road & Track on Triumph Sports Cars 1953-1967
Road & Track on Triumph Sports Cars 1967-1974
Road & Track on Triumph Sports Cars 1974-1982
Road & Track on Volkswagen 1951-1968
Road & Track on Volkswagen 1968-1978
Road & Track on Volkswagen 1978-1985
Road & Track on Volvo 1957-1974
Road & Track on Volvo 1975-1985
Road & Track - Henry Manney at Large and Abroad

BROOKLANDS CAR AND DRIVER SERIES
Car and Driver on BMW 1955-1977
Car and Driver on BMW 1977-1985
Car and Driver on Cobra, Shelby & Ford GT 40 1963-1984
Car and Driver on Corvette 1956-1967
Car and Driver on Corvette 1968-1977
Car and Driver on Corvette 1978-1982
Car and Driver on Corvette 1983-1988
Car and Driver on Datsun Z 1600 & 2000 1966-1984
Car and Driver on Ferrari 1955-1962
Car and Driver on Ferrari 1963-1975
Car and Driver on Ferrari 1976-1983
Car and Driver on Mopar 1956-1967
Car and Driver on Mopar 1968-1975
Car and Driver on Mustang 1964-1972
Car and Driver on Pontiac 1961-1975
Car and Driver on Porsche 1955-1962
Car and Driver on Porsche 1963-1970
Car and Driver on Porsche 1970-1976
Car and Driver on Porsche 1977-1981
Car and Driver on Porsche 1982-1986
Car and Driver on Saab 1956-1985
Car and Driver on Volvo 1955-1986

BROOKLANDS PRACTICAL CLASSICS SERIES
PC on Austin A40 Restoration
PC on Land Rover Restoration
PC on Metalworking in Restoration
PC on Midget/Sprite Restoration
PC on Mini Cooper Restoration
PC on MGB Restoration
PC on Morris Minor Restoration
PC on Sunbeam Rapier Restoration
PC on Triumph Herald/Vitesse
PC on Triumph Spitfire Restoration
PC on VW Beetle Restoration
PC on 1930s Car Restoration

BROOKLANDS MOTOR & THOROGHBRED & CLASSIC CAR SERIES
Motor & T & CC on Ferrari 1966-1976
Motor & T & CC on Ferrari 1976-1984
Motor & T & CC on Lotus 1979-1983

BROOKLANDS MILITARY VEHICLES SERIES
Allied Mil. Vehicles No.1 1942-1945
Allied Mil. Vehicles No.2 1941-1946
Dodge Mil. Vehicles Col. 1 1940-1945
Military Jeeps 1941-1945
Off Road Jeeps 1944-1971
Hail to the Jeep
US Military Vehicles 1941-1945
US Army Military Vehicles WW2-TM9-2800

BROOKLANDS HOT ROD RESTORATION SERIES
Auto Restoration Tips & Techniques
Basic Bodywork Tips & Techniques
Basic Painting Tips & Techniques
Camaro Restoration Tips & Techniques
Custom Painting Tips & Techniques
Engine Swapping Tips & Techniques
How to Build a Street Rod
Mustang Restoration Tips & Techniques
Performance Tuning - Chevrolets of the '60s
Performance Tuning - Fords of the '60s
Performance Tuning - Mopars of the '60s
Performance Tuning - Pontiacs of the '60s

BROOKLANDS BOOKS

CONTENTS

5	Chevrolet Takes the Challenge with Corvette Road Test	Motor Life	June	1954
7	Chevrolet Corvette	Road & Track	Aug.	1953
9	Retrospect — 1953 Chevrolet Corvette	Motor Trend	March	1983
12	From Dies to Driveways	Motor Trend	Dec.	1953
16	The Corvette	Automobile		1954
17	The Chevrolet Corvette	Road & Track	June	1954
20	New Fuel for an Old Duel Comparison Test	Motor Trend	June	1954
26	The Corvette V8 Road Test	Road & Track	July	1955
28	The Corvette V8 Drivers Report	Motor Life	Sept.	1955
31	Competition by Corvette	Autosport	Dec. 9	1955
34	Chevrolet Corvette Road Test	Sports Cars Illustrated	May	1956
39	'56 Thunderbird and Corvette Comparison Test	Motor Trend	June	1956
43	Corvette	Sports Cars Illustrated Annual		1956
44	Chevrolet Corvette Road Test	Wheels	July	1956
48	Corvette SR-2	Motor Life	Sept.	1956
50	1957 Fuel Injection Corvette Drive Report	Special Interest Autos	Feb.	1983
58	G M Project XP-64	Autocar	May 3	1957
60	A Fuel Injection Corvette Road Test	Motor Life	June	1957
63	The '58 Corvette	Sports Cars Illustrated	Jan.	1958
67	1958 Corvette	Road & Track	Dec.	1957
68	Sam Hanks Tests 4 Corvettes Comparison Test	Motor Trend	March	1958
75	1959 Corvette Road Test	Road & Track	Jan.	1959
80	'59 Corvette Road Test	Sports Cars Illustrated	March	1959
84	Corvette vs. Porsche Comparison Test	Motor Trend	April	1959
90	Corvette Road Test	Motor Life	Sept.	1959
95	1960 Corvette First Impressions	Sports Cars Illustrated	Nov.	1959
97	Corvette '60 Road Test	Motor Trend	July	1960
100	Corvettes to Order	Motor Life	Sept.	1960
108	1961 Corvette Road Test	Road & Track	Jan.	1961
112	Corvette Road Test	Motor Trend	Sept.	1961
116	3 Corvettes Comparison Test	Car Life	Sept.	1961
124	Big 'Vette Road Test	Hot Rod	Jan.	1962
130	Corvette Special	Sports Car Graphic	March	1961
136	Fuel-Injected Corvette Road Test	Motor Trend	Aug.	1962
142	Recapping the Road Tests	Corvette-An American Classic		1978
150	First V8 Years	Corvette-An American Classic		1978
162	Development Continues	Corvette-An American Classic		1978

BROOKLANDS BOOKS

ACKNOWLEDGEMENTS

Brooklands Books publish source books. There is nothing original within their covers and their purpose is to make available to today's owners the road tests and other technical stories that were printed about a model when it was in production.

Amongst our 350 titles is one other on Corvettes – High Performance Corvettes 1983-1989 – which covers the more powerful examples produced during the eighties. For some time we have been researching pre-'68 models and it is our intention to publish simultaneously with this book – Corvette Sting Ray Gold Portfolio 1963-1967.

Our books are printed in small numbers as works of reference for those that indulge in the hobby of automobile collecting and restoration. We exist firstly because there is a need by owners for this information and secondly because the publishers of the world leading automotive journals generously assist us by allowing us to include their copyright articles in these anthologies. We are indebted in this instance to the management of Autocar, Automobile, Autosport, Car Life, Hot Rod, Motor Life, Motor Trend, Road & Track, Special Interest Autos, Sports Car Graphic, Sports Cars Illustrated (Car and Driver), Wheels and Petersens Publications publishers of Corvette – An American Classic, for their continued support.

R.M. Clarke

ROAD TEST:

CHEVROLET TAKES THE CHALLENGE WITH THE *CORVETTE..*

By HANK GAMBLE

CHEVROLET stands alone in the American sports car field, with a *true* production automobile priced at a figure John Doe can comprehend. Despite this fact, MOTOR LIFE road testers were dubious of a so-called *compromise* vehicle; the tendency of American automotive engineers and designers is to come up with a cross-breed piece of transportation which barely *hints* at the handling characteristics of better sports cars.

Their problem, of course, concerns public demand; the small and compact, lightweight car which fits roads of Europe like a train on a track is out of place in America. The American public has variable needs for family transportation—no sports car manufactured *anywhere* can properly serve the multitude of purposes imposed upon it by John Doe and his wife, children, and visiting firemen from the old hometown.

A sports car is, frankly, a specialized "iron" (or more likely these days, as with the Corvette—a specialized "plastic"). This car is designed to serve a single purpose. That purpose is the transporting of one or two persons from one place to another in a very short time, with the *driver* enjoying the trip. Sports cars handle exceptionally well, often accelerate like Flash Gordon, and ride like the streets weren't paved. Relatively few Americans can afford the staggering prices asked for many imported models; if they could, there is still more money to shell out—for *another* car, one that can contain the family.

With this dare flung in their faces by the European invaders Chevrolet took up the challenge. The result is proof that a "compromise" car can be built; while the Corvette *won't* hold but two, this GM product combines the best features of a foreign sports car without its stark simplicity of purpose.

The Corvette *goes!* Aside from the standard performance-figure runs required of a sincere road test (with resultant

Profile of Chevrolet Corvette, with top up, is low and streamlined. Top is raised or lowered with ease by one person

Top lowers into concealed compartment behind seats. The instruments include tachometer and rev counter

Modified Chevy engine furnishes 150 hp at 4200 rpm. The power-to-weight ratio of Corvette is 19 to one

times to compare with those of competitors) the Corvette was driven side by side through acceleration and high speed runs against a well known and popular European make of sports car. Engine displacement put them in the same F.I.A. class (a competition common denominator).

From a standing start—*and bear in mind that the Corvette has automatic transmission*—the new member of the Chevrolet family took off like a scalded dog, left its competitor five car lengths behind at the end of a quarter mile!

With a standard transmission this remarkable performance would, of course, have been even more impressive.

Modified PowerGlide describes the Corvette transmission. To handle 223 lb-ft of torque the oil pressure has been increased. A shifter valve gives a full-throttle upshift at 4500 rpm (or 55 mph), and full-throttle downshift up to 47 mph. It has been modified for the Hotchkiss drive; a transmission oil cooler is not required.

Rumor has it that the Chevy people may, in the future, offer the Corvette with standard transmission; if true they might well be looking enviously at American sports car road race circuits—the Corvette is, in its present condition, very close to being competition material.

The standard and reliable Chevy 6-cylinder engine of 235 c.i. displacement, with modifications, makes the Corvette perform. At 4200 rpm it delivers 150 hp; the compression ratio is 8 to 1. Triple carburetion is stock, with manual choke. Some 8 to 10 lb-ft torque in the midspeed range was gained by use of a special exhaust manifold, a dual set-up which keeps the exhaust gases in the throat of each of the two downpipes always whirling in one direction. The two exhaust systems are separate. The engine, incidentally, as compared with the family Chevy, is located 3 in. lower and 7 in. further back.

A driving impression not entirely favorable concerns cornering. However, it must be explained first that for average driving the Corvette behaves itself around corners very nicely, turning flat, with a proper seat-of-the-pants feeling in the cockpit. When we tried to "break it loose" at high speed on a rather severe corner the Corvette complied, as any car will when centrifugal limits are passed—but it showed a definite unwillingness to "tuck back in." This could, undoubtedly, be corrected with improved rear shock absorber treatment.

An adaptation of the existing Chevrolet rear axle to a Hotchkiss drive, the Corvette rear suspension uses 2x51 in. leaf springs which are inclined to give about 15 percent roll understeer. The front suspension is standard but stiffer, with a fairly stiff front stabilizer.

The steering is correct for a sports car, with a steering gear ratio of 16 to 1. There is a positive-control feeling behind the wheel when maneuvering in town traffic or on the highway. Power steering is not necessary since the Corvette is comparatively lightweight.

The Corvette does not offer the riding comfort its more conservative Chevy family members do. However, this is not to be expected and next to impossible to achieve hand-in-hand with superior handling qualities. A certain amount of road bounce is experienced but is not objectionable as a "hard" ride.

The arrangement of the instruments on the dash is good except for the location of the tachometer; rather than in its present location in the center of the panel the tach would serve its important purpose better if relocated directly in front of the driver, next to the speedometer. An excellent added feature, with the tach, is a counter which permanently records revolutions as an odometer does with mileage. The speedometer is large, easy to read, and more accurate than most with less than a four percent error noted.

The cockpit of this two-seater is plush in the American fashion, with handy door compartments and plenty of space —maybe too much space. It is a pleasure not to rub elbows or shoulders with your passenger but the car *could* hold three if accessory space was cut down.

The GM curved windshield offers minimum wind resistance and no visual distortion, but a tall person has to slouch down a bit or the top beam over the windshield becomes a psychological hazard. Fender vision is good, especially to the rear, eliminating an oft-prevalent parking difficulty.

The car was driven with the top up and down. There is no feeling of being "closed in" with the top up. The top is manual, as with all sports cars, and slides neatly into a concealed rear deck compartment. No problems were encountered in raising or lowering the top; you don't need a passenger along to help you perform this minor task.

A question might be raised about the Corvette's inset license plate with glass over it, and the wire mesh headlight protectors; despite the fact that both are well designed and functional this treatment is illegal in some states.

The use of fiberglass as body substance is a revolutionary move — production-wise — on Chevrolet's part. The resin-glass combination is definitely out of the experimental stage and has proved a worthy successor to sheet steel, offering lightness and strength. The Corvette body is a laminar construction of glass fiber and plastic, weighs 411 lbs. It will not rust, takes a good paint job, and will not crumple in the event of a collision. It *is* easy to repair (fiberglass can be torn) but at this writing there is still a problem of *authorized* repair; few garage mechanics are as yet familiar with fiberglass and how to patch it.

To sum it up, the Chevrolet Corvette is a true sports car, offering the prospective buyer tops in performance. It has a few "bugs" as does any model first or last, but none are so extreme as to discredit the car to any degree. The Corvette is a beauty—and it *goes!* (Continued on page 24)

Photo of open door shows built-in compartment, located handily for driver. All the interior handwork is well done

Spaciousness of Corvette driver and passenger compartment is shown in overhead photo. Leg room is ample

Unlike many sports cars, the Corvette has a roomy and convenient-to-get-into trunk. The bumper is adequate, simple

Chevrolet Corvette

The Chevrolet Corvette will become the first volume-produced sports car made in America in over a decade.

Mr. T. H. Keating, Chevrolet general manager has announced that sample cars will be in the hands of principal dealers in 1953 and that about 3,000 units will be produced during 1954. It has also been stated that the Corvette is not intended to be a "racing sports car", but Jaguar said the same thing in 1949. Any sports car addict knows that if you can't race it, *it isn't a sports car!* The Corvette will be used in competition and it has every chance of its share of successes.

Trade gossip says the price will be about $3500 and it is an open secret that the entire contemplated production is "sold."

The powerplant is a modified 1953 assembly which has full pressure lubrication and aluminum pistons. The power output has been stepped up to 160 bhp at 5200 rpm by virtue of higher compression ratio, a special camshaft, side draft Carter carburetors, and a dual exhaust system.

The specification of a Powerglide transmission has met with considerable derision but a torque convertor has potential advantages for road racing which have not been fully explored.

The chassis is specially designed for this car and one notes that Hotchkiss drive is used, a drastic step for Chevrolet. There is independent front suspension and a special gear ratio of 3.27 is specified. The disc-wheels and ELP tires are not very functional, but if the number of accessories now available for the ubiquitous MG is any indication, this problem can be solved.

A close examination of the fiberglass body reveals excellent workmanship and careful attention to detail. The fabric top is much better in appearance than most imported cars and folds into a flush compartment behind the bucket type seats. The instrument panel is very neat and includes a tachometer placed in the center of the dash.

An estimate of the performance capabilities of the Corvette may be interesting —though premature. Top speed, 120 mph

The Corvette seats are well designed to eliminate "sliding about" when the car is maneuvered.

The Corvette engine. Cylindrical tank, just above the three side draft carburetors, functions as the radiator top tank, necessitated by the extremely low hood line.

Configuration is neat, although some criticism may be directed at the lack of bumpers.

at 4900 rpm; acceleration from zero to 60 mph, 11 seconds; standing ¼ mile in 18 seconds. The *Road and Track* performance index (based on a Cad-Allard = 100) is only 50.00 if our assumption of 195 ft/lbs. of torque is correct. This low figure may account for the employment of a torque multiplying convertor in the transmission. It also makes the possibility of installing a 302 cu in. GMC engine attractive in view of the present general use of F.I.A. regulations where Class C includes displacements from 183 to 305 cu in. —I.B.

Specitications

General: Wheelbase, 102 in.; Tread, front 57 in.; rear 59 in.; tire size, 6.70 x 15; curb weight, 2,900 lbs. approx.

Engine: Chevrolet, 6 cylinder ohv; 3.562 x 3.937; 235.5 cu. in. (3861 cc) 160 bhp at 5200 rpm. Torque (estimated), 195 ft/lbs at 2400 rpm. Three Carter carburetors. Dual exhaust system.

Transmission: Chevrolet Powerglide with floor mounted control. Overall ratios 3.27 and 5.97 plus torque convertor multiplication of 2.1 at stall.

Rear Axle: Hypoid gears with 3.27 to 1 ratio. Open driveshaft.

Suspension: I.F.S. with wishbones and coil springs. Rear, semi-elliptic leaf springs.

Brakes: Bendix duo-servo hydraulic with 11 inch drums.

Dimensions: Overall length 167 in.; width, 70 in., height to top of door, 33 in.

Clean functional lines of the Corvette reflect the fact that this is a genuine sports car, a refreshing contrast to the pseudo sports cars being shown by other divisions of GM.

1953 Chevrolet Corvette

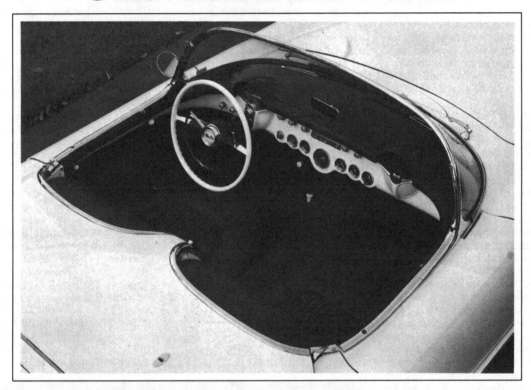

Out of Motorama by Blue Flame
—an unlikely thoroughbred

by Len Frank

PHOTOGRAPHY BY BOB D'OLIVO

The Bugatti people already have a book; they won't be reading this. Everything of interest to them, every engine, every chassis, every original body, owners, changes, a complete chronicle of who did what to whom—all in that book. No surprises for them. None allowed.

The Rolls-Royce people (sometimes "Royce" but never "Rolls" alone) have a book or two but they seldom consult them. It's not necessary—they just *know*.

But the Porsche guys and the Corvette guys have not just *a* book, or two books, but *books*—yards of shelves of books full of chassis and engine numbers, parts numbers, casting numbers, names of suppliers, complete text of the decals on oil and air filter housings for both early *and* late models. Trivia and minutiae, plants of origin, upholstery stitching materials, the correct negative luminosity of the matte finishes. More. Much more. It must be insecurity.

And that same presumed insecurity drives the Porschephiles and Corvette Cra-

zies to read all this stuff, magazine on left knee, poison pen poised above pad on right searching for the slightest slight, the least flake of error.

If one must choose between true believers, those with the brightest light of fanaticism shining in their eyes, the nod should go to the Corvette people. The Porsche types, you see, are much like the rest of us. They have selective memories. They view through the wrong end of a rose-tinted telescope. Each restored Porsche is more perfect than the last. No ripples, no asymmetry, no humanity.

The Corvette Berserkers, though, actually have a parts number for warts. And a sub-number for ripples, and one for waves in the fiberglass, warps in the panels, gaps between them. What a car, what an unlikely car to fall in love with.

Well, then, every legend, no matter how new and insecure, has its heroes. Those

here are Harley Earl and Maurice Olley, Bill Tritt, Ed Cole, Tom Keating, and, finally, Zora Arkus-Duntov. Oh—and Tony Kleiber.

More recently, we have, if not certified medal of honor winners, at least those deserving of the distinguished service cross: Noland Adams, Curtis Moran, all those other members of the National Corvette Restorers Club, all the patient authors and researchers who root out that trivia and minutiae, those 30-year-old wiring color codes, the correct "print" in the back side of the 'glass panels, the right sealed beam units and self-tapping screws.

Okay—hero No. 1, Harley Earl. Earl had been General Motors styling (really Colour and Design) since his 1927 LaSalle set the corporation off in new directions.

During the late '40s and very early '50s, Earl, engineering chief Charles Chayne (a Bugatti Royale owner), and corporation president Harlow Curtice cooked up the Motorama shows to keep high the excitement generated by those 1943 rotogravures and Sunday supplements. The Motoramas were an apology, really, for the 1946 product being identical with the '42. By 1948, GM had some new bodies but the cars underneath were pretty much the same. The Kettering engines—Cadillac and Oldsmobile—arrived in 1949 (Ed Cole worked on the Cadillac) but by 1951, sales were beginning to slide.

The LeSabre (and Buick XP 300) were GM's answer to the Tucker 48. They featured extensive light alloys in engine, body, and chassis, a rear-mounted transaxle, a supercharged dual-fuel V-8, and certain styling perks that were to become all too familiar.

In September 1951, Earl took LeSabre to Watkins Glen, then our premier sports car race. The crowds saw LeSabre, Earl saw Jaguars, Ferraris, Alfas, Allards. The result was a standoff. Road & Trackers laughed at the garish LeSabre and Earl saw automobiles in an entirely new light.

Back in Detroit, Earl started Bob McLean on a new concept. McLean had degrees in both engineering and industrial design and seemed a bit out of step with both of his peer groups. His approach was to start his layout with a side view from the rear axle. He located the seats as close to the axle as possible, the engine (the Chevy six) as far back and low as possible. So logical, so commonplace within just a few years, it was a radical departure at the time. Are—were—Turin, Stuttgart, Paris as parochial as Detroit?

Earl's styling ideas had come a long way since LeSabre, though perhaps not far enough. He insisted on the wraparound windshield that was to inflict Corvette styling for a decade. The "European" full-wheel openings were embellished by rocket-styled taillights, four little fins, and an incomprehensible dash layout. Really, though not as good as the best Italian designs, the original Corvette was better than some and as good as most. Indeed, with the exception of the aforementioned taillights, the whole design was very European—much more so than many European cars. Among those items left on the cutting room floor were plastic headlight covers and an exposed "Continental" spare.

Earl had a full-sized plaster mockup made and fully detailed and, in one of those political maneuvers known to GM's adepts, showed the model to President Curtice before the official showing. Before Curtice saw and approved it as a 1953 Motorama piece, Earl showed it to newly appointed Chevrolet Chief Engineer Ed Cole. Cole was said to have jumped up and down. Cole, of course, later went on to head Chevrolet, then General Motors. When he became enthusiastic about a project, it happened (Chevy small block, the Corvair, the Wankel rotary, air bags, and an uncounted number of show Corvettes

and Corvairs—the most exciting projects at GM—were his doing).

Maurice Olley, an ex-Rolls-Royce engineer who joined GM in 1930 (most famous for his investigations into ride rates and his development of short-long-arm independent front suspension), designed the frame in a remarkably short time. Cole, essentially an administrator at this point, was more than a little involved with the actual design, but the frame was really very much like Olley's original sketch.

Time constraints and Earl's desire to see the Corvette a production car should have dictated the use of more stock Chevy sedan pieces. The new frame was boxed with an X-member passing over an open driveshaft—all different from standard Chevy practice. The front swaybar was revised and the rear springs arranged to give additional understeer. Much quicker than normal steering (15:1 ratio) was specified, but standard brakes were assumed to be adequate for the sub-3000-lb weight.

At the time, Chevy had two transmission choices: a wimpy, wide-ratio 3-speed of no special merit and the division's 2-

The Motorama Corvette was a smash seen by 4 million people

speed automatic, Powerglide. Rather than revive the strong, closer-ratio LaSalle 3-speed or buy a gearbox from Siata (or another manufacturer), they chose the "Powerslide" and spent the next three years rationalizing their choice.

In 1952 there was only one engine choice, the "Stovebolt" 235cid iron six. The 235-incher was originally a truck engine. Its contemporary passenger car counterpart had, through 1950, cast iron pistons and splash oiling system. By '52 the 235 was used with Powerglide and had grown a proper oil pump, alloy pistons, and hydraulic lifters. It had a smashing 115 hp.

For the Corvette, compression was raised, a more radical solid lifter camshaft ground, dual exhausts added (with careful attention paid to the exact noise—rather than lack of noise), and triple Carter YF sidedrafts, similar to the carbs on the Nash Le Mans Dual Jetfire, added. On the early cars, bullet-shaped flame arrestors were used instead of air cleaners. The ignition system had to have a steel shroud enclosure to keep the radio static down. The 'glass body had no damping. The mighty Blue Flame now had 150 hp, it was later upped to 155 in '54. In fairness, the Olds 88 a few years earlier had 135 hp from 303 cu in.

Bill Tritt was an early L.A. fiberglass maven, a boat builder who turned to building bodies for kit cars. His firm, Glasspar, built the car that so impressed GM that the company built a standard 1952 Chevy convertible from polyester impregnated fiberglass mat and cloth.

The Motorama Corvette was a smash seen by 4 million people (GMs count). How many were over 16 is not recorded.

Sometime before production, GM still planned to use Kirksite dies to build steel bodies. The decision was made, though, to build an initial 300 plastic-bodied cars before going to steel. That decision was the result of what Chevy saw as overwhelming demand for an American sports car. At least that's what the division said. Perhaps it had more to do with dropping sales and an impending buyer's market. Who, at this late date, will ever know?

With an introduction planned for 1953, there was no chance for steel bodies. Engineers laid out a new body to be built of GRP (glass reinforced plastic) by either matched dies or the bag method. Time was wasting so they went with the bag.

The bag method involved the usual parting agent, gelcoat, polyester resin/mat sandwiched between wooden or composite molds, then a polyethylene "bag" was wrapped around the whole, the air pumped out, and the resin left to cure, sometimes for 24 hours. There were 62 separate pieces of all sizes used to make up the body. The pieces then had to be trimmed and glued together (more resin) with 'glass tape backing the joints. Assembly was slow and inaccurate. As quickly as possible production was switched to matched heated dies that produced better pieces faster.

Just before production began, Zora Arkus-Duntov, the man who was to direct Corvette fortunes for the next 25 years, revised suspension settings to make the car handle more predictably.

Quality control on the body was terrible. The production Vette had dips and waves, the famous lousy panel fit, and the equally famous stress cracks that appeared weekly. At least they didn't rust.

Harley Earl had wanted to keep the price as low as possible—below that of the standard sedan if possible. He felt that the car's real market lay among the college crowd and the young professionals, the same market Lee Iacocca discovered 10 years later with the Mustang. Unfortunately, the price was $3490 complete with

Powerglide, whitewalls, and a cigarette lighter. Release date was Sept. 29, 1953. It was a flop.

In the Corvette we have built a sports car in the American tradition. It is not a racing car in the accepted sense that a European sports car is a race car. It is intended rather to satisfy the American public's conception of beauty, comfort, and convenience, plus performance—Thomas Keating

Poor Mr. Keating. Jaguars were faster, Austin-Healeys nearly so. Sybarites hated the drafty, inconvenient side curtains, the rattles, the leaks. Enthusiasts hated the Powerglide, the dashboard, the whitewalls.

Chevrolet's plan was to sell Corvettes to the select few, the prominent, the visible. It didn't work. It was left to Cole's V-8 and Duntov's magic to save the Vette.

Curtis Moran sold our subject car to its present owner, Dorothy Clemmer. She hauled it to Oklahoma, hauled it back, finally called Curtis and asked him to restore it. He accepted, obviously. He also says he'd think twice about doing another. Between Mrs. Clemmer and the young Mr. Moran, they have owned, say, a couple dozen Vettes. That seems to be the pattern.

The man from whom Moran bought the '53 laboriously tracked it by looking through years of old *L.A. Times* classifieds, then making the frustrating phone calls. What did we say about fanatics?

Restoration began, typically enough, by taking everything off everything else. Most of the car was already in boxes so the adventure was in taking things out, looking at them while praying fervently.

The old cracked gelcoat was sanded off, the body reglassed. More than a little repair and refit was done. Engine, transmission, rear axle, radio, (a wonderful Wonder Bar AM signal seeker) instruments, front suspension, brakes were all overhauled. The frame was sandblasted, the old stenciled serial number applied in white, inverted (the cars were built upside down), over flat black Imron.

Moran says he did the restoration using Noland Adams' restoration book and an NCRS judging sheet. Fortunately, though this was his first '53, he had done, for himself, '54s—that *is* plural; Moran has owned a dozen and one '55 for good measure.

So naturally he had stockpiled parts, including some new old stock. But there's never enough. Upholstery came from Canada. Early cars had cotton stitching, later ones nylon. This one had cotton. Of course.

Mrs. Clemmer has a Pantera (her husband's choice) and a 1978 Corvette Pace Car replica that is her normal driver. But it's the '53 that occupies that special center. She says the house would go first.

Tony Kleiber? He was the first man to drive a production Vette. He drove No. 1 off the line—and into our hearts. (MT)

1953 Corvette

☑ SPECIFICATIONS

GENERAL

Vehicle mfr.	Chevrolet Motor Div., Detroit, Mich.
Body type	2-pass., 2-door roadster
Drive system	Front engine, rear drive
Base price	$3490
Major options on test car	Heater, Wonder Bar AM radio

ENGINE

Type	Inline 6, liquid cooled, cast iron block and head
Displacement	235.5 cu in.
Bore & stroke	3.56 x 3.93 in.
Compression ratio	8.0:1
Induction system	3 Carter YF sidedraft 1-bbl carburetors
Valvetrain	OHV
Crankshaft	4 main bearings
Max. power (SAE net)	150hp @ 4200 rpm
Max. torque (SAE net)	223 lb-ft @ 2400 rpm
Emission control	none
Recommended fuel	Super hi-test leaded

DRIVETRAIN

Transmission	2-sp. auto.
Transmission ratios (1st)	1.82:1
(2nd)	1.00:1
Axle ratio	3.55:1
Final drive ratio	3.55:1

CAPACITIES

Fuel tank	17.0 gal

SUSPENSION

Front	Independent, upper and lower A-arms, coil springs, hydraulic shocks, anti-roll bar
Rear	Solid axle, semi-elliptical leaf springs, hydraulic shocks

STEERING

Type	Worm and sector
Ratio	16:1
Turning circle, curb-to-curb	39.0 ft

BRAKES

Front	11.0-in. drums
Rear	11.0-in. drums

WHEELS AND TIRES

Wheel size	15 x 5.0 in.
Wheel type	Stamped steel
Tire size	6.70 x 15 in.
Tire construction	Cross ply

DIMENSIONS

Curb weight	2900 lb
Weight distribution (%), F/R	53/47 lb
Wheelbase	102.0 in.
Overall length	167.0 in.
Overall width	72.2 in.
Overall height	52.2 in.
Track, F/R	57.0/59.0

CALCULATED DATA

Power-to-weight ratio	19.33 lb/hp
Top speed	108 mph

ACCELERATION
(from 1954 Motor Trend)

0-30 mph	3.60 sec
0-40 mph	5.40 sec
0-50 mph	7.80 sec
0-60 mph	11.10 sec

from DIES to DRIVEWAY

Chevrolet's Corvette uses new Fiberglas construction methods

By Walt Woron

Last month, Walt Woron gave you his driving impressions of the Chevrolet Corvette. Now, to bring you right up to date on the story of the first Fiberglas car to be mass-produced anywhere, Walt went right to the assembly line to answer the question—"How is it made?"

TO UNDERSTAND the overall picture of the Corvette in construction, let's first review the groundwork that went into the car's conception. Fabricating a plastic-bodied automobile requires more time, more men, and more floor space than that needed for a steel body. On the other hand, the Fiberglas body offered these advantages: less weight, with resulting ease in handling;

elimination of heavy stamping presses; and quick molding of parts, affording short cuts in design processes.

A final analysis of Fiberglas, as opposed to steel, brought out a tooling cost favoring Fiberglas four to one. Fiberglas holds this edge largely because it can be molded into intricate shapes not possible with steel.

Before Chevrolet scheduled the Corvette for production, engineers made an experiment not only to determine possible production methods, but to test the physical characteristics of a Fiberglas body. The original plastic body was molded from a 1952 Chevrolet convertible. Reinforced plastic panels were built over the convertible's body sections; this

shell, when removed from the steel body, served as a female mold for the finished body to follow. Later, mounted on a stock Chevrolet chassis, this plastic body withstood many severe tests, including a roll-over.

Now in full production (with an expected 1954 output of 1000 units a month) the Corvette's breeding ground is nearly as active as the car-a-minute metal-body assembly lines. Located at Chevrolet's car and truck plant near Flint, the Corvette line is set up with body assembly in the center of the building, flanked by the chassis line on one side and paint booths on the other. In the body assembly area are the jigs in which body parts are joined.

Chevrolet uses the laminated — or "sandwich" — method to produce plastic bodies in 61 separate molds. The chief materials are glass fiber mats and polyester resins. ·When the liquid resin impregnates the glass fiber mats, it cures and it binds, and supports the filaments of glass to create a solid panel. (For a complete description of Fiberglas processing, see "How to Work With Fiberglas," August MOTOR TREND.)

In plastic fabrication, a mold substitutes for the steel die which fits into a metal-forming press. Chevrolet utilizes the so-called "bag method," where the curing process, under pressure, is accelerated by heat. When the mold is prepared with a parting agent (to permit ready separation of the cured panel from the mold) the first layers of Fiberglas are "laid-up" and coated with resin. A sheet of polyvinyl plastic is clamped over the mold, and the air between the mold and the sheet is removed; this causes a vacuum, and pressure is equal at all points. An application of heat speeds the curing process. When the part has been cured, it is removed from the mold and trimmed and ground to size on a band saw or sanding wheel.

This process is not too unlike that used by others working with Fiberglas, but Chevrolet engineers, with a high production goal in mind, have speeded up nearly every phase of the Corvette's construction. The Corvette, unlike many other plastic automobiles, has for its foundation a one-piece, reinforced plastic underbody that extends from the rear bumper through the dash panel. Its subassembled upper and front sections are bonded and riveted along a flange that later supports decorative moldings.

For maximum chassis strength, the car's driveshaft passes over, rather than through, the center of the X bracing the frame. The 51-inch rear springs are mounted outside the frame for stability. From bumper to bumper, the Corvette was designed for maneuverability, but its engineers nevertheless wisely demanded roominess not customarily found in a car of this type and size. For a car that is a true pioneer in its class (mass-production in Fiberglas by a major manufacturer) the Corvette is remarkably complete when it rolls from its six-chassis-long assembly line.

Still Chevrolet men aren't sitting back admiring their product, satisfied that they have their "baby" rolling smoothly off the line. E. H. Kelley, General Manufacturing Manager of Chevrolet, sums it up this way: "When we discuss produc-

Major Corvette components are (reading clockwise from "checker" at lower left): instrument panel, bulkhead and seatback, rear fender top panel, underbody, front end

One of the first steps in Corvette production was the construction of die molds for plastic body sections. Shown here is the mahogany die model for the underbody

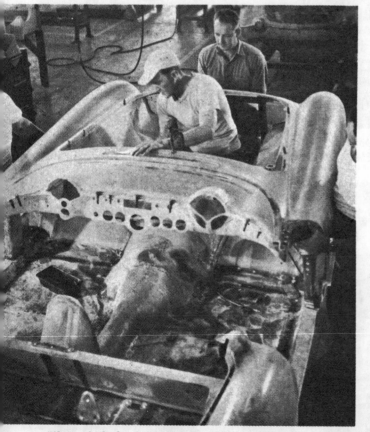

From DIES

tion of the Corvette body, we are speaking only as of today. Progress in manufacturing has been so swift that what is true now may be outdated tomorrow."

That could well be an echo from the past, referring to all the infant industries of America; but for now, it applies particularly to Fiberglas construction.

Few people doubt that Fiberglas has a future in the automotive industry, but whether or not it can compete on the same plane with steel is another matter. Although Chevrolet says that as far as

A drill jig, placed over the Corvette underbody section, serves as a guide for locating the holes needed when body is riveted

Typical of intricate shaping possible with Fiberglas, finned taillight housing is molded to fit the fender like a glove

The underbody, fitted with instrument panel and lower part of seatback, now receives the top-front Fiberglas body panel

Wired, and fitted with instruments and some of its trim, the Corvette body is lowered onto its chassis at the Flint plant

to DRIVEWAY

Fiberglas is concerned, they have "cast the dies," they also say cautiously that when a yearly productive capacity of 15,000 cars is reached, it's cheaper to produce bodies made of steel. Make of this what you will.

Whatever happens to the body, be it made of Fiberglas or steel, Chevrolet should be paid a tribute (as aptly put by C. A. Davison, Detroit sports-car enthusiast, at a recent S.A.E. meeting) "for taking time out from the work of putting out cars to play around a little."

Chevrolet's Corvette has a spacious trunk for its size — a rare feature in a sports car. Spare is stowed under trunk floor

Because a Fiberglas body will not shield the radio from interference, a housing is built around the entire ignition system

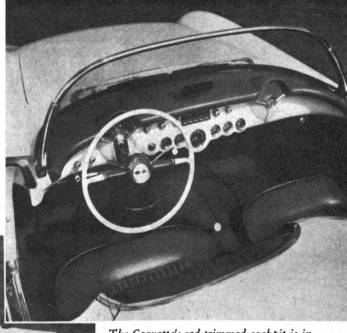

The Corvette's red-trimmed cockpit is in striking contrast to its white body. Instruments include a tachometer with cumulative rev counter like an odometer

The attractive interior sports handy parcel lockers in the doors. The white knob at the forward edge of door molding opens door; the other locks window

The Corvette

CHEVROLET'S PLASTIC SPORTS CAR

▶ Named after the naval patrol vessels of World War II, the new car has an engine which is basically a 1954 Chevrolet aluminum piston valve-in-head "Blue Flame" of 235 cu. in. displacement, but with added power obtained through modifications such as increased compression ratio, triple side draft carburetors and a dual exhaust system.

The transmission is 1954 Powerglide automatic with a floor-mounted quadrant in sports car tradition. It has Hotchkiss drive, independent front wheel suspension and a rear-axle gear ratio of 3.27 to 1.

The car carries an experimentally molded body, hood and fenders, and has a manually-adjusted lightweight fabric top that folds into a flush compartment behind the bucket seats of driver and passenger. The one-piece curved windshield is chrome bound, and its rakish 55° angle is set off by a slanted side pillar.

Headlights are recessed into the front of the fenders. Parking lights are inboard and below. Tail lights are circular and mounted high to complete the rear-fender jet type of styling.

The hood is front hinged and counterbalanced, as is the lid to the rear luggage deck. Spare wheel lies flat beneath the floor of the luggage compartment.

The driving compartment has two low doors which are wide in cross section and are equipped with saddle type compartments for driver's accessories. The doors are topped by chrome rails to which snap-on windows may be added with top up or down. Windows are stored in the luggage compartment when not in use.

The car's instruments include a center-mounted tachometer in addition to the usual speedometer, oil, water, fuel and generator gauges. ★

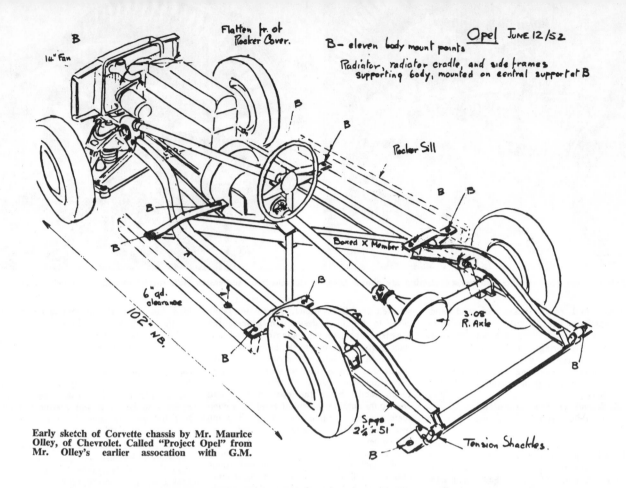

Early sketch of Corvette chassis by Mr. Maurice Olley, of Chevrolet. Called "Project Opel" from Mr. Olley's earlier assocation with G.M.

THE CHEVROLET CORVETTE

by John R. Bond

photographs courtesy Chevrolet Motor Division

As far back as 1948, *Road & Track* took-up the cause of the American Sports Car, with editorials and articles continuing through the years. Now we have such a car in the Chevrolet Corvette· During a recent trip to Chicago and New York it was discovered that very few sports car enthusiasts know much about this new car. There is also a very general feeling that the Corvette is not a genuine sports car. Maybe it isn't, though part of the difficulty can be traced to the lack of a universally accepted definition.

To enable each reader to evaluate the Corvette for himself, the following facts and information are presented. The basis for this report has been taken from an S.A.E. paper, presented by Mr. Maurice Olley, at Detroit, Michigan, on October 5, 1953.

The thinking behind the Chevrolet Corvette is based on the assumption that a sports car must have a cruising speed of over 70 mph, a weight/power ratio of better

(Continued on next page)

Final result, a well engineered sports car chassis.

Development of the new car enjoyed the advantage of G.M.'s vast proving grounds.

Bolt-on front cross-member and revised steering are shown here.   Corvette rear suspension with special springs and hotchkiss drive.

than 25 to 1, ample brakes, and good handling qualities. On this latter point Mr. Olley lists the following items as being desirable:

1. Quick steering with light handling.
2. A low center of gravity·
3. Minimum overhang with a low momoment of inertia relative to wheelbase.
5. Smooth yet firm suspension.
6. A quick steering response, but nó oversteer.

How the Chevrolet Motor Division achieved these obviously desirable sports car characteristics is very interesting. On June 2, 1952 Chevrolet engineers were shown a plaster model of a proposed car having a wheelbase of 102 inches. In seven months they were to design, build and test a chassis, using components of known reliability. It must have adequate performance, a comfortable ride and stable handling qualities.

On June 12, one of several sketches was

Manifold side of the 150 bhp Chevrolet engine. Flattened rocker cover allows low hood.

selected (see illustration). It remains fairly close to the final design. In general the chassis components were adapted from Chevrolet parts, but a hotchkiss drive was essential, since the short wheelbase would have required a torque tube so short as to produce excessive change of wheel speed on rough roads· Since the open body would contribute nothing to overall rigidity, a completely special frame was designed using box-section side rails and X-member. The X-member is low enough to allow the drive line to run above it, giving a very strong, solid junction at the "X". The low frame also required outboard rear spring mountings which places them close to the wheels, for stability. Weight of the complete frame is 213 lbs.

The front suspension uses many standard parts but is stiffer in roll by virtue of a larger diameter stabilizer bar. The coil springs are special because of the reduced

load, but their rate appears to be the same as the stock sedan. However the sprung weight is less than stock, giving the effect of "stiffer" springs with a faster bounce frequency. Static deflection is given as 7 inches, equivalent to a ride rate of about 105 lbs/in. and a bounce frequency of 71 oscillations per min. The front cross member appears to be stock and retains the excellent bolt-on, sub-assembly feature used by Chevrolet since 1934.

The steering idler arm (see photo) was redesigned because of the lower engine mounting and is carried on a double-row ball bearing. Steering ratio selected is 16 to 1. On this Mr. Olley says "We are aware of a preference in some quarters for a rack and pinion steering on cars of this type. However this involves a steering ratio of the order of 9 or 10 to 1· We regard this as too fast even for a sports car . . ." The steering wheel is 17.25" in dia., its angle is 13° from vertical and the turning circle is 38 ft.

The rear springs are 2" wide x 51" long, with four leaves. They are inclined (low in front, high at the rear) so as to give approximately 15% roll understeer. Quoting Mr. Olley, "This may appear excessive, but some of the handling qualities of a car depend on the amount it is allowed to roll on turns. When a car is designed to roll very much less than normal, and with a low c.g., so that the overturning couple on the tires is reduced, it may become necessary to put a strong understeering tendency into the rear axle control, to provide an adequate tail for the arrow." Tension type shackles are used to give a variable rate, but the static deflection at the rear is given as 5", equivalent to a ride rate at normal load of about 112 lbs/in., a ride frequency of 80 oscillations per minute.

The center of gravity of the Corvette is only 18" above the ground. This, in conjunction with a heavier stabilizer bar and stiffer, non-symmetrical rear springs contributes to greatly reduced roll angle when cornering.

Moment of inertia relative to the wheelbase of the car as whole is dependent on the distribution of the principal masses. A dumbell-like distribution, with weight concentrated at the ends, tends to give good riding qualities but a slow steering response. A sports car requires some compromise in this respect. In the Corvette the engine is

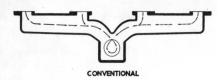

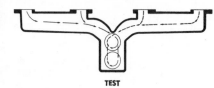

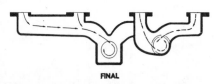

Dual exhaust adds to bhp, but thorough engineering resulted in over 4% better torque.

located 7 inches further back and 3 inches lower than a stock Chevrolet sedan. To avoid complexities, if we take the stock sedan's moment of inertia as 100%, the Corvette can be rated as 62%. Obviously much of this reduction in "dumbell" or flywheel effect comes about from the drastic reduction in body weight.

The net result of the suspension features just described more than fulfills the original design objective—smooth yet firm suspension. Again quoting Mr. Olley "A joggling ride is not acceptable, but a floating ride which appears to be divorced from the road is even more unacceptable. Excessive roll and vague handling characteristics will not do."

The question of weight distribution, fore and aft, should not be confused with mass distribution. A car could have its engine in the middle of the wheelbase and still have a 50/50 weight distribution. But its moment of inertia would be even less than the Corvette· Most engineers will agree with Mr. Olley that any deviation from 50/50 distribution should favor a slight nose-heaviness. There are many reasons for this, but

the most important one is that extra weight on the front wheels gives better directional stability at high speeds. The Corvette road tested this month (see page 10) weighed exactly 2890 lbs with full tank, spare tire, radio and heater. In this condition the fore and aft distribution was 1560 lbs front, 1330 lbs rear, or 54/46. With 320 lbs for driver and passenger added, the weights change by just over 2%, to 52/48. A mere 90 lbs of luggage over the rear axle changes the distribution another 2%, to 50/50. It is worth noting that every principal sports car manufacturer of note shows tendencies towards more weight forward. Allard's latest JR model is a complete reversal of previous policy with 57/43.' Even Porsche is "reversing" their engine location from just behind to just ahead of the rear axle, on their latest type 550 model.

Having dealt with the various aspects of the chassis design and its effect on the all-important handling qualities, let us examine the rest of the Corvette. Many people like to point out that "Chevrolet hasn't changed their engine since 1937" (when four main bearings and a new stroke/bore ratio were adopted.) This is however, a compliment for it attests to the excellence of a design which, though perhaps not exciting or dramatic, has stood the test of time. Actually, very little of the original design is left. Today all Chevrolets have a larger bore and stroke, pressure lubrication to the rods, aluminum pistons, insert type bearings, an even heavier crankshaft, very large ports and valves. The accompanying power curve data compares the 108 bhp 1953 Chevrolet to the Corvette. The Corvette engine is not changed radically over the 1954 115 and 125 bhp stock engines. Compression ratio is slightly higher at 8.0 to 1. Adjustable type valve tappets run on a revised camshaft having .005" more lift than the production 125 bhp engine. The following table illustrates the moderate changes made in valve timing.

ENGINE	I.O.	I.C.	E.O.	E.C.
115 bhp	1.0	39.0	42.0	9.0
125 bhp	10.5	53.5	49.8	15
150 bhp	19·5	44.5	59.0	5.0

The corresponding valve spring pressures on the three engines are 160, 182 and 207 lbs. The camshaft timing gear is aluminum

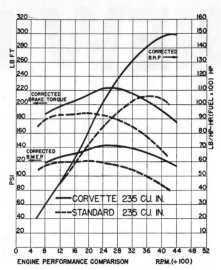

This shows the improved engine performance of the Corvette compared to the 1953 engine.

on the 150 bhp Corvette, to withstand the heavier loads and higher speeds.

There are three Carter side draft carburetors mounted on a cast aluminum manifold provided with suitable balancing passages. Automatic chokes were tried and abondoned because of choke valve flutter and fast idling. No exhaust heat is used or is necessary, but provision is made for extremely cold weather. The heat shield can be removed and the heat control valve spring reversed, if desired. The dual exhaust system (illustrated) is a special type to keep the gasses in the outlets always swirling in the same direction. This one feature added 8 to 10 ft/lbs of torque in the mid-speed range. On the mufflers, Mr. Olley says "A requirement in the minds of sports car enthusiasts is that the exhaust should have the right note. They don't agree what this is. Some prefer 'foo-blap' while others go for 'foo-gobble.' It is impossible to please them all. We hope we have achieved a desirable compromise."

The water pump is a special high-efficiency type running at .9 engine speed. Circulation rate is 27 gpm at 2000 rpm. The fan is 18 inches in diameter, not shrouded. Cooling tests show that the cooling system of the

(Continued on page 30)

The Corvette engine sits horizontal in order to get the drive-line over the X-member.

NEW FUEL

for an OLD DUEL

By Don MacDonald

AS LONG AS WE CAN REMEMBER, Ford and Chevrolet have battled it out for sales supremacy. Each has had a share of victory, but from our viewpoint, the important thing about the everlasting race is not who wins the various laps. Instead, just like road-racing, it sparks competition-bred improvements which tend to make all cars a better breed.

Nowhere is this more evidenced than in the recent revival of the *American-made* production sports car. It is easy to trace the

genesis, and from that you will understand our (and the manufacturers') seeming misuse of the term "sports car."

First came the post-war influx of foreign imports. In the beginning, these could be roughly grouped into three categories: road-racing cars, utility cars, and connoisseurs' (or vanity) cars. Detroit, fat in its seller's market, nevertheless watched closely, even though imported car sales never (even now) accounted for more than a fraction of the total market.

Road-racing cars (the true sports car) provided the key. Those marques, such as MG and Jaguar, which began early to cater to American standards of comfort even at the sacrifice of some performance potential, sold the best. Those that refused to conform found their sale limited solely to the "lunatic fringe," Detroit's tart (but really sympathetic) moniker for the true car enthusiast.

The pattern became evident. America was definitely interested in a *personal* car

NEW FUEL FOR AN OLD DUEL

that was *fun to drive* and *feasible to own*. The projected sales picture reached far beyond the roster of SCCA members to encompass the 17 per cent of American families who habitually own two or more cars. This is the market at which Detroit is aiming. Even though relatively high-priced (between $3000 and $4000), these cars are not intended to *replace* your Cadillac or Lincoln, but rather to be an *auxiliary* to them. The picture may change with the addition of new models to the lines, but that is the way it stands now.

The idea would still probably not have been budgeted if it had not been for something called "motivation engineering." This is simply the principle (see MT, Feb. '54) that showroom traffic is accelerated by the presence of a fancy display car. You have seen this principle in operation at auto shows (such as GM's Motorama) where the diet of standard production models is spiced with a liberal sprinkling of dream cars. However, these one-of-a-kind items are not of much help to the dealer in your home town. The production sports car solves this problem; each dealer can have his own dream car.

First on the scene was the Nash-Healey. This car qualifies in our category even though it is a sort of United Nations effort. The fact that its components have been exported and imported several times over in the process of manufacture and assembly probably has a considerable bearing on the inordinately high price which has limited its acceptance. Nevertheless, its publicity value to Nash can't be measured in terms of dollars and cents.

There is some argument as to who was next. Both the Kaiser-Darrin and the Corvette started out as solo dream cars. Kaiser now is seriously producing the KD-161, but this attractive car is considered by some to be underpowered in present form. Kaiser's analysis of the market seems to have missed on one vital point: potential

buyers of the production sports car don't want to be creamed at the traffic light by the average American sedan. It makes them feel a little silly, just like it makes an occasional MG owner (the one who cares little about 1½-liter class racing) question his investment. The obvious solution for Kaiser is the already engineered (MT, April '54) McCulloch-blown version.

Corvette, on the other hand, went to a lot of expense in souping up the standard Chevrolet engine. The result is a car whose performance matches its appearance. Up until recently, Sales Manager W. E. Fish's eyedropper distribution of this vehicle insured that it only got into the hands of the most prominent local citizen who wanted one. This was an almost psychic assumption that some boy remains in every man, especially those who can afford it. The boy wanted the sports car, but the man was afraid of ridicule. Thus, the Corvette has a performance capable of erasing the smiles of bystanders.

Only 315 Corvettes were built during 1953. Production facilities are to be moved from Flint to St. Louis, and as of presstime, output has jumped to 500 a month, which is only half of the ultimate goal. There is still a waiting list, but the long gap between initial publicity and availability has cooled the desires of many buyers. Chevrolet dealers (distribution is now in their hands) now find that they have to contact as many as six people on the list before they find one who will honor his original commitment.

Ford, with its Thunderbird in the offing, has learned a lesson from this. Now that the car has been announced for Fall production (deliveries starting in September), they are definitely averse to publicity until such time as adequate stocks are in dealer hands. This is a partial explanation why performance figures for the Thunderbird on page 18 are calculated by us. The other reason is that the car is still

Experts who forecast that the Thunderbird would seem stark beside a Corvette are pleasantly surprised by its luxury

undergoing engineering changes; some vital specs are not finally fixed. Ford will not let the car be driven by outsiders until the development program is completed.

Thunderbird features which will not be changed are adequate bumpers, three-passenger seat, wind-up windows, and an all-metal body. Ford feels that these are essential qualifications for any American car. The reasons for adequate bumpers and maximum seating capacity (for the body model) are obvious. Wind-up (power optional) windows and accessory hardtop are concessions to broaden the market. Not every state has the climate of Florida or California. Ford's choice of a metal rather than plastic body is equally simple to analyze, but has nothing to do with the

Looking skyward as a Corvette floats by, we see what is essentially a stock Chevy. Outrigger springs are an exclusive Corvette touch. Sturdy frame adds to practicality

Three carburetors and (not shown) shielded ignition are changes from stock

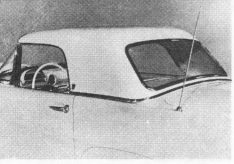

Exhausts end in bumper guards. Optional Fiberglas top is a courageous interpretation of the classic Continental's roof

Argentina's Juan Fangio smiles from the latest version of the Thunderbird (with new headlights). Both hardtop and convertible, below, feature a three-passenger seat, wind-up windows, all-metal body. Ford says all are essential for real sales volume

course taken by Chevrolet. Both cars came from the drawing board about the same time. The Corvette appeared first because a plastic car can be put into production in a relative hurry. A limited-production metal car, to be economically feasible, must utilize tooling common with its high-production brothers.

The Thunderbird is blood-relation, appearance-wise, to the forthcoming 1955 Ford. Although the body will be built by Budd (who recently leased Murray's Detroit facilities), it will alternate with Ranch Wagons on the same Rouge assembly line. Chevrolet, or the other hand, chose the plastic (Fiberglas) route frankly because General Motors wanted to gain experience with this new material. Although there have been statements that 15,000 units a year is the break-even point between metal and plastic, *the day the Corvette is made of metal will be the day when a forthcoming standard Chevrolet will look a lot like a Corvette.*

This last is the true contribution of the production sports car. It is safe to predict that both companies will expand their specialty line to include other body models. This will inevitably speed the day when there is at least a styling wedding between these and standard models. It is a happy, healthy future for the consumer—with or without gasoline in his blood.

Other aspects of the Fiberglas versus metal argument are pretty much secondary. Plastic, generally speaking, has an advantage in the strength-weight ratio department. On the other hand, it is an unfamiliar material to most body repairmen. Plastic, even when formed from matched-

metal dies, requires a lot of hand finishing which raises the cost considerably. Both materials can be engineered to hold up equally well in service, but plastic requires special manufacturing and repair facilities.

The basic difference between the Corvette and the Thunderbird is not so much the body material, but a conflicting analysis of the American market. The Corvette was patterned closely after the European concept of a competition car. *Conversely, the designers of the Thunderbird aimed at and achieved a California custom flavor.* This is why Corvette presently has an *almost* purist indifference to the problem of weather protection. It was easy for the come-lately Thunderbird to offer adequate coverage, but we predict that it will be equally easy for Corvette to rectify what may be an error by producing the car on our cover.

Performance-wise, neither car qualifies as a competition vehicle as it comes from the factory. Nor are they intended to be used for this purpose without extensive modification. However, both have sparkling *highway* performance, which is what the factories feel you want most. The Corvette we know handles well (see page **23**), and we presume the Thunderbird is equally agile. The famous race driver, Juan Fangio, managed to ride in (but not drive) the prototype Thunderbird and was impressed enough to sign up for the first to be sent to Argentina. Considering the fact that he is Buenos Aires' leading Chevrolet dealer, this is certainly a strong testimonial.

A peculiar paradox in this revival of real going road machines made in America

is the reluctance of the factories to talk concretely about their products' performance. The Thunderbird speedometer, for example, is graduated to 150 mph, but we predict that its true top speed will never be advertised except indirectly (such as a NASCAR win or one of our road tests).

The reason for this was almost enough to keep the Thunderbird and the Corvette from ever being born. Detroit is scared to death of well-meaning safety authorities who have branded horsepower as the cause of all accidents. Regardless of how unfair and untrue this is, it has placed performance figures in the same category as dirty jokes—something to be whispered in the back room amongst friends of the same sex.

In our opinion, the higher the power-weight ratio, the safer is the car. The production sports cars combine this advantage with exceptionally good handling characteristics. These features are inbred because of the market they seek to reach. In proper hands, they will harm no one, while improper hands can commit mayhem with a Model T.

Despite barbs and needles, Detroit is beginning to produce real automobiles once again—modern versions of the Bearcat and Mercer. Chevrolet, Ford, Kaiser, and Nash are to be congratulated for leading the revival. We think they'll succeed, and the measure of their success will be how soon they are joined by Plymouth with its Belmont, Mercury with its XM-800, Cadillac with its La Espada, and many other fine cars now being considered for production.

HOW THEY PERFORM

TEST CAR AT A GLANCE
FORD THUNDERBIRD

These figures are, of course, calculated; no Thunderbird had been driven at presstime by anyone not employed by the manufacturer. Ford is understandably not willing to release the figures that they have because the Thunderbird is not yet fully engineered. This is our educated guess on what we think the car will do in its present form. For the purpose of a valid comparison with the Corvette, our hypothetical Thunderbird is assumed to be equipped with a Fordomatic transmission. All specifications and options listed are those which hold as of presstime, but of course they are subject to change at any time.

ACCELERATION

The Thunderbird, with Fordomatic and a 3.31 to 1 rear axle, will probably have a slight edge over the Corvette, with Powerglide and a 3.55 to 1 rear axle, in initial acceleration. At higher acceleration speeds, Corvette has a slight advantage. These differences are almost entirely due to transmission characteristics
0-30 mph (Low) 4, 0-30 mph (Drive) 4.5, 0-60 mph (Low to 40, then Drive), 11, 0-80 mph (Low to 40, then Drive) 21.5

TOP SPEED

Here, axle ratio and engine friction take over, giving the Thunderbird a decided advantage. Our estimate with top and windows up:
112 mph plus or minus 2 mph

FUEL CONSUMPTION

The Corvette's rather astounding economy curve (almost a straight line from 20 to 70 mph) is probably due to erratic fuel flow at low speeds in the three separate carburetors. The Thunderbird, with its single four-barrel carburetor, should have better low-speed economy; high-speed consumption should be about the same for both cars.
23 mpg at steady 30 mph, 19.5 mpg at steady 45, 18.6 mpg at steady 60, 13.0 mpg at steady 80.

BRAKE STOPPING DISTANCE

Since both cars have the same loaded weight distribution and approximately the same size and type brake, there is no reason why the cars should not be equally good in this department. Incidentally, the Thunderbird's power brake option just reduces the effort; it doesn't improve braking ability.

Hubie Davis

CHEVROLET has produced a bucket-seat roadster that will hold its own with Europe's best, short of actual competition and a few imports that cost three times as much.

The Corvette is an exciting car to drive. First of all, thanks to eyedropper distribution and low production, the odds are very much against your seeing another one even once a day. Secondly, a poll of traffic-light comments showed nothing but admiration for its design and, incidentally, recognition—instead of the usual "what is it?" it was "what'll that Chevy do?" Here's what this one did.

Performance is best described as agile rather than startling. Several American sedans (the Buick Century in particular) can give the Corvette a hard time. A *good* Corvette will barely nose out an *average* Century on an unobstructed freeway.

From point to point on the usual two-lane, winding highway, nothing *now* made in Michigan will touch it. The car corners with gyroscopic steadiness. Even an amateur can set up a creditable four-wheel drift safely, because the rear end will break loose and give ample warning before there is any tendency to roll. This differs from other American production cars, which have a tendency to understeer or oversteer, but not both in happy combination. Our photographic records show some lean during high-speed cornering, but it is not noticeable while driving the car, probably due to the adhesive contour of the bucket seats.

The 16 to 1 overall ratio steering is ideal for normal American driving conditions. The nearly three turns of the wheel from lock to lock would tie the arms of a competition driver in knots, but the Corvette is not designed for tracing figure eights on an airport runway. For normal highway use, the steering is sensitive and practically shock-free.

TEST CAR AT A GLANCE
CHEVROLET CORVETTE

ACCELERATION

(In seconds, checked with fifth wheel and electric speedometer)
0-30 mph 4.9; 0-60 mph 11.5; 0-80 mph 20.2; 10-30 mph 3.2; 30-50 mph 4.1; 50-80 mph 11.2

TOP SPEED

(In miles per hour; clocked over surveyed ¼-mile with top up)
Fastest run, 108.2; Slowest run, 102.6; Avg., 105.3

FUEL CONSUMPTION

(In miles per gallon; checked with fuel flowmeter, fifth wheel, and electric speedometer)
17.5 mpg at steady 20 mph; 19.2 mpg at steady 30; 18.5 mpg at steady 45; 18.5 mpg at steady 60; 16.2 mpg at steady 70; 13.1 mpg at steady 80

BRAKE STOPPING DISTANCE

(To the nearest foot; checked with electrically actuated detonator)
38 feet @ 30 mph; 169 feet @ 60 mph

SPEEDOMETER ERROR

Car speedometer read 28 at true 30 mph; 58 at true 60 mph; 79 at true 80 mph

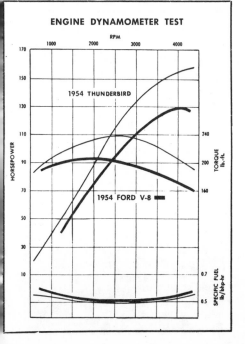

ENGINE DYNAMOMETER TEST

1954 THUNDERBIRD

1954 FORD V-8

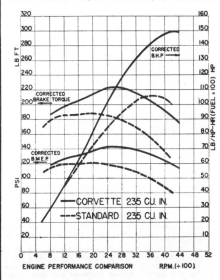

ENGINE DYNAMOMETER TEST
(Comparative data on Corvette versus standard 235-cu.-in. Chevrolet engine furnished by manufacturer)

CORRECTED B.H.P.

CORRECTED BRAKE TORQUE

CORRECTED B.M.E.P.

CORVETTE 235 CU. IN.
STANDARD 235 CU. IN.

ENGINE PERFORMANCE COMPARISON   R.P.M. (÷ 100)

New Fuel for an Old Duel

The nearly vertical wheel position seemed comfortable enough on our longest trip (350 miles at one sitting), but another styling feature of this car is definitely not. The editorial "we" in this case is six feet tall, which is not so unusual as to qualify him for a spare-time job in a circus. At least three inches of his head protruded above the stylishly low windshield. At any speed above 50 mph, "we" wondered whether or not what was left of his hair would stay with him.

We gave up and raised the top, even though it was a hot day for Michigan. This is no easy task, and Chevrolet makes no bones about it. Their conception of the Corvette market is that no owner will be caught in the rain without a spare Cadillac.

Actually, we are inclined to sympathize with the Corvette concept of motoring for the fun of it (not that we have a spare Cadillac sedan). The Corvette with top up and Plexiglas windows in place is as tight as a diving bell compared to most European sports car imports.

The Corvette ride is firm, but nowhere close to the springless "standards" of the true sports car. We bottomed once or twice on severe aberrations in the road, yet this is a small price to pay for comfort the bulk of the time. The relationship between car occupants and gravity is inevitably a compromise, at least until springs as we know them are outmoded. Be this as it may, we feel that the Corvette is of LeMans caliber in this department (it would be in all others if not for lack of power). Well, it should be, for amongst those who had a hand in its design were Maurice Olley of Vauxhall 30-98 fame, Zora Arkus-Duntov, who has driven many a LeMans on the Allard team, and Mauri Rose, who didn't need to cross the ocean to achieve his fame as a three-time Indianapolis winner.

The overall detail finish of the Corvette will stack up favorably with any show car—Italian or domestic. The instruments are plentiful, accurate, and readable, except we suggest the tach should trade with the speedometer for the place of honor. Anyone interested enough in cars to buy a Corvette knows how to govern himself by his tachometer. The hand choke is another welcome revival, although it is obviously made necessary by the three separate side-draft carburetors.

On the subject of options, we should mention the Powerglide transmission—normally extra but standard on the Corvette. The purist will turn up his nose at this (the better to catch the rain), but we found the beefed-up Corvette version highly satisfactory. If you manually drop into Low range for braking purposes at any speed between 30 and 50 mph, it does well enough to squeal the tires, which means that it's temporarily too efficient. Granted, placing the lever on the floorboards is imitative nonsense and serves only to confuse parking lot attendants. However, most of our objections to automatic transmissions in the past have been when they were combined with low horsepower. With adequate horsepower and automatic transmission, you can drive just as efficiently (if not more so) than the average manual speed-shift artist.

The rest of our comments about the Corvette would be incidental if printed. The gist of all of this is that if you want a car that is completely distinctive, performs with the best that you'll normally encounter, and can be serviced intelligently in any North American hamlet, put your name on the waiting list. Once your Corvette is delivered, you can worry about adjusting yourself to motoring for the fun of it, which, for taller-than-average people, is mainly building up a resistance to head colds.

—*Don MacDonald*

FORD THUNDERBIRD

GENERAL SPECIFICATIONS

ENGINE: Ohv V8. Bore 3⅝ in. Stroke 3 3/32. Stroke/bore ratio 0.857. Compression ratio 7.5 to 1. Displacement 256 cu. in. Advertised bhp 161 @ 4400 rpm. Bhp per cu. in. 0.63. Piston travel @ max bhp 2273 ft. per min. Max torque 238 lbs.-ft. @ 2200 to 2800 rpm. Max bmep 147.1 psi
DRIVE SYSTEM: STANDARD transmission is three-speed synchromesh, using helical gears. Ratios: 1st 2.78, 2nd 1.61, 3rd 1.0, reverse 3.64.
OVERDRIVE is planetary with standard gears, minimum cut-in speed 27 mph. Ratio: 0.7.
AUTOMATIC transmission is Fordomatic, torque converter with planetary gears. Ratios: Drive 1.48 and 1.00 x torque converter (max ratio @ stall 2.1); Low 2.44 x torque converter; Reverse 2.0 x torque converter.
REAR AXLE RATIOS: Conventional 3.90 standard, 4.10 optional; Overdrive 4.10 standard, 3.90, 3.31 optional; Fordomatic 3.31 standard.
DIMENSIONS: Wheelbase 102 in. Tread 56 front and rear. Wheelbase/tread ratio 1.82. Overall width 70.1 in. Overall length 175.2 in. Overall height 51.9 in. (top up). Steering ratio 20:1. Curb weight 2837 lbs. Weight/bhp ratio 17.7. Weight distribution 50% front, 50% rear loaded. Tire size 6.70 x 15.

PRICE

Not announced as of presstime, but said to be competitive with other cars in the same field; i.e., $3500-$4000.
ACCESSORIES: The list has not yet been finalized, but will most certainly contain these items: Overdrive or Fordomatic transmission, power steering and brakes, power windows and seat, plastic hardtop, radio and heater, and all the usual minor luxury items.

CHEVROLET CORVETTE

GENERAL SPECIFICATIONS

ENGINE: Ohv 6-cyl. Bore 3¹³⁄₁₆ in.; Stroke 3¹⁵⁄₁₆ in.; Stroke/bore ratio 1.11 to 1; Compression ratio 8.0 to 1; Displacement 235.5 cu. in.; Advertised bhp 150 @ 4200 rpm; Bhp per cu. in. 0.64; Max torque 223 lbs.-ft. @ 2400 rpm; Max bmep 143 psi @ 2400 rpm.
DRIVE SYSTEM: STANDARD transmission is Powerglide, torque converter with gears. Ratios: Drive, torque converter (max ratio @ stall 2.1) and 3.82 x converter ratio; Low, 3.82 x converter ratio; Reverse, 3.82 x converter ratio. Rear axle ratio, 3.55.
DIMENSIONS: Wheelbase 102 in.; Tread 57 front, 59 rear; Wheelbase/tread ratio 1.76; Overall width 72¼ in.; Overall length 167 in.; Overall height 52 in. (loaded, top up); Turning diameter 39 ft.; Turns lock to lock 3.9; Test car wet weight 2910 (factory shipping weight 2705 without radio and heater). Test car weight/bhp ratio 19.4; Weight distribution 50% front, 50% rear; Tire size 6.70 x 15.

PRICE

(Including retail price at main factory, federal tax and delivery and handling charges, Powerglide, white sidewall tires, windshield washers, direction signals, tachometer, and electric clock, but not freight) Roadster $3498.
ACCESSORIES: (It is difficult to obtain delivery without those listed) Heater $91, radio $145.

CORVETTE TEST
(Continued from page 6)

PERFORMANCE

TOP SPEED—
Average of two-way runs: 106.4 mph
Fastest one-way run: 107.1 mph

ACCELERATION—
0-30 mph: 3.7 sec.
0-50 mph: 7.7 sec.
0-60 mph: 11.0 sec.
0-80 mph: 19.5 sec.
Standing quarter mile: 18.0 sec.

FUEL CONSUMPTION—
18 mpg at continuous high speed;
16 mpg under test conditions and
20 mpg under normal driving conditions
Fuel used for test was Shell Premium

GENERAL SPECIFICATIONS—
Engine—6 cyl., 150 hp at 4200 rpm.
Power-to-weight ratio—19 lbs. per 1 hp.
Center of gravity—18" from ground
Overall Hgt.—47"
Weight Distribution—53% front, 47% rear (with 2 passengers and no load in trunk)
Weight—3210 lbs, test condition; 2890 lbs. normal, with full gas tank
Ignition—6 V.
Price—$3760, F.O.B. St. Louis

THE REAL McCOY

Here is the most remarkable car made in America today — the new Chevrolet Corvette.

Why remarkable?

Because it is *two* cars wrapped up in one sleek skin. One is a luxury car with glove-soft upholstery, wind-up windows, a removable hardtop (with virtually 360° vision), or fabric top, ample luggage space, a velvety ride and all the power assists you could want, including power-operated fabric top* and Powerglide transmission*.

The other is a sports car. And we mean the real McCoy, a tough, road-gripping torpedo-on-wheels with the stamina to last through the brutal 12 hours of Sebring, a close-ratio trans-

mission (2.2 low gear, 1.31 second) matched to engine torque characteristics, razor-sharp steering (16 to 1) that puts *command* into your fingertips.

Other people make a luxury car that has much the same dimensions as this. That's not so tough. . And the Europeans make some real rugged competition sports cars —and that's considerably tougher. But nobody but Chevrolet makes a luxury car that *also* is a genuine 100-proof sports car.

It's a wicked combination to work out, and we didn't hit it overnight. But you'll find, when you take the wheel of a new Corvette, that the result is fantastic — the most heart-lifting blend of all the things you've ever wanted a car to be.

If you find it hard to believe that one car could combine such widely different characteristics we can't blame you. And no amount of talk can tell you half so much as 15 minutes in a Corvette's cockpit — so why don't you let your Chevrolet dealer set up a road test of the most remarkable car made in America today? . . . Chevrolet Division of General Motors, Detroit 2, Michigan.

*Powerglide and power-operated fabric top optional at extra cost.

CORVETTE

Road Test: **The Corvette V8**

it may be "loaded for bear" but . . .

photography: **Ralph Poole**

Fiberglass top is not a factory option.

Last year, when we road tested the Corvette 6, the question was raised, "Is it really a sports car," Results to date are fairly conclusive, for the occasional rare appearance of a Corvette in competition has not been marked by any major upset.

For 1955 there are no changes in the car's specifications except that the new Chevrolet V-8 engine, tuned to 195 bhp, is optional, and the output of the 6 has been upped to 155 bhp (5 more). The V-8 powered version gives truly startling performance, as might be expected, but the transmission and brake deficiencies still will not satisfy the demands of either competition or of the true sports car enthusiast, no matter how loyal he may be to American engineering know-how. Furthermore, the theme "For Experts Only" can be applied only to those new to the sport, since the Corvette demands no unusual driver skill or special techniques. There is a rumor that a 3-speed manual transmission will be made available,

but no cars have been built with this equipment as yet.

Nevertheless, the fact remains that there is a small market for an open roadster which the lady of the house can use as smart personal transport without the necessity of learning how to manipulate one of those "funny old-fashioned gear shift levers." Chevrolet's Corvette fulfills the above need admirably, and if sales have been meagre it can only be blamed on the fact that a "female" personal car should also cater to the comfort demands of the sex and provide the usual assortment of power-operated gadgets (including side windows), three tone color schemes and frilly curtains.

The amazing thing about the Corvette is that it comes so close to being a really interesting, worth-while and genuine sports car—yet misses the mark almost entirely. Last June we said "The outstanding characteristic of the Corvette is probably its deceptive performance." Quite naturally the

more powerful V-8 gives vastly improved performance as the following comparison table will show.

	1954 Six	1955 V-8	
Top speed (best)	107.1	119.1	mph
0-30 mph	3.7	3.2	secs
0-60 mph	11.0	8.7	secs
0-80 mph	19.5	14.4	secs
0-100 mph	40.0	24.7	secs
SS¼ (avg.)	18.0	16.5	secs
Odometer	500	1450	miles

Despite the improvement in performance, economy has not been sacrificed; on the contrary the new low-friction engine yielded 2 to 3 miles more per gallon than last year's test of the 150 bhp 6 gave. The new V-8 engine is, incidentally, a stock passenger car unit with the four barrel "power-pack" carburetor. The only change is a special camshaft which alone accounts for the 15 extra horses. (The horsepower peaking speed and torque figures are our estimates, no official data being available). Reliability should be up to family sedan standards, and as a matter of interest the theoretical cruising speed, even with a 3.55 axle ratio, is nearly equal to the actual top speed—thanks to the shortest stroke in the industry (American). The new engine is very smooth and quiet, particularly on full throttle acceleration, whereas the 6 sounds a little on the "cobby" side under the same treatment. At idle there is some tappet noise, explained perhaps by settings slightly towards the high-limit, in anticipation of the high-speed runs. The 8 does idle much more quietly than the 6, however.

Last year we also mentioned that "The second most outstanding characteristic of the Corvette is its really good combination of riding and handling qualities." We added, "It may not be suitable for road-racing

A minor change in the script lettering on the side identifies the 1955 Corvette V-8.

Corvette cockpit is spacious and luxurious.

as it comes from the factory—but . . . it should be easy enough to strip the car down to a better weight". Watching a Corvette in an airport race coming into a corner with fast company, we have observed that the brakes show up poorly, but the actual cornering is done just as fast, flat and comfortably as several imported sports cars we could name. Coming out of the corner, the Corvette 6 seems to accelerate on a par with an average 2-litre production sports car (as it should on the basis of performance tests) but not nearly as well as cars in its own engine-size class having four forward speeds and approximately the same power-to-weight ratio. The new V-8 powered car still will need "brakes", but it handles very well and should now accelerate more on a par with machines of its class. Worth mentioning is the fact that the brakes are more than adequate for ordinary usage, with 158 sq. in. of lining area for only 2900 lbs of machine (109 sq. in/ton).

Chevrolet says the Corvette has "quick" 16:1 steering, but 3¾ turns, lock to lock, is not quick-steering "for experts", nor fast enough for a sports car which merits our whole-hearted and unreserved recommendation. The steering is actually very light at all times and could easily be reduced to 3.0 turns lock to lock and still be parkable, especially if power-steering were available for the frailer type of driver.

Riding qualities are excellent and directional stability at high speeds is near-perfect. One does wonder why the much advertised ball-joint front suspension of the

(Continued on page 30)

The V8 engine is 41 lbs lighter than the 6.

ROAD & TRACK ROAD TEST NO. A-4-55
CHEVROLET CORVETTE V-8

SPECIFICATIONS

List price	$2901
Wheelbase	102 in.
Tread, front	57 in.
rear	59 in.
Tire size	6.70-15
Curb weight	2880
distribution	52/48
Test weight	3200
Engine	V-8
Valves	pohv
Bore & stroke	3.75 x 3.0 in.
Displacement	265 cu in. (4344 cc)
Compression ratio	8.00
Horsepower	195
peaking speed	4600
equivalent mph	103
Torque, ft/lbs.	260
peaking speed	2800
equivalent mph	63
Mph per 1000 rpm	22.5
Mph at 2500 fpm	112.5
Gear ratios (overall)	
Drive	3.55
Low	6.46
Low + converter	13.57
R & T high gear performance factor	72.5

PERFORMANCE

Top speed (avg.)	116.9
best run	119.1
Max. speeds in gears—	
low (5500 rpm)	68

N.B.—Powerglide transmission normally shifts from low to high at 62 mph, under wide-open throttle.

Mileage	18/22.5 mpg

ACCELERATION

0-30	3.2 secs.
0-40	4.4 secs.
0-50	6.4 secs.
0-60	8.7 secs.
0-70	11.3 secs.
0-80	14.4 secs.
0-90	18.9 secs.
0-100	24.7 secs.
Standing ¼ mile—	
average	16.5 secs.
best	16.3 secs.

TAPLEY READINGS

Gear	Lbs/ton	Mph	Grade
Low	600	35	32%
High	380	50	19%

Total drag at 60 mph, 152 lbs.

SPEEDO ERROR

Indicated	Actual
10	11.0
20	20.4
30	29.7
40	39.5
50	48.6
60	58.0
70	67.3
80	77.0
90	86.1
100	97.1
118	119.1

CHEVROLET CORVETTE V-8
acceleration through the gears

ROAD and TRACK

Corvette V-8 makes a top-speed straightaway run. Driver found car exceptionally stable, without sacrifices in cornering.

The addition of two extra cylinders under the hood has made a big difference in the performance of this production American sports car

SPECULATION began immediately after the introduction of the Chevrolet V-8 as to whether or not it would be offered in the Corvette. It looked like a natural combination, so no one was greatly surprised when Chevrolet announced that the new engine *would* be available in the Corvette. There were a few raised eyebrows when it was reported it would be rated at 195 hp, however; this is 15 hp higher than the regular Chevrolet engine with power pack.

At the first opportunity arrangements were made with Chevrolet to use a Corvette for several days and report our impressions. I picked the car up in Detroit and drove it for four days, taking it up to Lansing one day where Roger Huntington and I put it thru a number of performance tests. My impression can be summed up like this:

The Corvette V-8 is an outstanding performer and is a lot of fun to drive. In this sense it's a real sports car, although the purists will argue this point. It is still not quite a serious competition car, although it probably could be modified to give some of the more expensive foreign iron a rough time in road races.

It has some flaws—it's not the ideal car for driving in a heavy rain, I found. However, for those interested in a car of this type, the virtues should make up for any minor shortcomings.

Now for the interesting part: the way it performs! To give you an idea, it turned 0-60 in an average of 8.5 seconds, with a couple of runs being even a couple

of tenths of a second less than that. It made it from 0 to 80 in less than 15 seconds. And these were actual speeds, not just indicated figures. Other acceleration figures were: 0 to 30, 3.4 seconds; standing quarter-mile, 16.9 seconds. The car was turning in the neighborhood of 85 at the end of the quarter-mile, incidentally.

On top speed runs the best we could get was 110. These runs were made with the top down and a relatively low tire pressure of 27 psi. If we had had time to experiment with different tire pressures, the top up and only the driver in the car, I feel we could have improved the top speed by about five mph, however.

One thing that surprised us was the very small speedometer error. Up to around 50, the error was almost negligible—amounting to only about one mile per hour or so. At an indicated 60 the error was about 2½ or three mph. This held true on up through 80. At the top end speedo readings were about four mph more than actual speeds. This is excellent. The tach, however, didn't seem to be too accurate to us, although there was no way of checking it to be sure.

Mentioning the tachometer, by the way, brings up one of the flaws mentioned earlier. This very important instrument is small and is placed very poorly. It's mounted low and in the center of the instrument panel and it's next to impossible for the driver to see it easily. You have to take your eyes off the road for too long a period to get an rpm reading. Actually the person riding in the

passenger seat can see the tach much better than the driver. Otherwise, instrumentation is good, although spread out a shade too much for easy reference.

One of the things that contributes to the Corvette's excellent performance is its relatively light weight. The registration tag for the car we had listed the weight at 2715 lbs. As a check we put it on a scale. With two passengers (total weight about 325 lbs.), a half tank of gas and a few other odds and ends aboard, the car weighed 3075 lbs. This was the way we tested it. For competition this could be cut down by removing the top, radio and heater (the car we used was equipped with the latter accessories). With a standard transmission instead of Power-Glide the weight would be dropped still more—and be better for competition.

While talking about the transmission, perhaps I might pass along a few observations I made in this respect. First, the car we had did have the Power-Glide automatic, but standard and overdrive units are supposed to be available. Roger and I agreed that the ideal setup, other than a four-speed box, would be overdrive. However, the automatic drive was not at all bad.

Down-shifting into low range for corners helped slow the car down and made it easy to power out of bends in very fine style. You can kick-down for an extra burst of passing speed up to about 62 mph—and this kick-down gear really gives you a kick! Starting in low range offers little appreciable advantage over

DRIVER'S REPORT

THE CORVETTE V-8

By KEN FERMOYLE

V-8 engine is 28 pounds lighter than the inline six it replaced. Abundance of chrome makes layout attractive.

drive range, except that you can hold it in low a little longer. With wide-open throttle in drive range, you go into top gear at about 62; about the maximum you can run up to in low range is 68, so there isn't a tremendous amount of difference.

In handling and roadability the Corvette V-8 rates very high. Steering ratio is 16-to-1 and it's very light. In fact, it's hard to understand why it should require the 3¾ turns lock-to-lock this car is set up for. However, the steering and feel of the car was one of its highlights and was a special joy in these days when power steering is coming to be regarded as almost a necessary accessory.

In corners the Corvette felt great. It can be whipped around with ease and remains remarkably flat in the tightest turns. I had a real ball bending it around corners at speed and, when I got back in my own passenger car later, I felt like I was wheeling a truck around by comparison.

The ride is good by sports car standards, rather hard by normal passenger car standards. You bounce a bit more than you would in a stock Chevrolet sedan but this is more than compensated for by the security and stability you feel even at top speed. Roll and sway are practically non-existent. Even when going flat out there is no wander.

Visibility is, of course, terrific with the top down. Even with the top up it's not bad. The rear view mirror on the car I had vibrated a lot, making it difficult to use at high speed. However, there was a side mirror mounted, too, and this was very handy—particularly when driving with the top up.

The top can be put up by one person, but it's a lot quicker and easier with two working. There are no windows, of course; two plexi-glass side curtains lock securely into place on the doors. Frankly, I preferred not to use them unless necessary. Even with them on, the car does leak in a heavy rain. With the top down,

however, you ride in comparative comfort as far as wind is concerned. The wrap-around windshield deflects the wind over the passenger compartment quite success-

The seats are comfortable and roomy. Although designed for only two, three people can ride in it for short distances without too much discomfort—if the two passengers aren't too big. The Corvette isn't meant to be a family car but I took my wife and two small daughters, one four, and the other eight months, for several rides. We even crowded in our full-grown Collie with us for one short hop!

The trunk is large compared to those in most sports cars, but naturally is not as roomy as our regular passenger cars. There seems to be ample space for luggage for two in it, however.

As mentioned earlier, the V-8 engine is basically the stock Chevrolet mill—with added goodies. Displacement is 265 cubic inches and compression is 8-to-1. It has

Corvette instrument grouping places tach to the right of the driver's line of vision. Speedometer is very accurate.

Fermoyle raises Corvette top singlehanded, a fairly easy job—this is not a common characteristic of most sports cars.

Underhood accessibility of the Corvette engine is excellent, since the mechanical arrangement is more compact than most.

CORVETTE V-8

the four-barrel carburetor and dual exhaust system that make up the optional power-pack, plus the special cam. Installation of the compact V-8 in the Corvette is very neat; the engine fits so nicely, in fact, that one suspects that the possibility of using a V-8 was considered when the Corvette was designed. Chrome has been used generously on some of the engine components, rocker covers, racing-type air cleaner, etc., adding to the attractiveness of the engine compartment.

Incidentally, after we finished our acceleration tests, Roger and I made some runs using a PerfOMeter to get an idea of what kind of horsepower was being delivered at the clutch. Roger took the figures home, worked for awhile with his slide rule and came up with a curve showing peak power to be 147 at 4600 rpm. He figured maximum torque to be 215-220 lb.-ft. at about 2800 rpm. These figures are not based on dynamometer tests, of course, but Roger has run many tests using a PerfOMeter and has found it to be a pretty reliable and useful tool for this type of work. At any rate, you can take these figures for what you will.

Appearancewise, how you react to the Corvette depends on your own personal tastes. I must confess that I wasn't too impressed by the lines of this car at first. I found that it grows on you, however, and now I like it very much. The one I had was yellow and I think this is the color that looks best on the car for some reason. The workmanship and finish of the fiberglass body was very good.

We weren't able to run fuel consumption tests, but the mileage seemed to be very good. Driven normally, the Corvette should deliver more than adequate fuel economy. I would estimate very roughly that a full tank of gas should give you a range of from 250 to almost 300 miles, depending on the way you drive.

Whether addition of the V-8 engine—which weighs 28 lbs. less than the inline 6—will hypo Corvette sales remains to be seen. After a fast initial start following introduction, sales of the car sagged. When Ford's Thunderbird appeared it diverted some of the potential market for this type of car. The blazing performance the Corvette now offers should attract more buyers. It will also be interesting to see how it fares in competition now. It could well be that enthusiasts will modify the chassis and brakes to a point where it will show up better in competition than it has in the past with the six-cylinder.

Whatever else happens, one thing is sure: the V-8 engine makes this a far more interesting automobile and has upped performance to a point at least as good as anything in its price class. I certainly enjoyed driving it and I'm sure that anyone else who has a chance to do so will feel the same way. •

CORVETTE

(Continued from page 19)

Corvette (pressurized at 4 psi) is far above normal passenger car standards.

The ignition system is 6 volt, with a special coil, condenser and distributor cam. Voltage reserve is ample for speeds well above 5000 rpm. Standard spark plugs are 14mm AC 44-5, but the AC 43-5 is recommended for continuous high speeds.

As a result of these engine modifications the maximum output has been raised to 150 bhp at 4200 rpm. More power has been developed experimentally, but only at a higher peaking speed, and accompanied by a serious loss in torque. As it is, the bhp gain is 20%, yet torque has also gone up by 11.5%. The net result is a vastly better acceleration curve, and a smooth idle at 475 rpm.

For reasons of wider appeal, a modified Powerglide transmission is used on the Corvette. Mr. Olley says on this: "The use of an automatic transmission has been criticized by those who believe that sports car enthusiasts want nothing but a four speed crash shift. The answer is that the typical sports car enthusiast, like the 'average man', or the square root of minus one, is an imaginary quantity. Also, as the sports car appeals to a wider and wider section of the public, the center of gravity of this theoretical individual is shifting from the austerity of the pioneer towards the luxury of modern ideas . . . there is no need to apologize for the performance of this car with its automatic transmission." That statement, from Chevrolet, should get a rise from 100,000 *Road & Track* readers!

The rear axle is essentially stock, but the housing and pinion gear are special to provide an oil seal and universal joint flange. The open drive shaft is only 36 inches long and check straps are used to prevent too great an angle at full rebound. The spring pads are also different from the stock rubber bushed pin used with the torque tube.

The first Corvette shown at G.M.'s New York Show in January 1953 had a fiberglass body, as is well known. What isn't so well known is that the 1954 production schedule of 10,000 units were to have steel bodies made from Kirksite dies. But, the demand for immediate delivery was so great that it was decided to build 300 Corvettes in 1953, with fiberglass bodies. As experience was gained with the new material, so also did confidence increase. The result was the decision to build the entire contemplated 1954 production in fiberglass, and the Kirksite dies were never cast.

Chevrolet sums up the experiment this way. "What we get for all this is a very usable body, somewhat expensive, costing a little less than a dollar a pound, but of light weight, able to stand up to abuse, which will not rust, will not crumble in collision, will take a paint finish, and is relatively free from drumming noise."

Finally it is worth noting that it is amazing to find a great mass production organization willing and able to step out of its normal role of producing over 500 vehicles an hour, to make 500 specialized vehicles in two weeks. The Corvette is more than just a new sports car. It is all of that, but perhaps more important it heralds an entirely new approach, offers new hope, for the individualist. ●

Corvette . . .

(Continued from page 27)

1955 passenger cars was not applied to the sports car to give the reduced brake dive, easier maintenance and longer life of the ball joints. However, the ball type i.f.s. would have meant an extensive re-design in order to incorporate it—for 1955.

This year we were not "favored" by inclement weather for the purposes of testing, but judging from the number of letters we have received, the average Corvette of 1954 was not notable for its freedom from water leaks during a downpour. There is no reason to believe that the 1955 model will be any better. Our test car was equipped with a fiberglass top which is not a factory-approved extra (made by Plasticon, $225) but it smooths up the car's appearance and is almost instantly removable with the aid of four toggle type clamps.

Externally the Corvette scores heavily because it has well-executed sports car styling. There has been ample criticism of the fiberglass body material employed, but most if not all of this can be traced to the lack of adequate bumpers—a strange complaint to be applied to an American car. The weight-saving advantages of a fiberglass body should appeal to sports car people, and the new V-8 engine weighs 41 lbs less than the 6. However, our test car weighed only 10 lbs less than last year's car, since two tops were carried.

The instrument panel layout of the Corvette commits a cardinal sin by using a very small tachometer and placing it in the center of the panel rather than alongside the speedometer. Real oil-pressure and ammeter gages are a saving grace in this day of warning indicators.

The seats are beautifully done and very comfortable but no provision has been made for seat belts. A large central transmission cover is expected in a sports car, and the Corvette's is typical. Knowing the compactness of a Powerglide transmission unit does raise a question as to why this cover had to be so large, even though there is ample pedal room.

Finally, to divert an avalanche of Technical Correspondence, let us mention that the Chevrolet V-8 engine can be (and has been) installed in last year's Corvette. For that matter, so can many other V-8 engines including Cadillac, Buick and Oldsmobile. However, even the lightest of these 3 (the Buick) adds over 100 lbs to the front end weight.

Touring in a sports car was never like this.

Addison Austin in the Chevrolet Corvette at Thompson has left the Thunderbird far back, beyond the parked car inside the circuit. This, the sharpest bend on the course, demonstrates that the Corvette does not lean unduly.

what would happen to a well-prepared car in serious U.S. competition.

Meanwhile, the sound of Detroit war drums changed in tone and America is told loudly of Chevrolet's stock car success in winning virtually every NASCAR event entered this year. Next comes word of a 1956 Dodge, setting 306 new A.A.A. records on the salt of Bonneville, stressing speed runs of 114 m.p.h. in addition to 31,244 miles of endurance. No sooner said, when a 1956 Chevrolet,

COMPETITION BY CORVETTE

Experiences at Thompson, Watkins Glen and elsewhere establish raceworthiness of Chevrolet's 4·3-litre V8 sports car

IT is with intense interest that your writer watches the complete reversal of American automobile manufacturers' sales policy in regard to competitive events. Chevrolet first introduced the Corvette sports car in 1953 and advertised it as a non-competitive car in which the owner could enjoy merely the "fun of driving". The first Corvette to be delivered on the eastern seaboard of the U.S. was ordered by Briggs Cunningham and it was this car that I tested for a New York motoring magazine. Frankly, the car had many faults, suffering mainly from quite poor cornering adhesive qualities on rough road surfaces and consequently being a far from ideal proposition for the speed-seeking average U.S. motorist. I thoroughly agreed with the factory, thinking that these cars were not intended for racing.

Luckily, I happened to meet the famous Indianapolis "500" race driver, Mauri Rose, at General Motors' remarkable Motorama a few weeks after my experiences with that original six-cylinder Corvette. Mr. Rose is given to extreme

tact but none the less managed to inform me that there was much in store for the U.S. sports car as offered by General Motors, where he is employed as a director-engineer of the Corvette division. Knowing Mr. Rose as a fine sportsman and brilliant driver, I decided thereupon, to follow the Corvette programme most carefully.

By BENJAMIN WEST

I have not been disappointed. And luck again is at my side. A close friend of mine is, of all fortunate combinations, a first line S.C.C.A. competition driver, an owner of a local Chevrolet agency of considerable size, and a man willing to allow me to drive his new specially ordered V8 Corvette to my heart's desire. In fact, the Corvette was ordered by this Mr. Addison W. Austin for the express purpose of demonstrating to ourselves and AUTOSPORT readers exactly

driven by Zorra Duntov, set production car records in climbing Pike's Peak, a feat advertised on TV, by folk singer Burl Ives, and in every major U.S. newspaper and magazine . . . all before the car was publicly shown. And a beehive of activity is Ford's new proving ground, now being rushed to completion at the foot of that famous Pike's Peak run. The next item should be—factory-prepared teams at Sebring, Le Mans, and onwards.

So much for trends "Mercedes". . . . Let's get to the facts on our particular Corvette. Ordered 1st June, the car finally arrived 22nd July. This delay was due, no doubt, to strict stipulations by Mr. Austin to omit "luxury" equipment. Almost all Corvettes come from their special assembly line burdened with extras, hence a wait is standard if one orders "no radio, heater, white wall tyres, etc." Austin forgot to say "no windshield water squirt equipment," so this was factory fitted. It did not weigh enough to remove, however.

In stunning red, the car body lines

WELL-TAPED: For racing purposes the headlights and various body joins on the Corvette were carefully taped-up. As a production American sports car, the Chevrolet attracted many fans before the start of the Thompson meeting.

miles, and came in with a stock left front "shoe" completely gone through to the casing fabric—and was subsequently refitted with the best Pirellis.) The new Corvette does howl a bit on sharp, low speed bends, as do the best Mercedes of passenger type. But it has been my experience that such tyre noise at polite speeds can mean excellent traction at full tilt if the geometry and so on are right. And it is thus with the Corvette.

The Corvette 16:1 steering requires 3¼ swings lock to lock, is pleasantly light and just right for the novice driver who is encountering a helm system somewhat better than the 20:1 sort prevalent on most of our stock vehicles, including the Thunderbird. Note particularly that this vastly improved Corvette does not have ball-joint suspension (standard on all other 1955 Chevrolets) but uses an adaptation of their 1954 stock car A arms i.f.s. design. A further note is that the new V8 engine weighs at least 100 pounds less than the old 6. And some careful parts-catalogue searching tells that Corvette aero type dampers are not stock passenger items.

Austin's first competitive trial of the car was to have been a stiff hill-climb event up Mount Washington, New Hampshire. Heavy rains made mess of the road and the cars were offered an acceleration trial on a nearby airport runway instead. This consisted of about a 1¼-mile sprint from standstill to a pylon marker and return. The Corvette ran against many Jag. 140Ms and placed second in its class following a 120M (fitted with special gears) by two seconds. Considering that Austin made a rather wide tour in rounding the marker on his first run, this performance seemed promising.

Next came a race at Thompson which showed how not to race-start a Corvette. One must realize that, in order to compete with cars having conventional 4-speed boxes, the GM two-ratio "auto-

were virtually unchanged since the pioneer o.h.v. six. But it was very apparent that much development has been carried out by the fibreglass division of G.M. Gone entirely were the wavy surface faults found in all early Corvettes. The door latches and trunk fastenings were in good alignment and stayed so through some very rugged going. The lacquer was of excellent quality and well sprayed on, as some severe flying stone tests were to show. As usual, the handsome white and red leather-plastic upholstery was neatly installed and of unusually fine quality. Comfortwise, the cockpit and its two individual seats are ideal for man-sized pilots, Austin tipping the scales at some 210 pounds.

Seat belts were installed impromptu, no deliberate provision having been made for such items. As there is no side contouring of the seat base cushions to secure one's thighs, a wide belt is in order, as is a facia grip for the passenger.

The windscreen proved impossible to remove quickly, in fact requiring almost an hour of shop work. So all events were entered with this "wind brake" in effect. As the car does quite well at speeds over the century, it seems not out of place to reckon Austin one position better for each race run, had a race screen been fitted. But I must write this secretly, and know what Austin will remark upon reading.

The o.h.v., 4,344 c.c. V8 stock (four-throat carburetter and special cam) engine was found in perfect tune upon delivery. Austin's own excellent shop test equipment verified our ears and spine sensations after trial runs. A slight resetting of the float level was required after some 3,000 miles and several events, and the factory specified sparking plugs (A.C. 43-5s) were too cold for modest motoring. Going to A.C. 44-5s cured such

minor fouling and it was later proved that the car would race on either type plugs. When the car was well run in, the 43-5s were left in place for all usage. Further changes were to Firestone Champion 6.70 x 15 tyres *with tubes*. (This grade tyre is the most inexpensive Firestone, chosen by many drivers "who know" for the reason that such shoes have less synthetic rubber content in the tread mixture and consequently provide superior adhesive qualities. They wear out sooner, but grip better while they last.)

My own first trial of the car proved that the Corvette engineering staff have indeed succeeded in improving the road-holding of the V8. True, the car does not have the soft ride of its American competitor, the Ford Thunderbird, but neither does it break away on all four wheels at low speeds with consequent appalling tyre wear. (A Thunderbird raced at Thompson early in the season made the required 10 laps, about 15

SPECIFICATION OF THE CORVETTE

Car Tested: Chevrolet Corvette sports 2-seater. Price $3,200 delivered (approx.).

Engine: V8, 3¾ ins. x 3 ins. bore and stroke, 235.5 cu. ins. (4,344 c.c.). Pushrods to overhead valves. 8:1 comp. ratio. 195 developed b.h.p. at 4,200 r.p.m. Carter 4 throat carburetter, automatic choke. Delco Remy coil and distributor.

Transmission: Powerglide automatic type, reverse and bottom gears are planetary top direct, all through torque converter. Ratios: top, 3.55; low, 6.46; low plus converter, 13.57. Central control lever. Hotchkiss drive, semi-floating hypoid gear rear axle.

Chassis: Box section steel frame passing above rear axle. I.f.s. by wishbones and helical springs with rack and pinion steering. Semi-elliptic rear springs. Telescopic type dampers. Bolt-on, pierced disc wheels. 6.70 x 15 tubeless tyres. Bendix hydraulic brakes, 11 ins. drums, 2 ins. F., 1½ ins. R. width.

Equipment: 12 volt Delco lights and starting, speedometer, rev. counter, ammeter, water temperature, oil pressure, fuel level gauges. Self-parking wipers. Optional: radio, heater, demister, water squirt screen clearer, WW tyres, directionals.

Turning Circle: 43 ft. to left, 39 ft. to right. Weight, 2,800 lb. at kerb. 48 per cent. load on rear. Ground clearance, 6½ ins.

Performance: Maximum speed, 123 m.p.h. Speeds in gears, 62 m.p.h. is shiftpoint for low to top in HI range setting of control lever. Speeds to 76 m.p.h. were obtained by use of LO (LO may be safely engaged at such speeds for engine brake by use of "double clutch method" wherein control is pulled into neutral while engine is revved up). Acceleration (approximate average taken over three-month period of tests), 0-30 m.p.h. 3.1 secs., 0-40 m.p.h. 4.2 secs., 0-50 m.p.h. 6.1 secs., 0-60 m.p.h. 8.5 secs., 0-70 m.p.h. 11 secs., 0-80 m.p.h. 14.1 secs., 0-90 m.p.h. 18.5 secs., 0-100 m.p.h. 24.5 secs. Standing quarter-mile, 16 secs.

Fuel Consumption: Driven hard, 16 m.p.g. Average 20 m.p.g.

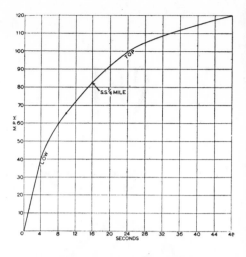

Acceleration Graph

"matic" gearbox requires special techniques. One trick is starting. Analyse a low gear coupled with converter giving a 13.57 bottom gear effect, with final drive 3.55 : 1, torque at 3,000 r.p.m. rated 260 ft./lbs. and race weight, with driver, of approximately 3,000 lbs. Being remarkably sturdy, the "Powerglide" box will withstand revving to some 3,000 r.p.m. and whipping into low range at standstill. On road surfaces with excellent adhesion this can whisk the car away neatly. The start line at Thompson resulted in some of the most magnificent wheelspin seen in years. A lesson was learned, but the only other U.S.-built entry, a lone 'Bird, was easily led to the finish.

We then set sights for the big race at Watkins Glen, and found over 20 140MC "Jags." sharing the class with no Thunderbirds entered. Starting (properly) in 10th row, Austin easily held position with a Mercedes 300SL directly astern, and overtook two of the Jaguars before entering the first bend. Here was a hell-for-leather event, in which the Corvette hounded many excellent drivers in top-tuned cars and showed 123 m.p.h. on the straight. The technique of passing "Jags." was by now well established and is as follows. Hold the low gear direct (6.46) up to around 6,000 r.p.m. and listen for the "Jag." ahead to change up from second to third (or watch his smoke if you like). As the "Jag." changes, whip into high ratio (3.55) with full throttle and pull ahead if all goes well. Once leading, the Corvette will hold its own through any bend . . . *if* the brakes are not cooking.

But consider the day's warmth at this last Watkins Glen. The tarmac on the bend in front of the grandstand was melting to a point where the flag marshal soon stuck his slow flag deeply into the road surface and any giddy young pilots who insisted on speed at such points provided unpleasant thrills on each lap. Such experts as Sherwood Johnston, overall winner in Cunningham's D Jaguar, were very content to motor through much of this event . . . Bill Lloyd remarking that his Maserati would have done better in a swamp. The Corvette brakes were factory-fitted Delco and were proving that passenger car equipment has its limits. Austin was making do with his expert downshifting of the Powerglide and an "occasional"

brake pedal. The Corvette eventually took two rapid bends in very far-reaching fashion and lost a place or two so doing. Finishing position was 10th overall, and seventh in class. The best Jag. was third in the class and it can be mentioned that the 300SL "Merc." passed Austin finally at the 10th lap when the Corvette brakes were very sad indeed.

Hereafter, the stock brake linings were removed and the 158 square inches shoe area relined with Raybestos heavy duty. The brake efficiency improved enormously and no further trouble was encountered. It is calculated that the Corvette brakes have 109 square inches to the ton . . . more than adequate for all ordinary usage. The safe tyre loading is theoretically 900 lb. above kerb weight, and the car weight figures 13.71 lb. per h.p. (The Thunderbird is listed 425 lb. tyre loading, 15.55 lb./h.p.) Following Watkins Glen came an S.C.C.A. event at Thompson, in which the Corvette took third place behind two beautifully piloted Jag. 140MCs. Another big time race was entered at Hagerstown, Maryland, in which the Austin entry was awarded "Best Performance in a U.S. car" and again proved itself able to catch other class runners on the long runways. Ending up the season, Austin ran once more at Thompson and won first in class, third overall. A Porsche Spyder 550 was first, an Austin-Healey 100S was second, and a hurried 300SL spun out after Austin rode its tail-lights for some laps. Behind Austin came a Jaguar 120M, an Austin-Healey 100, one or two 140 Jaguars, and a Lotus Mark 9 which did not last to finish. Thus ended the season.

Before closing this review some mention should be made of the everyday features offered by Corvettes. The unpadded facia is still grievously laid out with a much-too-small tachometer well out of easy eye scan at panel centre, and the oil pressure dial virtually forgotten at extreme right of the horizontal cluster. Perhaps we should be grateful that it *is* a dial with needle and not a light.

Speaking of lights, one can never, never drive off in a Corvette without releasing the hand-brake, as a dazzling ruby diamond lamp virtually blinds the eyes in mid-day as warning. This startling device is nicely located dead ahead

of the driver, above the steering column.

Rather like old-time vehicles of sport, one finds the glove compartments to be in the windowless doors, that the nylon and Plexiglass side curtains are not ideal for side vision, that the nylon top rubs one's cap busily on slight bumps, and that the vision line upwards ahead is sharply cut off by said hood. This completely disappearing top may well be called a one-man affair . . . for only the man who has fully practised putting it up can manage the job neatly. The very tidy trunk space must be cleared if one must seek tools or the spare wheel, and the deeply recessed licence plate oft becomes conveniently obscured behind its plastic window by misting, mud or dust . . . to the baffled constabularies' deep concern.

Much has been said concerning the disadvantages and advantages of fibreglass bodyshells, but few actually know what it costs in time and money should one be shattered . . . and *shattered* is exactly what happens. One case occurred where an owner creamed the entire side of his Corvette from the door rearwards. A factory team of three was required by the local dealer to fix things up and the job took a total of three weeks, counting waiting time. The bill rendered was some $900 and the owner's insurance company took loud exception, saying that the panelbeating of ordinary metalwork in similar mishaps would have totalled under $200. The factory was sorry but could do nothing. That was the price of fibreglass repair.

I think the much rumoured-about 1956 Corvettes will doubtless turn out fine cars minus many of these minor defects, and that fibreglass repair charges will be lowered. One thing I know for sure. The 1956 Powerpack V8 four door pillarless salon Chevrolet has acceleration *phenomenal*, due to a 9.2 compression ratio, improved breathing, and a slightly altered cam, gaining smoothness throughout the power range. This atomic-like engine, dropped into a Corvette, should put it well ahead of many very expensive creations and bring the American sportsman a truly good sports car. Let's all pray that the new GM pride and joy is just that and not a beast burdened under automatic window raisers and useless chrome adornments. If Mr. Rose has his way our prayers will be answered.

SCI

ROAD TEST:

Chevrolet

Here the author takes a long, fast turn at 60 mph. Note that the rear dips more than front, giving car an understeer effect. Stiffer shocks and springs on the back end would add stability on bends.

BY KARL LUDVIGSEN

CHANCES are that by the time you read this the '56 Corvette will have made a profound impression on the whole sports car world, and after having had one under me for a couple of days I will be the last to be surprised. This very early production model showed a willingness and ability to be driven fast and hard under almost all conditions and demonstrated an even greater potential for competitive use. In my opinion, the Corvette as it stands is fully as much a dual-purpose machine as the

Although automatically raised and lowered, the top's back window has to be pulled down by hand. This is no problem since the well fitted top clamps down quickly sans fuss.

Photos by Don Typond

Cruising at 85, the Corvette produces wind noise over top. However, at such speeds there's bound to be wind disturbance on any car.

Corvette

The Halibrand type knock-offs look like the McCoy, but are actually wheel discs. The real thing is being planned as possible optional equipment.

stock Jaguar, Triumph, or Austin-Healey. Without qualification, General Motors is now building a sports car.

Unfortunately, at this writing accurate information both on the Corvette itself and on their future plans is not available, and the air is rife with rumor. SCI's test car was chassis #1002, and was obtained from the Chevrolet Motor Division through the combined efforts of Shelly Spindel and Alvin Schwartz Chevrolet of Brooklyn, N. Y. Finished in two-tone turquoise with a matching hard top and a white convertible top, it was a real traffic-stopper, and was specifically destined to make a New York TV appearance. As such, it had the full range of options, including whitewalls, the hard top, power windows, radio, heater and windshield washer. To our joy it had the close-ratio stick shift, but less happily had the higher, 3.27:1 rear end ratio. It was, all in all, a lot of car and I regret that at this time Chevrolet was not ready to discuss prices. There is little question, though, that it is to be competitive with the Thunderbird.

Now that the "dual-purpose" claim has been made, it should be backed up. Those accustomed to GM products may tend to take the creature comforts for granted, but any owner of an older Corvette will readily testify that those cars could be uninhabitable at times. Much effort has been expended to rectify this, and it has paid off in full.

Entry and exit over the wide sill on the passenger side is easy, for a sports car, but as the driver slides under the steering wheel he becomes aware of one of the car's few major faults. While it is handsome, and provided with more than enough finger ribbing, the wheel is too close to the driver and is non-adjustable. Ex-Jag drivers may find the position natural, but I personally felt that more arm room would be useful, particularly for competition. You also sit close enough to the door for the integral arm rest to be in the way.

The seats themselves are very handsome, and very deceptive. They look like a true bucket type, and the seat bottoms are comfortable enough, but the backs are bolt upright and provide no lateral support for the torso. Adjustment of rake and a more definite "bucket" would improve

them greatly and would obviate a certain amount of fatigue that now occurs. Fore-and-aft adjustment is not extensive, there being just enough room for a six-footer. Leg room is excellent; the left foot can roam about under the suspended pedals, and the brake and throttle are well-placed for heel-and-toe downshifting.

Headroom is also at the bare minimum for six feet of height, with slightly more room under the soft top. In general, the Corvette has very little interior room for such a large car, and it seems that neither GM nor Ford have yet completely solved the sports car seating problem.

Driving the Corvette with the top down is very pleasant, the windshield giving good protection to the top and side. You sit high enough to rest your elbow comfortably on the door, if so inclined. The power windows are handy and reliable, but the power-operated top qualifies as the most fascinating mechanism I have seen on any car. The lid rises, the top emerges, and the lid closes again as the control button is pressed. You must then pull down and clamp the back window section by hand, and close two front latches. It's all very easy, and the finished product is attractive and tight. It can be stowed away just as simply.

The hard top is also easy to install, having two clamps at the front and three bolts and two locating dowels at the rear. It is well finished and padded, and provides unobstructed vision. Light and easy to transport, the top's main fault is arbitrary sealing at the sides of the rear deck.

Instrument panel layout is identical to last year's cars, and has many of the same faults. All the secondary instruments, including the tachometer, are very difficult to read

Twin four-barrel carburetors squat on power plant ready to help deliver 225 bhp at 5200 rpm. At low speeds, only rear carburetor functions. BELOW—Hood raises from rear, reducing possible lifting at high speed. Engine compartment is more accessible for shop work.

A lack of bumpers at the rear will make any Corvette driver over-cautious when backing. Exhaust tubes are in for abuse.

SPECIFICATIONS
CHEVROLET CORVETTE

ENGINE

Cylinders	V8
Bore and stroke	3.75 in x 3.00 in (95 mm x 76 mm)
Displacement	265 cu in (4340 cc)
Compression ration	9.25:1
Max. horsepower	225 bhp @ 5200 rpm
Max. torque	270 lb ft @ 3600 rpm
Max. b.m.e.p.	154 psi

CHASSIS

Wheelbase	102 in
Front track	57 in
Rear track	59 in
Curb weight	2980 lbs
Front/rear distribution	52/48
Test weight	3250 lbs
Turns lock to lock	3.6

Gear ratios:

Gear	Standard	Optional
3rd	3.55	3.27
2nd	4.65	4.28
1st	7.84	7.22
Rev	7.84	7.22

Tire size	6.70 x 15
Brake lining area	158.0 sq in
Fuel capacity	17 gal

PERFORMANCE

TEST CONDITIONS

40°F, light wind, dry concrete surface at sea level.

SPEEDS IN GEARS

Gear	True mph	(Car) mph
1st	64	(60)
2nd	108	(102)
3rd	118.5	(110)
Best run	120.0	

ACCELERATION

Range	Time, Seconds	Gears Used
0-30	3.4	1st
0-40	4.6	"
0-50	6.0	"
0-60	7.5	"
0-70	10.0	1st, 2nd
0-80	12.5	" "
0-90	15.8	" "
0-100	19.3	" "
50-70	4.5	2nd
50-70	5.8	3rd
60-80	4.7	2nd
60-80	7.0	3rd
Standing ¼ mile	15.9	1st, 2nd
Speed at end of quarter	91 mph	

FUEL CONSUMPTION

Hard driving	12 mpg (tank mileage)

Instruments are well balanced for eye-appeal, but not practical. Reading them at any speed over forty is difficult. Note simple design of steering wheel.

Small luggage compartment makes long trips restrictive. Jack fits inside spare to conserve space. Larger trunk would destroy line, increase weight.

View shows sleekness of new Corvette. Except for phony air-scoops and knock-off type discs, the car is functional in design.

Fully automatic, the top slips out of the well after the lid raises. Convenience of automation makes added weight of unit bearable.

Corvette interior is well appointed, with leg room for the six-footers. Wrap-around windshield makes getting in and out a bit awkward.

at the bottom of the dash, even if you can take your eyes from the road long enough to find them. The speedometer is well-placed, but quick correlation between the numerals and the divisions is impossible, as they are on different planes. Dial lighting is very good, with rheostat control, and the interior lights are perfect for rallying, being placed under the cowl.

Other interior shortcomings are the dearth of storage space, save for the between-seat compartment, and a conflict between the heater and the passenger's feet. The view forward is very impressive, and clever psychologically. The hood bulges, long fender lines, and cowl vents (which, incidentally, can easily be made functional for dry climates) combine to give an impression of great forcefulness. Vision over this snout is adequate, but not outstanding. The heater and defroster are well up to their jobs,

and the only other irritant might be a very awkward and stiff interior door control.

In spite of numerous open car details, the passengers can be kept warm and dry, and can set their own climate at a literal touch of a button. I can imagine no greater contrast than between this and the forced exposure of the gutty old J2 Cadillac Allard, but the fact is that such an Allard in stock trim would be left behind at the quarter by this incredible Corvette! The figures speak eloquently for themselves, and with the lower 3.55:1 ratio things should happen even more rapidly. As a matter of fact, our speedometer was so very slow that it probably was geared for use with that ratio. Also, the engine was nothing like wound out at the top end, and the lower gearing would probably improve top speed by five to seven miles per hour.

SCI Road Test: Corvette

Precision balancing after assembly may have accounted for the clean, smooth running of the engine, and its ability to rev freely to around 5500. For about the first half inch of throttle travel only the rear one of the two four-barrel carburetors is working to prevent overcarburetion at low speeds. When the front quad cuts in the previously unobtrusive exhaust note sharpens and the car starts to move. When backing off at higher speeds there is a not unappealing rap from the duals. Idling is at 1000 rpm when the automatic choke is working and 600 rpm when warm, and the powerplant is tractable enough to lug down to a 12 mph in high.

Featuring special cooling and nine coils instead of the old diaphragm spring, the clutch took a lot of punishment without complaint. It is not easy to get a potent car off the mark with such very high gearing, and this component took the brunt of the effort without signs of heating or slippage. The gearbox wins similar praise for its well-chosen ratios and effective synchromesh. Shifting linkage is smooth and direct, the heavy-knobbed lever being spring-loaded to the right-hand side of the conventional "H" pattern. The synchro can be beaten by a very quick move from first to second, but the movement between the two top gears is impeccable. Synchromesh on low would be a useful boon, but a noiseless downshift can be made by double-clutching.

Due to the high ratios, the standard-shift Corvette is not really at home in town, and Powerglide might be better for urban use. Out on the road, though, as second gear takes over from first at around sixty and keeps the seat in your back 'til over a hundred, you learn what this car was made for. Cruising is effortless at 85 or 90, though with enough wind noise over the soft top to render the radio unintelligible.

It is in the handling department in particular that the Corvette proves itself the only true American production sports car. The steering is far from perfect but it is fast enough to allow right angles to be taken without removing the hands from the wheel, and this virtue will make up for many vices. The latter include an inch and a half of play, beyond which a strong caster action gives the wheel a springy feel. This little "no-man's-land" in the middle causes some trepidation in tight spots. Once the wheel has been set for a bend, and the car has assumed an initial roll angle, the steering and throttle response are fast and consistent enough to allow very precise control.

Like most American cars this Chevrolet is a very strong understeerer, and requires a lot of helm to keep it on line in a bend. The stock rear end damping is a little weak; too much so to make a full-blooded drift a stable proposition. Cornering speeds and behavior were markedly improved by tire pressure five psi higher than the standard of 25 psi front and 27 psi rear. Raised pressures plus stiffer rear shocks could combine with an already broad track, good weight distribution, and low center of gravity to make the Corvette a real fiend on corners. These criticisms, it will be noted, are minor, and apply equally to many imported machines.

Of course, tire squeal is not entirely absent during these high-speed direction changes, but the car stays in the corner so there can be no real complaints. The Corvette is at its best on a winding open road, and, like the Jaguar, is dramatic but uncomfortable on a twisty back lane. The test car would have been much handier there if the driver had had more arm room and the optional seat belts. He tends to be thrown around more than necessary, but is not as conscious of the car's roll angle as is the passenger.

Brakes are still by far the weakest link, and it must be admitted that they faded almost into oblivion during the performance tests. They recovered very quickly, though, and pulled the heavy car up with a minimum of slewing even when very hot. I sincerely feel that the substitution of harder Moraine linings or some of the foreign competition brands will improve high-temperature durability and perhaps modify the present spongy feel of the pedal. No power booster was fitted, and required pedal pressure was on the high side.

Very sensibly for a high speed car, the hood is hinged from the front, and opens well out of the way. The battery and brake master cylinder are easy to reach, and the small air cleaners ease access to the engine as a whole. Most awkward feature is the shielding for the ignition wiring, necessary to eliminate radio interference in a Fiber-glas body. Wingnuts quickly free these shields and bare the double-breaker distributor and all but the two left front spark plugs, which are tucked in behind the steering box.

The hydraulic system for the top mechanism is powered by a separate electric motor, which allows operation with the engine off and avoids direct absorption of any engine power. Individual motors operate the door windows.

Well finished and fitted, the trunk is usefully large for a sports car. All luggage must be removed to extricate the spare from its wooden-lidded compartment, which also houses the jack. One carrying feature of many imports that is missed in the Corvette is that handy space right behind the seats for coats, hats, lunches and other items that you don't want to store in the trunk. In the Corvette you either live with them or lock them away.

In almost every respect, the 1956 Corvette is a very satisfying car on the highway, and supplements astonishing performance with a high level of road-holding. Even as it stands, power equipment and all, it has become a serious competitor for Jaguar in Production Class C, and this is by no means General Motors' highest goal. In international events this year the car will be equipped with an optional cam providing 250 bhp at the sacrifice of present low-end smoothness. Also on the fire for either this or next year are engine boosts to 275 bhp, extensive use of light alloy in both body and chassis, and the development of suitable disc brakes by GM's Moraine Division.

It seems likely that the standard Corvettes will remain much as they are, with work on the competition versions proceeding simultaneously as has been the case with Jaguar and their C and D models. Another two or three years could probably see a racing Corvette with as many standard parts as the D retains from the Jaguar line, shrouded in advanced coupe bodywork. GM will learn an incalculable amount from these cars, much of which will be passed on to the standard Corvette and to the passenger car. They've already learned quite a lot, as a matter of fact, most of which shows up in the all-around excellence of the 1956 Corvette.   #

DRIVING AROUND

with WALT WORON

'56 THUNDERBIRD AND CORVETTE ROAD TEST

photos by Bob D'Olivo

THE ANNOUNCEMENT BY CHEVROLET that the '56 Corvette would have more power, wind-up windows, and better weatherproofing has, among other things, served to add still more fuel to an old duel. Where the Corvette may not have competed on across-the-board terms with the Thunderbird, the scales are now more evenly balanced. But don't get the idea that Ford has been lulled into a no-progress policy by their sales leadership with the Thunderbird; the No. 1 sales position is hard to come by and is jealously guarded.

To give the best possible comparison between these 2 Detroit-based "sports cars" we thought it best to drive the Thunderbird and Corvette side by side. We wanted the cars to be as alike as possible, but our plans didn't work out quite right: the T-Bird had more initial break-in mileage, which was partially compensated for by its also having power steering and the standard power brakes. It came with the standard plastic top and no soft top, so we (one person can't lift it off without marring the finish) took the top off and then kept both tops down during all testing.

Test crew stops at Mt. Wilson to discuss handling of rival cars

Trunk space is somewhat greater in the Thunderbird, at left, but the continental wheel gets in the way. Compartment is much deeper than the Corvette's

Corvette trunk has flat floor with spare tire that is awkward to remove without bumping your head. Despite easy access, there isn't much room

With some prior acclimation to the 2 cars under our belts, 3 of us (Paul Sorber, our new staff member, and Bob D'Olivo, our ace photographer, and I) climbed into the cars before dawn one day and rode off to our desert test site. Alternating between the 2 cars we followed a route that led us thru traffic, over a winding mountain road to the top of 5710-foot Mt. Wilson, then dropped down onto the 2000-foot flatlands of the Mojave Desert. Thru the mountains we were pleased that the heaters worked as well as they did; with tops down we might have otherwise chilled ourselves into going back for the T-Bird's top.

Behind the Wheels the 1st Time

Our 1st reactions to the 2 cars, of course, were those on getting in and out. They are pretty much alike in this respect, with the wraparound support cutting into your kneeroom as you snake in under the wheel. With the top up, it becomes more difficult, for you have to bend down, throw in a leg, duck to miss the top, scoot under the wheel and again avoid the wraparound with your left knee. You should be under-6-foot tall and like setting-up exercises if you'll be driving either car much with the top up.

Once you get in the T-Bird, you'll find the seat is well-padded and comfortable, even for a long trip. On this particular T-Bird the seat rose, lowered, slid forward and backward by electrical power at the touch of a finger control on the door. Within a back-and-forth range of 3 inches, you can adjust the low-set wheel to your liking. Headroom, legroom, and shoulder room are good, but not exceptional.

The Corvette's seat is firmly padded and fits your back contour snugger than the T-Bird because of its semi-bucket shape. Each seat manually adjusts forward and backward, allowing you slightly less legroom than the T-Bird. You're also closer to your passenger, with less shoulder room, but you don't rub against each other. The non-adjustable racing-type, plastic-covered wheel sits close to you and is fairly high.

The T-Bird's instrument panel setup appears to have been thought out with more concern for driver seeability, what with the semi-circular speedometer high on the crash-padded panel, the tach close by and to the left, and the fuel and water temperature gauge below the speedometer.

The Corvette's speedometer, in its above-the-column position, is legible, but the position of the smaller tachometer in the center of the panel makes it almost useless. To see the fuel and water temperature gauges, you have to take your eyes well off the road. The advantage of having oil pressure and ammeter *gauges* instead of warning lights is somewhat lessened by their location on the far side of the centrally located tachometer.

Glove compartments are about a toss-up: the smallish T-Bird's compartment is a far right reach for the driver; the Corvette's upright box, in the center between the seats, is not useful except for the few things you can stack in it.

Chevrolet seems to have come closer to curing windshield distortion, tho some was noticed on the Corvette, the amount in the T-Bird was more annoying. Possibly because of our being closer to the windshield, there seemed to be even more distortion than on Ford sedans. Except for that complaint, and the bubble on the hood of the T-Bird, the cars have equal forward vision. Naturally, with tops down, all-around vision is excellent, marred only by the T-Bird's swivel-type rear view mirror, which can be pushed around to where it doesn't get in the way of forward vision. Glare caused by the blazing sun was noted only occasionally from the T-Bird's spokes. Driving into the sun we praised Ford's foresight in providing narrow, padded visors, and complained about the Corvette's lack of them.

Taking Them Thru Traffic

Our test Thunderbird was more of an in-town car because of its power steering, but if you're of a mind to taint the Corvette's attempt at simon-pure sports car design, you can have it equipped with power steering too. The stiffer steering of the Corvette is one of the features I like about it, tho I dislike winding the wheel 3¾ turns to make a U-turn. Many undoubtedly prefer the driving ease (with a surprising amount of road feel) that the T-Bird's power steering gives it.

Whipping in and out of tight traffic situations, the cars do equally well. Unlike the feeling you get in many small foreign sports cars, you aren't domineered by the big Detroit bullies. The Corvette and Thunderbird are not as small as most sports cars, being little less in width and only a few feet shorter in overall length than their sedan counterparts.

Driving either car in traffic can't be termed an enjoyable experience, for you should have room in front of you to occasionally tromp down hard on the throttle. Not only is this dangerous in town, it'll cause a screech of rubber and possibly more than a raised eyebrow from the local gendarmes. It's more practical to wait until you get to open stretches where it's legally and safely possible to succumb to the urge of getting pushed back in your seat.

How They Go

It took quite a bit of experimenting by all of us to arrive at the best possible shift method for the utmost acceleration. More experimentation, as you would do with a Corvette or T-Bird if it were yours, might possibly trim some time off the figures we got. Those shown in the table indicate the most we could get out of these particular cars using this procedure: revving to 1500 rpm in LOW, holding the car back with the foot brake, then suddenly releasing it and at the same moment stomping the throttle, shifting to DRIVE at 4000 rpm in the T-Bird, and at 5500 rpm in the Corvette. By this method we shaved almost a full second off the 0 to 60 times with the T-Bird using just DRIVE, while we didn't improve the Corvette's time at all. In either car, DRIVE will obviously suffice for normal driving.

From scratch the T-Bird surges ahead, but 2 shifts (from LOW range to intermediate to high) against one (from LOW to DRIVE) for the Corvette allows the latter to catch and barely nose out the T-Bird at the quarter-mile mark. In the passing speed ranges, the Corvette was the Thunderbird's master, even when we tried a manual upshift from LOW to intermediate at 3800-4000 rpm instead of the normal 3400, and higher rpms than the normal upshift at 3800 from intermediate to high. Valves float in the Thunderbird at 4400, not until much over 5600 in the Corvette.

It's a surprising, but undeniably true, fact that neither our test '56 Corvette or Thunderbird had better acceleration across the board than its '55 counterpart. From a standing start neither of them gets off the mark as quick, apparently because of a loading up of the engine by over-carburetion, a characteristic common to most 4-barrel-carbureted engines. When the engines clean out, they make up for some of the time they've lost; thus they get to the quarter-mile quicker, tho they're not going so fast. In high-speed passing the '56 Corvette is faster than the earlier model, but not so the T-Bird. With both '56 cars it could have been a matter of lesser tune, or perhaps the '55s were hotter cars—cars that were made to run like clockwork by each factory's technicians.

The floor-position shift on both Corvette and T-Bird seems quite natural after driving sports cars, which was probably the thinking in placing them there. Both quadrants are well marked; the T-Bird's is lighted at night, tho without driving both cars intermittently as we did, there's not much to confuse you. In the Corvette you can shift from L to D and from D to L with no strain and can't accidentally shift to R because you have to consciously press the lever to the left side and push all the way forward. The T-Bird has an added safety factor in that a knob on top of the lever must be pressed down to allow you to go from D (or N) to R. Unfortunately, this latch permits you to overshift into N when holding the lever in L and manually upshifting to D in trying to get better acceleration times. A modification could be made that would prevent you from going into N without pressing down the button.

An advantage the position of the T-Bird's lever has over the Corvette's is that you can rest your leg against it, at least until it gets too warm. In the Corvette, your throttle foot gets tired because you naturally rest it against the transmission hump, and since the throttle is straight up and down, you're pressing on it with only the ball of your foot. The T-Bird's lever jumped quite a bit on rough roads and vibrated some even on level roads, like the engine mounts were loose. Upshifts and downshifts were quite smooth in both cars.

During these acceleration runs, neither engine detonated and hot starts were easily made. Cold-morning starts were usually quick in the Corvette and took a little cranking in the T-Bird. Neither car heated up, or even got up to 180°F.

Acceleration runs, and mountain driving, always bring out the shortcomings of the brakes, if any. Both systems were quite responsive and could be easily applied with left or right foot. There was some brake fade in the T-Bird, with quick recovery.

Who's Tops in Roadability?

The general feel of the Thunderbird is unlike what you might expect from the car's size and appearance. Thru turns it leans considerably, but after it reaches its maximum point of lean, it settles down and takes the corner quite well. When it breaks loose, which it does after an initial 4-wheel drift, it takes considerable wheel correction and more power to pull out. Despite power steering, it retains a good feel of the road, enough to generally keep you out of trouble.

The Corvette, on the other hand, feels more like a sports car, with more steadiness and not as much apparent lean. The complaint leveled at it in cornering can't be laid to the suspension, which is good and firm, but rather at the carburetors, which starved the engine on a hard left turn; the right bank gets its share, but not the left one. This generally happens about midway in the turn, where you really need it. On right turns it was not quite as bad. The same was noted on the Corvettes at Sebring, except that they starved out in either direction.

When the Corvette's rear end does break loose, it's easier to correct than the T-Bird, tho there are still too many turns from lock to lock for a "sports car." With just one less turn, making it 2¾ lock to lock, you could get thru most turns without changing your grip on the wheel.

To really compare the cornering abilities of both cars, we took them thru the same posted 20-mph right angle (to the right) at 40-45 mph. To compensate for any driver familiarity or error, Sorber and I switched between the 2 cars. For both of us the Corvette stuck in the groove exceedingly well, while the T-Bird drifted across the road, finally breaking loose and several times going off the asphalt.

The Corvette and T-Bird alike have a good sense of direction on perfectly flat, or even crowned, roads. When each leaves the asphalt there is just a slight whipping. Hard frontal and side wind gusts had little effect on either car. Stiffer shocks on the T-Bird would be welcomed by drivers who push their cars more, tho it would stiffen the ride. The wallowing at extremely high speeds (90 and above) makes it somewhat uncomfortable for driving; at lower speeds there's little to concern you. The difference between the 2 cars seems to be in the shocks, for the spring rates of both cars are quite similar.

On choppy asphalt you'll get some wheel vibration in both cars, but you won't hear nor feel any thud in the column. There's no tendency to swap ends on dirt washboard.

How They Compare in Ride

The ride of the T-Bird is definitely softer. The Corvette's ride is more prone to transmit road noises to the driver and

At the same position in the curve, and at identical speeds, the Corvette's better cornering shows up. Thunderbird's greater lean in corners could stand improvement

Dual quad setup dom nates Corvette's somew at roomier rnder-bood compartment

Thunderbird's engine, hampered with power equipment, is no direct comparison

passenger. The T-Bird has a tendency to "float" over dips and bumps, which is comfortable at low speeds and not as likable at higher speeds.

Both cars bottom on intersection drainage dips if they're driven over at 30 mph or above. After a dip of this type the Corvette recovers its composure quicker. Each had a considerable number of body rattles, while the Corvette also had a vigorous cowl shake on rough roads.

The individual bucket seat of the Corvette is more comfortable for one passenger, but the T-Bird has the advantage of carrying an emergency 2nd passenger in the middle, if he (or she) doesn't mind the transmission hump. The armrest of the Corvette is positioned somewhat better for the passenger, tho with either car it's pleasanter to rest your arm on the doorsill; of course, this isn't the safest practice.

What About Fuel Economy?

Driven over the identical 650 miles, at identical speeds and in identical fashion, the Corvette and T-Bird got virtually identical overall gas mileage. Tho 12.8 and 12.7 may seem unusually low, it's important to remember that we drove the cars hard and fast. Under less strenuous conditions you might expect up to 14-15 mpg, tho if you're like most persons who drive such cars, it will be of little concern—except possibly

for the next time you bench-race. Few competitors are so alike.

And Their Construction?

Fit of the panels on the T-Bird was quite good, except for an occasional ripple in the body. The bumpers are sturdy, more like those of a sedan than those of the Corvette. The workmanship of the Corvette seemed to be on a par with that of the T-Bird. Common to Fiberglas, there were a few cracks in the Corvette's body paint at a few stress points.

Some Final Conclusions

The Thunderbird is pretty much what Ford claims it is—a "personal car," suitable for the bachelor, for the young or "young iu heart" couple, or for the husband or wife as a 2nd car. Its sales indicate that the people who are buying it are not necessarily concerned with its sports car attributes, nor are they overly impressed with unbeatable performance. A fact that's sometimes easy to overlook is that pretty big strides have been recently taken by Detroit manufacturers; since the introduction of the T-Bird in the fall of '54, several sedans have surpassed it in acceleration and will stay with it in the handling department. As a "personal car" it meets its requirements. For those who want to make it into a sports car, we would suggest firming it up, adding a good close-ratio gearbox, putting on bigger brakes, and lightening it considerably.

The Corvette is less of a personal car and closer to being, or easily becoming, a sports car. The sales philosophy of Chevrolet seems to have been more to compete with the foreign sports car market—at least until the Thunderbird came along. Now it appears that they're trying to split down the middle by providing more highway comfort for the average guy and/or the ability to make the car into a sports car by the addition of the modification kit (finned brakes, limited-slip differential, disc brakes, and heavy-duty springs).

Which one for you? Within $2.60, you can have your choice. Each performs a slightly different function, and each does right well for itself.

P E R F O R M A N C E

	'56 THUNDERBIRD	'56 CORVETTE
ACCELERATION	From Standing Start 0-60 mph 11.5 seconds ¼-mile 18.0 and 76.5 mph	From Standing Start 0-60 mph 11.6 seconds ¼-mile 17.9 and 77.5 mph
	Passing Speeds 30-50 mph 4.6 seconds 45-60 mph 4.4 50-80 mph 12.8	Passing Speeds 30-50 mph 3.6 seconds 45-60 mph 3.8 50-80 mph 11.0
FUEL CONSUMPTION	Used Mobilgas Special Stop-and-Go Driving 12.7 mpg city and highway average for 650 miles	Used Mobilgas Special Stop-and-Go Driving 12.8 mpg city and highway average for 650 miles

S P E C I F I C A T I O N S

THUNDERBIRD

ENGINE: Piston speed @ max. bhp 2637 ft. per min. Max. bmep 156.6 psi. Additional data in table on page 48.

WEIGHT: Test car weight (with gas, oil, and water) 3600 lbs. Front 1780 lbs. Rear 1820 lbs. Per cent distribution 49.4 front, 50.6 rear. Test car weight/bhp ratio 16.00:1.

PRICES: (Including suggested retail price at main factory, federal tax, and delivery and handling charges, but not freight.) $3147.60.

ACCESSORIES: Fordomatic $215, Overdrive $146, power brakes $34, power steering $64, power windows $70, power seat $65, radio $107, heater $84, convertible top alone $75, with Fiberglas hardtop $290, safety packages $22, $32.

CORVETTE

ENGINE: Piston speed @ max. bhp 2600 ft. per min. Max. bmep 153.6 psi. Additional data in table on page 48.

WEIGHT: Test car weight (with gas, oil, water) 3020 lbs. Front 1610 lbs. Rear 1410 lbs. Per cent distribution 53.3 front, 46.7 rear. Test car weight/bhp ratio 13.42:1.

PRICES: (Including suggested retail price at main factory, federal tax, and delivery and handling charges, but not freight.) $3145.

ACCESSORIES: Prices not yet released for publication.

CORVETTE

Corvette—A new direction in American motoring.

FROM the ever popular Chevrolet division of General Motors the Corvette is among the first on the American market to emphasize the "sports" aspect of motoring. Although its weight and soft suspension are not ideal for competition, the machine is often raced. Fully automatic transmission gives a great deal of ease, and combined with the sporting look the car is proving very popular.

CORVETTE

SPECIFICATIONS
Engine . . . . V8cyl.
Valves . . . . ohv
Displacement . . . . 235cu.in.
Horsepower 160hp
Curb Weight . . . . 2,900lb.
Wheelbase . . . . 102in.

Chevrolet *Corvette*

The first road test ever conducted in Australia, exclusive to

"Wheels" of one of the most noteworthy cars of the decade.

CHEVROLET'S Corvette was planned in 1952 and was running on the road by mid-1953. Production was scheduled for all-steel bodies, but due to the delay on the dies and the demand for immediate delivery of the car by enthusiasts, the first cars were made with fiberglass bodies This was continued with most of the first series Corvette.

The car tested was a 1954 model, imported by plastics manufacturer Roy Hargreaves for research. Hargreaves, whose business is in Sydney, is enthusiastic about plastics and about the Corvette. He believes that plastics have not yet begun to arrive and that the Corvette foreshadows a world-wide

change in automobile manufacture.

Or interest in the car was more mundane: How did this first sports car by the world's largest manufacturer of motor cars perform? The answer is that General Motors have done a good job.

The Corvette gives an exhilarating sports car, but a fast tourer. This was true of the early Jaguar XK-120's, but it didn't stop them being used as sports cars. And it hasn't stopped the Corvette being used as one in the U.S., either.

The Corvette gives an exhilirating performance because the power is high (150 b.h.p.) and the laden weight low (28¾ cwt. with two passengers and fuel). It is inevitable that it should have found

its way into competition.

The fiberglass body sounds unusual, but it would not be noticed unless one was told. The finish is indistinguishable from all-steel cars. There are no ripples on the large body surfaces, the doors shut with a comforting slam, there is no working or rattling when running. The lot is sprayed with a paint job which shames most of our local ones.

There is sprawling room for two people inside on individual seats. One more could be carried—somewhat uncomfortably—on the wide propellor-shaft tunnel between them.

In terms of feet and inches, the Corvette is quite compact, although

44

considerably bigger than its British counterparts, the Austin Healey and the Triumph TR3.

The overall length is thirteen feet eleven inches, and the height at the top of the wrap around windshield, three feet eleven inches. At the top of the door, the Corvette stands a mere two feet nine inches.

The Corvette is typically American in at least one aspect — the width. It is five feet ten inches wide overall, giving it a peculiar "squashed look" when viewed from either end.

Some idea of the Corvette length-height ratio can be gathered by comparing it with the Austin-Healey.

The British car has an overall length of twelve feet eight inches, and height at the top of the windshield of nearly four feet.

The Corvette, therefore, is sixteen inches longer than the Healey, and slightly lower on to the ground.

The front tread of the Corvette is 57" and the rear tread 59".

The seats and door trim are high quality leather and have the best finish we've seen for a long time. The doors, which are thick and follow the body curve, have a recess at the top and a large pocket under it. The recess makes do as an arm-rest and has an ashtray, too. The access to the pocket is via a hinged lid.

The hood is neatly hidden and appears from behind the seats like a conjuring trick. It looks neat when in place and is set off by well styled side-curtains, one of their attractions being adjustable venti-panes.

There is a large uninterrupted boot space with more than enough room for two persons' luggage. The spare wheel is placed in the open underneath the boot in the normal petrol tank place on most cars. The Corvette's petrol tank is set vertic-ally, immediately behind the seats and gives a big capacity without much bulk.

Finish is luxurious-looking and of good quality. Rev. counter is obscured by steering wheel. Vision, seating, is excellent.

The Corvette is roomy enough to get in and out of easily. Once in, the driver sits low, but has a fine view. He sees around the car with a minimum of distortion through the steeply sloped and curved wind-screen. There are virtually no blind spots.

A standard Chevrolet speedometer

Engine has three Carter carburettors, but only two air cleaners. Body panels are obviously fiberglass when bonnet is lifted, but impossible to pick from outside.

sits on top of the facia in front of the steering wheel. This is legible, more accurate than we at first believed, and free from float. It is shielded to prevent reflections on the windscreen.

The remaining instuments are spread in a line across the centre facia. These are for petrol, oil, engine revs. (a little larger than the others), heat, and amps. We found most of these awkward to read, particularly revs., when travelling at high speeds.

The first thing the enthusiast notices is the lack of a clutch pedal. The Corvette is fitted with "Powerglide", a two-speed automatic system which is used in Chevrolet saloons. The Corvette's, however, is modified. It is also operated from the floor, sports-car-fashion, with a stubby lever.

The transmission's low-range is manually selected and gives a speed of 55.6 m.p.h. at the engine's 4,500 r.p.m. limit.

Drive-range switches automatically to Low when the accelerator is floorboarded and holds it to 45 m.p.h. before changing to the higher "top-gear" ratio.

Drive is used for all normal work, Low being mainly for engine braking on long descents.

We feel that the Corvette's performance would be vastly improved by a close ratio, four-speed manual gearbox (allowing a 3rd-gear speed of 80/85 m.p.h.), but admit that the Powerglide is ideal for fast touring. Its only fault is a leisurely automatic (and manual) shift to the higher ratio and lack of a suitable accelerating ratio between 60 and 80 m.p.h.

As is usual in cars with automatic transmissions, the Corvette is fitted with an extra large brake pedal. The left foot uses this as a clutch when edging the car in 1st or reverse.

Our first impression of the Corvette was that it seemed sedate. We expected it to go like a rocket but were lulled by its easy, extremely quiet, running. And there is little wind noise to give an audible impression of speed.

A stop-watch soon showed how wrong we were. The Corvette *does* go. What we thought was a fast speedometer was, in fact, near enough correct. What we thought was merely "indicated" cruising between 90 and 100 m.p.h. was, in fact, actual cruising.

The acceleration is smooth and rapid all the way to 90 m.p.h., when it fades a little, making the car run for some distance before it hits top speed. The standing ¼-mile time is a gratifying 18.8 sec. — fast enough to leave nearly every car behind, but so smoothly accomplished your mother-in-law wouldn't take her eyes from her knitting.

This performance comes from a big six-cylinder (3,861 c.c.) engine. The engine has been very little modified since it was introduced in 1937, but has long been a favourite with hot rodders in the U.S.

However, the recent years have seen some detail changes in its design, mainly pressure lubrication (instead of splash), insert bearings,

and a heavier crankshaft. The Corvette's engine goes further with three side-draught carburettors, 8 to 1 compression, and a hotter camshaft.

By sports-car standards it is a low revver (150 b.h.p. at 4,200) and its torque reaches the high figure of 200 lb./ft. at an extremely low 1,200 r.p.m. Torque does not fall substantially until 3,600 r.p.m. — the speed at which most sports engines are beginning to bite.

The engine idles evenly, never seems to work, even at high revs., and makes no noise whatever. This latter is probably the result of the fiberglass body's excellent sound dampening properties. The Corvette's exhaust has a big-engine chuffiness at low speeds and a low tenor note when travelling flat out. It is the only clue as to where the power is coming from.

The handling gives an interesting sidelight on the thoughts of American manufacturers towards sports cars. To put it bluntly, the Corvette gives high-speed motoring to the public. This may or may not be commendable, but it certainly means that the Corvette has to do what the public wants — go fast on good roads.

This is achieved by building in a considerable amount of understeer (achieved with the rear wheels steering by roll), more even than is used with most stock U.S. saloons.

It makes the Corvette remarkably steady at speed on an open highway corner, but a little touchy when travelling flat out in a straight line (the rear wheels also steer under bump deflection).

On top of these properties, the steering is slow at 3.7 turns from lock to lock on a 38 ft. turning circle.

It adds up to the fact that the Corvette has to be driven forcibly

on a twisting road and man-handled on right-angle corners. It will keep up with the best or even leave them on open highway roads, but would be at a disadvantage on twisting ones.

But there is no doubt that the Corvette is a very safe car and ideally suited to first class roads, for which job it was designed.

The brakes readily cope with fast highway cruising and a light pedal pressure pulls off speed with commendable sureness. However, hard stops from extreme speed bring on pedal loss and some fade. The trouble probably comes from the enclosed body shape and the wheel shrouding embellishers. Harder linings (and higher pedal pressures) would help the trouble, but we feel that some fade would be inevitable.

We found the Corvette a most interesting and entertaining car to drive. The model we tested has proved popular enough in the U.S. for G.M. to produce a second-series car. This newer model has a few points we would have liked in the test car and shows that U.S. manufacturers are willing to learn by comment and experience.

Our look at the Corvette told us that U.S. manufacturers are interested in faster, better handling cars. The Corvette with its looks and performance, yet with its production-car engine and suspension units, heralds that future — at a moderate price.

However, interested parties might not have to wait for manufacture here or imports to own one. Now that Roy Hargreaves, normally a Rolls-Royce driving businessman, has finished his experiments he has no more use for the Corvette. An offer to buy to Box 23, Rockdale P.O., N.S.W., might bring pleasant results.

Lines are plain and functional. Chrome rubbing strip isn't bent—reflections from road give optical illusion.

SPECIFICATIONS:

MAKE:

First series Chevrolet Corvette, 2-door, 2-passenger roadster. Our test car from Mr. Roy Hargreaves, Sydney.

PRICE AND AVAILABILITY:

Car is 1954 model and not for sale in Australia.

DIMENSIONS:

Wheelbase, 8' 6"; track: front, 4', 9", rear 4' 11"; length 13' 11"; width 4' 10"; height, 3' 11'. clearance 7".

ENGINE:

6-cyl. o.h.v., 80.5 x 100 mm., 3,861 c.c., comp. ratio 8 to 1, 150 b.h.p. at 4,200 r.p.m., 2.55 b.h.p. sq. in. piston area, 223 lb./ft. torque at 2,400 r.p.m. Three Carter carburettors with twin-oil-wetted air cleaners. Capacities: Radiator, not quoted; sump, 9 pts.; petrol tank, 16 gal.

TRANSMISSION:

"Powerglide" automatic operated by floor shift-lever; open propellor shaft; hypoid bevel final drive, ratio 3.55 to 1. *Overall ratios*: Low range, 13.57 to 6.46; Drive range, 6.46 to 3.55; reverse, 13.57 to 6.46. *Drive range m.p.h.* (3.55:1): 22.5 m.p.h. at 1,000 r.p.m; 86 at 2,500 ft/min. piston speed.

CHASSIS AND BODY:

X-braced box-section frame; separate fiberglass body. Dry weight, 25 cwt.

SUSPENSION:

I.f.s. by coils and wishbones; rear suspension by semi-elliptic leaf; telescopic shock absorbers.

BRAKES:

4-wheel hydraulic (Bendix duo-servo); mechanical hand linkage to rear wheels from facia mounted lever; transmission parking brake. Friction lining area not quoted. Footbrake at 30 m.p.h. in neutral, 33.1 ft. Handbrake at 30 m.p.h. in neutral, 78 ft. Fade, nil with normal cruising.

ELECTRICAL EQUIPMENT:

6-volt ignition; 90 amp. battery; 35/45-watt headlamps; automatic courtesy lights; cigar lighter, dual wipers.

STEERING:

Worm-and-wheel, ratio 16:1; 3.7 turns from lock to lock; turning circle, 38 ft.

WHEELS AND TYRES:

Pressed-steel disc with 5-stud attachment; 6.00-16 tyres; fast driving pressures, 30 p.s.i. front and rear.

PERFORMANCE:

MAXIMUM SPEEDS:

Average of test runs .... 100.5 m.p.h.
Fastest one way .... 101 m.p.h.

MAXIMUM SPEEDS ON GEARS:

At 4,500 r.p.m. (*see text*): Low range, 55.6 m.p.h. *Recommended shift points*: 0-55.6 m.p.h. in Drive range depending on throttle opening (see text).

MAXIMUM ENGINE PERFORMANCE:

135 b.h.p. at 4,200 r.p.m. (Drive-range equivalent, 94.4 m.p.h.); 208 lb./ft. torque at 2,200 r.p.m. (Drive-range equivalent, 49.5 m.p.h.).

ACCELERATION:

Standing ¼-mile: Average, 18.8 sec.; fastest, 18.7 sec. *Acceleration through gears*: 0-10 m.p.h., 1.1 sec.; 0-20 m.p.h., 2.0 sec.; 0-30 m.p.h., 3.8 sec.; 0-40 m.p.h., 5.5 sec.; 0-50 m.p.h., 8.0 sec.; 0-60 m.p.h., 11.7 sec.; 0-70 m.p.h., 15.4 sec.; 0-80 m.p.h., 21.7 sec.; 0-90 m.p.h., 29.0 sec. *Drive-range acceleration*: 10-30 m.p.h., 2.9 sec.; 20-40 m.p.h., 3.5 sec.; 30-50 m.p.h., 6.2 sec.; 40-60 m.p.h., 6.2 sec.; 50-70 m.p.h., 7.4 sec.; 60-80 m.p.h., 10.0 sec.; 70-90 m.p.h., 13.6 sec.

BEST HILL CLIMBING:

Low range: Better than 1 in 3 at constant 30 m.p.h. Drive range: 1 in 5 at constant 50 m.p.h.

SPEEDO CALIBRATION:

10 m.p.h. (indicated)—10 m.p.h. (actual); 20 m.p.h.—19.9 m.p.h.; 30 m.p.h.—29.7 m.p.h.; 40 m.p.h.—39.1 m.p.h.; 50 m.p.h.—48.7 m.p.h.; 60 m.p.h.—58.0 m.p.h.; 70 m.p.h.—67.6 m.p.h.; 80 m.p.h.—77.3 m.p.h.; 90 m.p.h.—87.0 m.p.h.

TEST WEIGHT:

Driver, assistant, full tank, and gear: 28¾ cwt. Distribution: front, 15½ cwt.; rear, 13¼ cwt.

PETROL CONSUMPTION:

Hard driving, 17.6 m.p.g.; normal cruising, 22 m.p.g. Premium grade fuel used.

Bubbles over headlights are used when racing to protect glass from breaking from action on course, removed for street.

Front detail with headlight bubbles removed shows how car would look in road condition. Extended nose improves style.

CORVETTE SR-2

The only changes to the rear of the Corvette are the addition of the fin and the new faired glass covering tail light tunnels.

Magnesium knock off racing wheels with Firestone racing tires are used on the SR-2. The aluminum scoop on the door

Custom Corvette from the factory could be the forecast of things to come from Chevrolet, and if it is, they've got a winner

BY ART DEAN

SR-2 looks terrific from most any angle and especially this one as seen from the photographers platform for the press.

ONE WOULD think that the most talked about car at a sports car race would be one of the more exotic, high priced foreign machines such as Ferrari, Maserati or possibly the D type Jag.

This however, did not seem to be the case at the recent Elkhart Lake ROAD AMERICA race. It appears that the Corvette shown here stole the show from the transatlantic machinery.

Basically a stock 1956 Corvette, this beautiful metallic blue custom model is the result of many hours' labor by a crew of General Motors stylists and engineers. Owner of the car is Jerry Earl, son of Harley Earl who is Vice-President of G. M. and head of its vast styling section.

Modifications, most of which can be readily seen in the accompanying photos, include an extended nose section (in which a stock Corvette grille is mounted) which fairs nicely into the stock body and hood configuration.

The elongated teardrop hood bumps which, on a stock Corvette, are round on top (in cross section) have been "peaked." Between these are 18 louvers, which run almost the full distance between the two fairings, set into the hood for letting hot air out of the engine compartment.

This is the most advantageous spot for that purpose as the hot air rises and gathers at the back of the engine compartment, but it makes me wonder what would happen if the engine should catch fire. It seems the driver might get a face full of flames.

As can be seen in the photos, the concave section of the body side has been formed from aluminum and the addition of a functional air scoop in the door at the rear of this concave portion now admits cooling air to the rear brakes. This is accomplished by a duct through the door jam and in to where it can be directed at the backing plates.

Two small racing windscreens set in a special cowl panel replace the normal full size windshield usually seen on the Corvette. Although these are not very high, they do better than one would expect in directing air around, or up and over the driver and/or passenger.

The upholstery and floor mats are done in blue leather to match the metallic blue paint and a highly polished fire extinguisher is mounted in brackets atop the transmission housing.

At the rear of the car we see a beautifully faired, but unnecessary, tail fin in the center of the body. Starting at a spot between the two seats and going straight back to a point almost a foot behind the body, then cutting back sharply into the deck lid.

Beneath the fin, the rear of the Corvette appears to be stock with the exception of the tail lights. The stock tail lights which were set in semi "tunnels," now have red glass covering them completely and fairing perfectly into the fender profile. This car is an excellent example of factory customizing. •

actually scoops in air which is directed through a duct in the door jamb to the rear brakes. Fin is nonfunctional.

49

1957 FUEL INJECTION CORVETTE

283 cubes = 283 horsepower

by Dave Emanuel
photos by Roy Query

THIRTY YEARS have passed since Chevrolet Motor Division apprehensively introduced their first sports car. During the intervening years, economic, political and sociological turmoil has wrought immeasurable change upon the face of the nation, often obscuring the priorities that were paramount during previous decades.

So it is with the Corvette. In the beginning, it was little more than an experiment to determine whether a homegrown sports car could successfully compete with the European imports. In 1953, there was precious little indication that a long-term market existed for such a vehicle, but at least some of GM's executives had vision of sufficient acuity to read between the lines of market research reports. And over the years, their confidence in the Corvette project has been vindicated. The car is now a national institution.

Although it continues a tradition begun in 1953, recent incarnations are separated from their antecedents by a broad conceptual chasm; early Corvettes are sports cars, later models are grand touring machines. Given the current state-of-the-art, and immense popularity achieved by the Corvette, it is difficult to imagine that the marque once struggled for mere survival and almost died in infancy. Further, the significance of the engineering developments that set the Corvette on firm footing has been muddied by the waters of time.

During its embryonic years, America's only sports car suffered more than a few teething pains. Equipped with a six-cylinder engine and two-speed automatic transmission, and perched on a modified sedan chassis, the first models offered less than spine-tingling performance. And while the division's decision to cloak the car in a fiberglass, rather than steel body was laudable, quite some time was required to iron out production problems associated with the new material. Thus in attempting to lure sports car buyers with a product that lacked refinement, Chevrolet was knocking heads with relatively sophisticated European makes, specifically Jaguar, Austin-Healey and MG. The advantage enjoyed by these marques was further enhanced by a legacy of racing success, something the

Model year 1957 was when Chevrolet truly got the Corvette's act together. By combining the nicely restyled '56 body with the fire-breathing option of fuel injection they built a car which had begun in 1953 as a hesitant pussycat and transformed it to a snarling tiger.

Right: Many enthusiasts of the marque consider the '57 Corvette to be the most attractive car ever to wear that badge. Below: Taillamps are sunk in chromed nacelles; "bumpers" offered little protection from close encounters of the parking kind. Below right: Vette's dual exhausts exit through the bumpers. Bottom: Concave body side sweepspears began in 1956 and continued with some trim modifications through 1962.

1957 CORVETTE
continued

Corvette was too new and anemic to achieve. This situation undoubtedly induced more than one buyer to opt for a British, rather than American two-seater.

On road courses, the 1953 and 1954 models were 98-pound weaklings, capable of little else besides having sand kicked in their faces. Muscles began to ripple during the following two years, but it wasn't until 1957 that the Corvette, now with broad shoulders and bulging biceps, began kicking its competition off the beach. Zora Arkus-Duntov, commonly known as the father of the Corvette, had begun working his engineering magic. And the United States had finally produced a world class sports car.

Among Corvette aficionados, 1957 stands as a high water mark and well it should; there can be little to dispute

Fuel Injection

 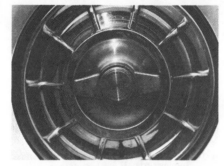 

that the quintessential Corvette was produced in that year. It was in 1957 that the original 265-cubic-inch V-8 was enlarged to 283 cubic inches, and fuel injection, a close ratio four-speed transmission, a special suspension and braking package and Positraction were all added to the option list. But of even greater significance, in its fuel injected form, the new 283 became the first American production engine to achieve a ratio of one horsepower per cubic inch of displacement. Chevrolet, seeking to capitalize on this fact, announced in its ads, "It is with considerable pride that Chevrolet invites you to examine an engineering advance of great significance, available on the 1957 Corvette. It is fuel injection, and in the Corvette V-8 it permits a level of efficiency hitherto unrealized in any American production car: *one horsepower for every cubic inch of displacement...283 hp!*"

Seeking to drive home the fact that the Corvette was indeed a thoroughbred sports car, the ad continued, "This is another major step in the creation of a proud new kind of car for America: a *genuine* sports car, as certified by its record in competition. But a *unique* sports car in its combination of moderate price, luxurious equipment and low cost maintenance with fiery performance, polo-pony responsiveness and granite stability on curves."

While the advertising copy smacks of hype, it was, in actuality, not far off the mark. The 283-hp fuel injected engine

did provide "fiery performance." In combination with a 4.11:1 rear axle and four-speed transmission, the powerplant propelled the car from zero to 60 mph in 5.7 seconds and from zero to 100 mph in 16.8 seconds. Standing start quarter mile figures were equally impressive as the car sprinted the distance in 14.3 seconds, reaching a speed of over 96 miles per hour. These performance figures were compiled by *Road & Track* magazine which went on to report, "An engine speed of 6500 is easily reached in fourth gear, equivalent to 132 mph with no allowance for tire expansion. With suitable gears the Corvette can approach 150 mph, as has been proven at Bonneville and at Daytona."

But in order to earn its bars within the sports car fraternity, the Corvette had to prove its mettle on the race track. Chevrolet was sensitive to this fact and

Top: The two magic words that mean one horsepower per cubic inch appear on the trunk lid. Above left: Gas filler is hidden away in front of left rear wheel well. Above center: High-styled wheel covers with "knock off" spinner added to Vette's sporty image. Above: Convertible top and optional hardtop were secured on the deck by chromed clamps. Left: Huge radio speaker outlet complements shape of speedo housing.

offered a $725 option tailored specifically for road racing. Known as Regular Production Option (RPO) 684, the package included higher rate front springs (340 as opposed to 300 pounds/inch), five-leaf rather than four-leaf rear springs, 13/16-inch-diameter front anti-roll bar, specially calibrated shock absorbers measuring 1⅜ inches rather than one inch in diameter, quicker steering (16.3:1 as opposed to the standard 21.0:1 ratio), Positraction rear axle, finned brake drums and ceramic/metallic brake linings. Wider wheels measuring 5.5 rather than 5.0 inches were available under RPO 276. By specifying the proper options, it was possible to order a car virtually race-ready, directly from the factory. (How times have changed.)

The race car image was further enhanced by the Corvette's record in competition—a first in GT class and a

specifications

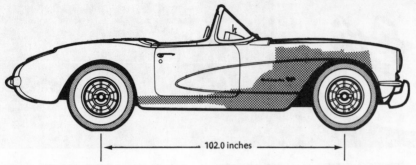
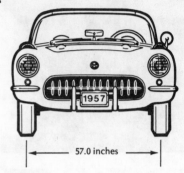

102.0 inches   57.0 inches

1957 Corvette

Base Price	$3909.52 f.o.b. St. Louis, MO
Optional equipment	Fuel injection, four-speed transmission, hardtop, "two-tone" paint, radio

ENGINE

Type	V-8 ohv
Bore & stroke	3.875 x 3.00
Displacement	283 cubic inches
Horsepower	283 @ 6200 rpm
Torque	290 @ 4400 rpm
Compression ratio	10.5:1
Induction system	Rochester Ramjet continuous flow fuel injection
Exhaust system	Dual, 2.0-inch o.d. exhaust pipes
Electrical system	12-volt battery/coil

TRANSMISSION

Type	4-speed manual
Ratios: 1st	2.20:1
2nd	1.66:1
3rd	1.31:1
4th	1:1

DIFFERENTIAL

Type	Hypoid semi-floating
Ratio	3.70:1 (3.55:1, 4.11:1 and 4.56:1 optional)

STEERING

Type	Semi-reversible, worm and ball bearing roller
Ratio	16.0:1 overall
Turns lock to lock	3.9
Turning circle	37 feet

BRAKES

Type	Hydraulic duo-servo cast iron drums 11 inches x 2.00 inches front, 11 inches x 1.75 inches rear
Total swept area	157 square inches (121 with H.D. brake option)
Lining material	Molded asbestos standard, sintered metal and ceramic optional heavy duty

CHASSIS & BODY

Construction	Welded box section frame with "X" crossmember
Body	Fiberglass 2-door roadster

SUSPENSION

Front	Independent SLA, coil springs, double-acting tubular shocks, anti-sway bar
Rear	Live axle with semi-elliptic leaf springs, double-acting tubular shocks, anti-sway bar with optional heavy duty option
Wheels	15-inch x 5-inch slotted steel disc
Tires	6.70 x 15-inch 4-ply rayon

WEIGHTS AND MEASURES

Wheelbase	102.0 inches
Overall length	168.0 inches
Overall height	51.9 inches
Overall width	70.5 inches
Front tread	57.0 inches
Rear tread	59.0 inches
Curb weight	2849 pounds

PERFORMANCE

Maximum speed	132
Acceleration 0-50	4.7 seconds
0-60	5.7 seconds
Standing start ¼ mile	14.3 seconds and 96 mph
Fuel economy	11-16 mpg

1957 CORVETTE

continued

twelfth and fifteenth overall at the 1957 edition of the 12 Hours of Sebring. A Corvette also won the season-opening sports car race at New Smyrna Beach, Florida, defeating a Jaguar XK-140, a Thunderbird and a Mercedes-Benz 300SL in the process. Other victories included a 1-2-3-4 finish in the stock production category at Nassau Speed Weeks, the SCCA B Production class championship, and at Daytona Beach, the car dominated the C Production class placing first, second and third in both standing start acceleration and flying mile competition. A winning speed of 131.941 was posted in the latter category.

By mid-year the 1957 Corvette, especially the fuel injected version, was well on its way to becoming a classic.

Obviously, 283 horsepower @ 6200 rpm was not every buyer's idea of nirvana and for the more effete driver, Chevrolet offered several alternatives. The base engine, which was fitted with a mild hydraulic cam, Carter WCFB four-barrel and 9.5:1 compression ratio, bore a rating of 220 hp @ 4800 rpm; with optional dual WCFB carburetors, the horsepower rating rose to 245 @ 5000 rpm. Just as all the lower horsepower engines shared the same hydraulic cam, the top options were fitted with the identical "competition" mechanical lifter grind. When combined with dual Carter WCFBs, the "Duntov" cam was responsible for 270 hp @ 6000 rpm; with fuel injection, the rating jumped to 283 hp @ 6200 rpm.

All engines were available with either three or four-speed manual transmissions or two-speed Powerglide automatic. Both of the manual gearboxes

were of the close ratio variety with gear sets of 2.21:1, 1.32:1 and 1:1 and 2.20:1, 1.66:1, 1.31:1 and 1:1 respectively for the three and four-speed models. A tubular driveshaft connected the transmission to the rear axle where ratios ranged from 3.55:1 to 4.56:1 with either conventional or Positraction differential carrier.

In all, six exterior colors were offered —Onyx Black, Venetian Red, Polo White, Arctic Blue, Cascade Green and Aztec Copper. An optional paint treatment consisted of either Shoreline Beige or Silver Metallic, rather than the body color, being applied to the scallop which extended along the doors and front fenders. Interior colors were listed as Shoreline Beige or Venetian Red.

With exceptional performance, handling capability and visual appeal, the 1957 Corvette has fulfilled the prophecy of its builder: "It is our intention to

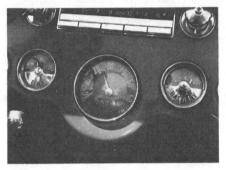

Left: Good looks aside, the true allure of the '57 fuelie is in the driving. Breathtaking performance all the way through the power band awaits the command of your right foot. Below left: Doors open with convenient push-pull knob. Below center: Tachometer occupies exact center of dash; not the most convenient spot for a quick reading of the revs. Below: With all the power on tap a four-speed box seems almost unnecessary, but it was in keeping with the desire to make the Corvette a thoroughbred sports car. Bottom: The durable 283 V-8 could be ordered with a relatively tame 220 hp all the way up to the unprecedented one horsepower per cubic inch version.

make of the Corvette a classic car, one of those rare and happy milestones in the history of automotive design." Chevrolet had indeed created a classic—distinctive of line, limited in number and revered by serious collectors and casual enthusiasts alike. It's a sad fact that a mere 6339 samples of the 1957 edition were produced (only 240 with fuel injection), and of these, many have long since departed for the great wrecking yard in the sky. But somewhere, tucked away in a barn, a star is waiting to be discovered.

Driving Impressions

Whenever conversation turns to fuel-injected Corvettes, my memory flips back to an evening in 1963 when a 1957 "fuelie" went head-to-head with a high-powered motorcycle. The image of the bike has long since faded from my cerebral cavity; I can't even remember what make it was, although I'd bet it was a Harley. But I remember the black and silver 'Vette as if I had seen it just yesterday. With the paint shimmering beneath the street lights, the Corvette rolled out of its parking space and moved alongside the bike. Waiting to enter the road, its fuel injection unit emitted that unmistakable whistle while the mechanical lifters clattered like so many cymbals in a symphony of machination. It is the sight and sound of the car more than the race itself that remains so strongly implanted in my

memory—it had a certain, unforgettable charisma, somewhat akin to that of a mythical princess. And it beckoned as coyly, staying close enough to touch, but always just out of reach for all but a fortunate few. This is perhaps the reason that fuel injected Corvettes in general and 1957 models in particular have achieved such great popularity.

As I climbed behind the wheel of the driveReport car, the memories of that night 20 years ago came flooding back. All the right sounds and sights were present; the only things lacking were the motorcycle and some of the hair that used to call the top of my head home.

But if the 'Vette was impressive in 1963, it must have been awesome the year it was built. Letting my mind wander, I could envision what it must have been like when a proud owner had just taken delivery of a brand new 1957 fuel injected, four-speed Corvette. At the time it had to be the fastest production car on the road, and I'm sure it was displayed all over town with the pride and enthusiasm usually demonstrated only by a new mother showing off her progeny. The mind games were fun, but when I began to seriously evaluate the car in practical terms, I noticed that the princess had more than a few warts.

Carburetion versus Injection

A few years ago, before the Corvette restoration movement shifted into high gear, Rochester fuel injection units were readily available for $75-$150. Generally, all other things being equal, the older the model the lower the price. This state of affairs was brought about by a lack of understanding on the part of Corvette owners. As soon as an injection unit became the least bit troublesome, it would be replaced with a carburetor and intake manifold. The fuel injection equipment would subsequently be sold for whatever it would bring. Today, those same units bring from $1500 to $2000.

An alternative to fuel injection, available from 1956 through 1961, was twin four-barrel carburetors. Equipped with the same mechanical lifter cam as the injected engine, the dual four-barrel arrangement was rated at 270-horsepower. Some people have disputed that rating stating that Chevrolet, seeking to spotlight fuel injection, was overly conservative when applying horsepower figures to the carbureted engine.

While it may not have all the charisma of fuel injection, a dual four-barrel induction system has a magical ring all its own. Since the carburetors were relatively trouble-free, many original 270-horsepower Corvettes have survived intact. One example is the 1957 model owned by John Brock of Houston, Texas. An active member of a local Corvette club, Brock raced his concours-winning '57 in autocross competition until quite recently. "It was a real kick," says Brock. "All I had to do was change wheels and tires and go. I think that part of the fun of owning an older car is driving it—not just letting it sit around like a hangar queen. I did fairly well with the '57, but it began to pick up a few too many rock chips, so I don't race it anymore. But I still enjoy driving it."

1957 CORVETTE

continued

While it is now quite in vogue to excoriate the caliber of newer automobiles vis-a-vis their ancestors, there is much to be said for later model Corvettes. Certainly with air conditioning, AM-FM/stereo tape and a plethora of power accessories, they lack the simplicity of the older models. They also lack the throttle response and raw feel of horsepower that is characteristic of a Chevy small block fitted with a mechanical lifter camshaft. But the newer Corvettes are generally much more enjoyable to drive. They offer more room in the cockpit, demonstrably superior handling and ride comfort and significantly better braking capability.

Much of the 1957 models' handling potential is compromised by original equipment type bias ply tires. The car does go around corners well, albeit with more lean than should be present in a sports car, but a set of high performance radial tires, although viewed as anathema by purists, would make a world of difference.

Then again, one doesn't usually expect a 26-year-old car to live up to current state-of-the-art standards. The fact that the '57 Corvette comes so close as to invite comparison is testimony to the high caliber of its design. But the true essence of the car is not in its undercarriage but its under-hood equipage. With the exhaust pipes reverberating to the engine's 750 rpm staccato idle, the whistle of air flowing through the fuel injection and the rat-a-tat of pushrods rapping against rocker arms, anyone who appreciates the beauty of a highly tuned powerplant is immediately enraptured. And as you spend more time behind the wheel, the captivation grows greater, prompting

Upper right: There's plenty of leg room inside, and the "waffle" pattern semi-bucket seats are much plusher than the Corvette's European counterparts. Right: Push-button on metal band between seats allows access to top storage area. Below: Vette has one of the most symmetrical dashboards ever designed.

Left: All graceful, sweeping curves in the rear, it looks like it's going 100 even when standing still. Below left: Grille design on '57s was carried over from original '53 Corvette styling. Below: Fuel injection identification plates are also carried in sweep spears. Center left: Airscoops in front fenders are non-functional; they're perhaps the only piece of styling gimmickry in an otherwise sensationally sleek design. Below center: Installing or removing optional factory hardtop is a two-person operation. Bottom: Rear appearance is "just right"; smooth, sensual and purposeful.

you to forget the world of emissions controls and emasculating government regulations.

Pulling away easily from a dead stop, the engine's responsiveness and eagerness to accelerate leaves no doubt that the true performance potential has been barely tapped. Moving the shift lever through the gears as you accelerate, the feeling of power diminishes only slightly thanks to the closeness of gear ratios. Once in fourth gear, 60 miles per hour is quickly reached, even though you've conservatively applied your right foot to the accelerator pedal. With a more vigorous driving style, 0-60 mph times fall in the low six second range and after 17 seconds of full throttle driving, the speedometer is swinging past the 100 mile per hour mark. The engine, transmission and rear axle seem to enjoy a symbiotic relationship, all working in harmony to yield a result that's greater than the sum of the parts.

Although a removable hardtop was optionally available, it borders on sacrilege to drive an early model Corvette in anything other than open roadster form—to do otherwise is analagous to dressing Bo Derek in baggy overalls. Driving with the top down may leave you wind blown and feeling a bit gritty, but that's all part of what driving a classic Corvette is all about—it's a matter of essentials, a man and his machine. Once the bond is made, nothing else seems to matter.　□

Acknowledgements and Bibliography
The Best of Corvette News, *edited by Karl Ludvigsen;* Corvette America's Star-Spangled Sports Car *by Karl Ludvigsen;* Road & Track, *various issues;* Corvettes Technically Speaking, *by Michael G. Harrison. Special thanks to Bob McDorman, Bob McDorman Chevrolet, Canal Winchester, Ohio; John Brock, Brock's Collision Repair, Houston, Texas; and Bob Fitch, Houston, Texas.*

GM Project XP-64

SPORTS-RACING

CHEVROLET

CORVETTE SS

By Jesse Alexander

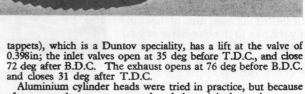

The SS Corvette with Arkus-Duntov at the wheel. He is well known for his racing experiences with Porsche, and was formerly chief engineer for Allard

Moss, who tried the car, discusses its merits with Duntov (left) and Fitch

HOPES for a genuine, completely American sports-racing car were raised when the Chevrolet Division of General Motors rolled their new SS Corvette to the starting line of the Sebring Twelve Hours. Rumours had been circulating for some time concerning a new competition Corvette that was reportedly under construction at the GM Research establishment in Warren, Michigan; no one knew exactly what was in the wind, but inasmuch as the production glass fibre Corvettes were doing not too badly in American races in the hands of competent drivers, and knowing that both Zora Arkus-Duntov and John Fitch were on the payroll at Chevrolet, the creation of the SS was really no surprise.

The decision to undertake the project was made last August, and design work commenced in October. General Motors had given up the annual Motorama show, and the funds normally allocated to it had been handed to the Chevrolet Research Division to build this car; on the O.K. of General Manager E. N. Cole, both Duntov and Fitch put their heads together with the engineers, and in five short months the new car was being trucked down to Sebring in company with the "mule"—a prototype rolling test bed to be used in practice.

To any student of racing car design the features of the Corvette SS are not new; the power plant is the regular Chevrolet vee-8 engine, slightly modified to give a horse-power rating of about 310 at 6,000 r.p.m.; stock Corvettes put out 275 b.h.p. on carburettors, 283 b.h.p. on injection. The inlet valve has a head diameter of 1.85in and the exhaust 1.625in, both with 30-deg valve seats. The camshaft (in combination with solid tappets), which is a Duntov speciality, has a lift at the valve of 0.398in; the inlet valves open at 35 deg before T.D.C., and close 72 deg after B.D.C. The exhaust opens at 76 deg before B.D.C. and closes 31 deg after T.D.C.

Aluminium cylinder heads were tried in practice, but because of warpage they were removed and the original cast iron ones used. From examination the aluminium heads would appear to be identical with their cast iron counterparts and probably produced from the same pattern equipment, for the valves seated direct on the aluminium without inserts, and the stems operated similarly directly in the castings. If this presumption is correct then the distortions experienced are not unexpected.

Other special features include aluminium clutch housing, water pump and radiator core; the oil pan is of magnesium; the specially prepared crankshaft runs on five main bearings. The Rochester fuel injection unit fitted to the SS is virtually the same as is found on production Corvettes, with the slight difference that the air metering valve is remote from the injector plenum chamber and is fed by a duct from the front grille; the ignition system is of Delco manufacture, with a special aircraft-type 12-volt generator.

An approximate torque figure for the competition engine is 295 ft/lb at 4,400 r.p.m. Drive to the rear wheels is by an open shaft running from the special Chevrolet 4-speed fully synchronized gear box, installed in an aluminium alloy case that cuts the weight down to 65 pounds; steering is a modified Chevrolet recirculating ball-type with a 12 to 1 ratio; stock Chevrolet ratio is 16 to 1.

The Corvette SS differs from the production car chiefly in its chassis. Instead of having classic side members in pressed steel, it consists of a chrome-molybdenum space frame, very similar to that of the 300SL and weighing 180lb; the magnesium-alloy body is not stressed over the frame, except for the cowl; the body is hinged both front and rear, to give easy access.

Front suspension has an orthodox wishbone layout, the suspension arms being in pressed steel, similar to but smaller than those of the production car. Spherical joints are used and they are arranged to provide a high roll centre at the front of the car. The suspension units at the front and rear are of the same type, being helical coil springs surrounding telescopic direct-acting dampers.

A de Dion axle in conjunction with inboard brakes is featured at the rear. The input passes underneath the differential assembly to a pair of quick-change spur gears for varying the final drive ratio, so that the hypoid pinion drives forward to the crown wheel. The de Dion tube passes behind the frame-mounted final drive unit and is located by four arms. There is an upper one at each side parallel to the chassis frame and attached to the tube close to the hubs. Each lower arm is positioned obliquely from the centre of the de Dion tube to an attachment point on the chassis frame immediately below the upper arm. The layout is such that the height of the roll centre can be modified and the position of the axle altered slightly to give variable anti-roll characteristics.

The SS brakes are good; oddly enough, they are very similar in design to the Chrysler Center-plane units; individual vacuum servos are standard and, in addition, a unique feature, a mercury switch that is sensitive to deceleration, is coupled to the inboard rear brakes to limit rear wheel braking to a predetermined amount; linings are cera-metallic, and these, in conjunction with the Center-plane-type mechanism, make for most efficient braking; it is indeed too bad that the car was not driven the full distance at Sebring so that the brakes could be given a valid assessment. It's interesting to note, in passing, that neither Ferrari nor Maserati fit servos to their sports car brakes.

Several Ferrari drivers and one Maserati driver were complaining after the race of the terrific physical effort required to apply the brakes on these cars during a long race; it is so great that they had lost all feeling in the middle toes of their right foot—the nerves being pinched from the continual pushing on the brake pedal. Ferrari have indicated that they will begin to use a brake servo on the big 3.5 and 3.8 machines beginning this month.

How does the new Corvette handle? Remarkably well; this observation is borne out by not only watching the car in fast corners, but also by the fact that both Fangio and Moss recorded amazingly fast lap times in practice, driving the prototype car (which is exactly the same as the No. 1 SS which started in the race). Fangio turned 3min 27.2sec without really trying; his best time in the 4.5 Maserati was 3min 25sec. Stirling Moss turned 3min 28sec, and, when he got out of the car, thought he could do 2 or 3 sec better. So, without a doubt, Chevrolet have a car that could win Le Mans in the hands of the right driver, and, given a proper share of luck. Piero Taruffi was

in the Corvette team at Sebring, but he never really seemed at home in the car; his lap times were much slower than those of Fangio and Moss.

The No. 1 car was not even completely built by the time they got down to Sebring in one of the big GM Motorama trucks; around the clock activity in an airplane hangar at Sebring was the order of events, so that the car could do a little practice; it finally appeared during the first night-time session in the hands of both Duntov and Fitch; the body had to be cut somewhat when it was found that the exhaust tubes were heavily shrouded —resulting in a parboiled driver.

Its baptism of fire at Sebring was short and not too impressive at that; Fitch got off to a mediocre start and circulated well in the middle of the pack for some time; then, as he began to move up, troubles set in. First it was a locking brake; then a defective coil which he repaired out on the circuit, but finally, a rubber bushing in the rear suspension gave up the ghost and the Chevrolet team manager decided to withdraw the car after it had completed 23 laps.

Now, it's most certainly an over-simplification to brand the SS as a typically GM publicity stunt and leave it at that; first of all, it's not true—at least not the whole story, anyway; there is a core of men at Chevrolet who want to go racing—international racing; but top brass at GM are terribly afraid of failure and whether Project XP-64 will be allowed to continue is a matter of conjecture at the moment. Under proper guidance, a team of three or four of these machines with top drivers could put the United States on the sports-racing car map—figuratively and literally. The 64-dollar question of whether or not the Corvette team will come to Le Mans is as yet unanswered; apparently Briggs Cunningham has made a firm entry of at least one car along with his C-6 now powered by the latest 3.8 Jaguar engine. All we can do at present is hope that Mr. Cole at Chevrolet will give an unqualified go-ahead to Briggs.

A dished steering wheel on a sports car is unusual to European eyes. The electrical box to the right of the starter key is a mercury switch sensitive to gravity, which limits rear wheel braking

Upper right: The Rochester fuel injection system, with a dual section trunking supplying air to the engine and the front brakes. Note the take-off from the plenum chamber for the brake servo mechanism

Left: The aluminium cylinder heads which proved unsatisfactory in practice show the relative sizes of valves and the wedge type combustion chamber

Right: The rear brake drums are cast iron on the rubbing surface, and have heavily finned, shrunk-on aluminium cooling rims

CHIEF ADVANTAGE DISCOVERED WITH INJECTION WAS LACK OF SENSITIVITY TO MOTION. FULL POWER WAS MAINTAINED IN HARDEST TURNS.

FIRST ROAD TEST OF

A FUEL-INJECTION

CORVETTE

FUEL injection, apparently the magic words in automobile advertising today, has created a furor which has the engineers burning the midnight oil, the ad agencies looking for new adjectives and the ultimate buyer completely confused.

It was, therefore, with a great deal of anticipation that the MOTOR LIFE crew looked forward to the test of the fuel injected Corvette. Due to the new-ness of the injection, and the fact that Corvette chassis and body has not changed appreciably since 1956, this is actually more a test and report of the injection than of the car.

Praise and criticism are both to be found in the report, and should not be interpreted to mean that the injector is either perfect, or a failure. One thing is certain; driving a car that will reach 100 mph in the length of time it formerly took (a few years ago) to reach 60 mph, left everyone who drove it in a high state of excitement.

Basically the Chevy injector system is quite thoroughly planned. A great deal of thought was apparently given to all the conditions that had to be met. The numerous control and compensating devices incorporated in the unit indicate that a strong effort was made to design something that was more than just a substitute. This term has been used by many who feel that timed injection, similar to the Bosch system used on the Mercedes, is the only method that has merit.

When viewed in the proper perspective it will be found that port injection will do just as well, in most cases, as the more expensive timed, cylinder injection. And by this it isn't meant to infer that the Chevy injection in its present state of development is on a par with Mercedes.

Despite all the talk, few car buyers would be willing to pay the price necessary to get a cylinder injection system on their 1957 Detroit products. Even though the Chevrolet injection price of $485.00 is much less than a cylinder injection system, public opinion says it is still too much. The majority of purchasers feel that the advantage over a carburetor isn't worth quite that much.

Higher production will naturally reduce the cost of the Chevy system considerably, but it will still cost more than a carburetor. In view of this fact it can readily be seen that the engineering department at Rochester, had definite cost limitations imposed. It is apparent that these limitations were strongly instrumental in the selection of the low fuel pressure employed. A higher fuel pressure would have made possible a much better unit, but the cost of a high pressure pump and drive would further reduce public enthusiasm.

Future engine design may make it possible to drive a high pressure pump without a great increase in cost. If another accessory drive was added to the camshaft, the pump could be driven by something more substantial than the "jumbo speedometer cable" presently used. This new drive could be at the front end of the cam, leaving the already over-taxed drive at the rear to drive the oil pump and distributor. The present cable drive is very indicative of something that was expedient rather than preferred. A different type of pump would also be necessary. A higher quality, more precise unit.

"Why a higher fuel pressure," you may ask. There are many answers to this question, the most important of which is a slower idle. The present idle speed is about 900 rpm unless you want the engine to die every time you remove your foot from the throttle pedal. This fast idle has, probably, been mistakenly blamed on the Duntov cam by many observers. There are many hot cams being used today that are more radical than the Duntov and they idle at 450 to 500 rpm. Of course they don't idle smoothly, but the engine continues to run despite the roughness. The fuel injection Corvette road test car had a mildly rough idle at 900 rpm, even after the idle mixture screw was adjusted properly. Adjustment for a slower idle met with failure because the engine would die on the slightest provocation.

A check of the fuel pressure being delivered to the injector nozzles at an idle speed of 900 rpm revealed that there was only ¾ pound pressure. This apparently indicates a lower pressure would effect distribution to such an extent that some cylinders would become starved and others would load up, thereby killing the engine.

If the engine will idle on ¾ pound pressure at 900 rpm, it will also idle at 450 rpm if the pressure is ¾ pound. The big difficulty with this situation lies in the fact that in order to get ¾ pound at 450 rpm the nozzle orifices will have to have their area reduced by 50 per cent. The present size of the nozzle is .011 inch diameter so halving the area would require approximately an .008 inch hole.

Cutting the orifice area in half would require that the pressure be four times greater at higher rpm. This is due to the fact that fluid friction goes up on a square progression. When flow rate is doubled, pressure must be quadrupled.

Close examination of the nozzles reveals the startling fact that they very much resemble simple carburetors. Again there is a concession being made to low fuel pressure. In this instance it involves an ingenious combination of holes that solves an otherwise difficult problem.

As was noted before, the fuel pressure at idle was only ¾ pound, but if we add the 15 inches of vacuum which exists in the manifold at idle there'll be another 7½ pounds pressure differential to add to the ¾ pound for a total of 8¼ pounds attempting to force the fuel through the .011 inch orifice in the nozzle.

Needless to say, this would result in a fuel flow that would literally drown the engine if the pump didn't limit the flow. This condition is further eliminated by nearly complete separation of the manifold's vacuum from the fuel orifice. To accomplish this, atmospheric air is bled into the nozzle just below the fuel orifice. At this point, there are four .100 inch holes drilled at right angles so that they join directly under the orifice. These holes receive atmospheric air through the combination insulating block and air manifold. The air is piped to the air manifold through tubing that connects with the air cleaner. Immediately downstream from the fuel orifice and on the opposite side of the air bleed holes, is located another orifice. This one is roughly .040 inch in diameter. At idle the air flow will be greatest through this hole due to the high vacuum at the intake port, being that the four .100 inch air bleed holes upstream from this orifice have a much greater area than the orifice itself, the pressure in the air bleed is very close to atmospheric. This arrangement almost completely eliminates the tendency to have a vacuum under the fuel orifice. Coincidentally this air flow has a tendency to break up the fuel at low fuel flow rates and is sort of a bonus benefit.

Probably of greatest importance is elimination of the vapor problem in the fuel line. If the vacuum wasn't eliminated at the fuel orifice, there would be a tendency for the fuel to boil in the nozzle delivery lines even at moderate temperatures. The reduction in pressure would try to induce a fuel flow greater than the pump output so the whole line would be under reduced pressure. A further deterent to fuel boiling is the plastic insulating block that doubles as an air manifold for the nozzle air bleeds. The insulating block reduces the flow of engine heat to the nozzles and lines.

Many people, upon viewing the large air intake manifold on the Rochester fuel injection unit, associate it with a conventional fuel and air type manifold. This reasoning leads them to believe that it contains the usual twisting passages that cross over and wrap around each other.

This concept is completely wrong, because the manifold actually contains eight, individual, nearly straight ram passages that are joined on top with a plenum chamber. This chamber is essentially a box that connects the ram tubes to the air meter which contains the throttle valve.

These ram tubes have somewhat the same purpose as those used on the Hilborn system, that of using the inertia of the incoming air, at high rpm, to pack more air into the cylinders than they would normally breathe. Despite the criticism of manifolds, this one actually helps performance.

Even though the manifold is good and the fuel/air metering system is supposed to be very efficient, the venturi of the air meter seems to offer the greatest resistance to air flow. Under full throttle and load at 6,000 rpm drivers found the plenum chamber had 1½ inches of vacuum. This is a higher vacuum than is often experienced with carburetion but is apparently necessary with a mass air flow type of metering.

Although the Rochester injection system shows evidence of a great deal of development work, there are indications that its present state could change somewhat. The use of sand castings for many of the small parts indicate plans for alterations, or a rush to get on the market. Sand castings are less expensive than die castings if a very limited production run is anticipated, and patterns for sand castings are quicker to produce if an early production deadline is to be met.

After driving the fuel injection Corvette many miles and under all sorts of conditions, it was very evident that this new fuel system has great possibilities with further refinement. Its present appeal would not be to the majority of the motoring public. The sporty individual, who enjoys instantaneous throttle response and a surge of power that never seems to run out,

no matter how tight you wind the engine, will be enthusiastic in his praise of the fuel injection unit.

However, grandma wouldn't be the least bit impressed with the necessity to shift into second gear at crusing speeds under 30 mph. And, even the sport would object to the hard starting encountered when poor throttle and clutch coordination on the part of the driver causes the engine to die. This lack of foot dexterity always seems to cause a loading-up condition that requires long starter cranking with the throttle wide open. Normal starts however, are much quicker than those experienced with carbureted engines. Even in 29 degree weather, with the car standing outside all night, the engine would fire up immediately, but often would not keep running until after two or three restarts.

The greatest praise for the Chevy fuel injection unit (from the driver's standpoint) comes from its insensitivity to motion. This was appreciated more than any other driving characteristic because of long experience with four barrel carburetors in turns. A tight turn causes a great power loss with many four barrel carburetors.

Quite often such power losses can be frightening during high speed cornering, when variations in power can cause one to lose control of a car. No matter how violent the maneuvers of the fuel injection Corvette, no variation in power output was experienced. Even though the horsepower rating of the fuel injection engine is only 13 higher (a portion of this figure can be attributed to the half-point higher compression ratio of the injection engine) than the one with dual four barrels, this insensitivity to motion makes the injection worthwhile for competition minded buyers.

The fuel-injection engined Corvette looks no different, on the outside, from the standard carbureted model. Body, chassis, interior, all look the same. The only identifying feature, from the outside, are the words Fuel Injection on each side of the body and on the rear deck.

Performance however is another matter. The acceleration and top speed of this car is fantastic for a stock car that is available to the public. In either low or second gear, 6,000 rpm could be reached with rediculous ease. At this rpm the speedometer registered 60 mph in low and 90 mph in second. Rear end ratio of the test car was 3.54 to 1.

Timed acceleration runs in two directions resulted in an average of 0-to-30 in 2.8 seconds, 0-to-45 in 4.3 seconds, and 0-to-60 in 6.35 seconds, all done without shifting from low gear.

The Corvette has all the makings of a wonderful sports car, and it is very gratifying to see Chevrolet developing this model to the extent which they have. but, the stock brakes are woefully inadequate to cope with the power and speed built into the engine and the stock suspension leaves a lot to be desired. The suspension of a car should be as good as, or better than, the engine and the Corvette suspension definitely is not. One simple item that would help immensely would be the addition of a torque reactor on the rear, something on the order of the Traction Master, to cut down wheel hop on acceleration and braking. •

CORVETTE TEST DATA

Test Car: Corvette
Basic Price: $3950.00
Engine: 283 cubic inch ohv V-8
Compression ratio: 10.5 to 1
Horsepower: 283 @ 6200 rpm
Torque: 290 @ 4400 rpm
Dimensions: Wheelbase 102 inches, Length 168.01 inches, Overall height (hardtop) 50.98 inches, Tread 57 inches front, 59 inches rear, Width 70.46 inches.
Curb weight: 2850
Transmission: Three-speed floor shift
Acceleration: 0-30 mph 2.8 seconds, 0-45 mph 4.3 seconds, 0-60 mph 6.35 seconds
Speedometer corrections: actual speeds were 28, 42 and 56 at an indicated 30, 45 and 60

by Stephen F. Wilder

SCI LOOKS AT THE '58 CORVETTE

CHEVROLET'S 1958 Corvette incorporates several improvements to the body and a few minor ones to the engine. The plastic body has the aluminium reinforcements in the dash structure, which were introduced in 1957, extended back under the door openings. The front and rear bumpers are now bracketed to the frame in conventional American style, but they can be removed should the car be used for racing, so saving just under 100 lb. in weight.

Uncowled dual headlights show how attractive most American front ends would be if they would forget the "I'm longer than you are" idea. Just below them are really large holes for blasting air onto the brakes, but on the test car, alas the "holes" were painted black!

Further production experience with the fuel injection nozzles and metering controls permits closer control over the fuel-air ratio than previously. The hot spot diaphragm is more sensitive and the air-filter is also changed. On all Corvettes, the dynamo is now on the right so that the fan belt engages the water pump pulley over a far greater arc, reducing slippage at high revs. Common to all 1958 Chevy's with the 4,638 c.c. engine are a new distributor rotor and a cap with longer sides to help keep out moisture.

Like most manufacturers, Chevrolet are none too happy about some of the attempts to make "boulevard" engines produce such high power outputs. More is required than just a Duntov high-lift cam and solid pushrods, although the factory is not too specific as to what is. What they have done is to clarify the picture of available options.

First of all here is what an absolutely standard Corvette would have: a 4,638 c.c. V-8 engine with a normal camshaft and hydraulic tappets (limiting revs. to about 5,500 r.p.m. as on the test car), a single four-barrel Carter carburetter, a "close-ratio" three-speed transmission (also used on other Chevy's with the 4,638 c.c. engine), a 3.7 : 1 crown wheel and pinion, 6.70 × 15 tyres (tubeless or not, to choice) on 5K × 15 steel wheels, and a choice of either a hardtop or a hand-operated folding one.

Options that do not change the basic car's essentially "boulevard" character include: Powerglide transmission and with it, a 3.55 : 1 rear end; electric operating window equipment; a hydraulic mechanism for the folding top; and for the belt-and-braces types, both the hard and soft tops may be ordered on one car.

To improve performance, one can order either two Carter four-choke carburetters or fuel injection (we had the latter)

the manifolds differing slightly between Powerglide and manual-change cars. But for the most in "go", there is the "D" fuel injection engine, which features a 10.5 : 1 compression ratio, a high-lift cam, solid pushrods, an air intake extension to bring in cool outside air, a reputedly "more efficient radiator", and a tachometer reading up to 8,000 r.p.m. Maximum output is 290 b.h.p. at 6,200 r.p.m. Especially designed for this engine, but available separately, as on the test car, is a really delightful, all-synchromesh, four-speed gearbox.

In much the same category are the "Positraction" limited-slip differentials available with either the 3.70, 4.11, or the 4.56 ratios. The Standard Chevrolet 3.89 gears will fit the carriers of either the 4.11 or the 4.56 Positraction differential, although this cannot be specified in the order. To give slightly better side-load characteristics, wider ($5\frac{1}{2}$K × 15) rims are available for fitting 7.10 or 7.60 × 15 tyres, racing or otherwise; the difference between the two enabling last minute "gear" swaps to be made at races.

For the man who is really serious about racing, a heavy-duty brake and suspension specification is offered in an all

The boot space shows the American influence on sports car design; it's huge

or nothing deal. To get this you must also order the "D" engine and the limited slip differential. But what a package! Stiffer front coils give a spring rate $13\frac{1}{2}$ per cent higher. The anti-roll bar is 40 per cent stiffer. The rear springs, with an extra leaf, have a $9\frac{1}{2}$ per cent higher rate. The shock absorbers, with 88 per cent larger working area, have different valving and finally, the steering ratio is changed from 21 : 1 to 16.3 : 1 by lengthening the third arm idler.

The famous Cerametallic brakes are fitted and it is interesting to note that although the drum diameter remains at 11 in. and the shoes are a full half inch wider, the total braking area is actually reduced by 20 per cent because the leading shoes are lined over only half of their length. To reduce the amount of braking done by the rear wheels, the rear brake cylinders are only $\frac{7}{8}$ in. diameter instead of 1 in., whereas the front ones remain at $1\frac{1}{8}$ in. The drums have cooling fins cast on the rim, and as a further option, vented backing plates with air scoops are available. Those large holes in the front mentioned previously may then be opened up and a duct will carry air back, not only to the front brakes, but under the door sills all the way to the rear ones, too.

The Cerametallic brakes are definitely not intended for all types of driving. Corvettes so equipped are delivered to the customer with a placard on the windscreen which reads, "This car is not for street use". Until warmed up, they are quite apt to pull strongly to one side or the other; not quite the thing for Grandma on her shopping jaunts.

Faced with the realities of the American scene, Chevrolet now follows tradition in marketing two apparently similar, yet actually quite different sports cars, one for the every day sort of user who might occasionally go racing, and another for the serious competitor in the Production category. However, in this case, the engine mods from the racing model are readily available without the heavy duty brake and suspension kit which may seem rather the wrong way round. But at least you can't get the "D" engine with the Powerglide transmission. That would be too much!

One of the pleasanter aspects of this test was that, being in the nature of a sneak preview, the entire operation was conducted on General Motors' Proving Grounds at Warren, Michigan. After the brake fade and acceleration tests were completed on the 1½ mile level straight, we turned the Corvette loose on a sample road circuit with a multiplicity of turns of varying radius, camber, and surface. A visitor is said to have remarked naively that GM, with all it's money, certainly could have afforded to build better roads than these. Be that as it may, we were able, in a very short time, to discover how the 1958 Corvette behaves in nearly every conceivable road situation. It may be summed up as "very well indeed."

There are no tricks at all to the steering, which is amazingly light at all times. We went through a series of S-bends at

(ABOVE) *The fuel injection equipment is mounted beween the cylinder head rocker boxes*

(LEFT) *During a brake fade test the Corvette dips its nose sharply, but braking efficiency remains high*

(BELOW) *Under the bonnet accessibility is good although the injection pump takes up a lot of room*

speeds ranging from 40 to 70 m.p.h. The only time the car felt at all uncertain was on a special piece of road featuring ridges running parallel to our direction of travel. The reaction here was pretty typical, the back end wanted to walk out when we crossed them on a diagonal. Elsewhere on the track, when we abruptly crested a sharp rise in the middle of a 70 m.p.h. bend, the front of the car moved out only slightly, a tribute to a well-arranged front suspension and the high polar movement of inertia. On really tight hairpins, tighter ones than you have any right to be going that fast on, the steering lock seems to call for rubber arms. (The HD kit reduces the 3.7 turns lock to lock to under 3.)

Whether on fast bends or slow, when you reach the limits of adhesion, the back starts to come around in a calm, unhurried manner that leaves you plenty of time to get off the throttle a bit. On really rough surface, it is rather more ruffled, for the rear axle is a heavy item of unsprung weight. After finishing the tests we were told, that the car we had been driving was not equipped with the HD suspension options. We were suitably impressed.

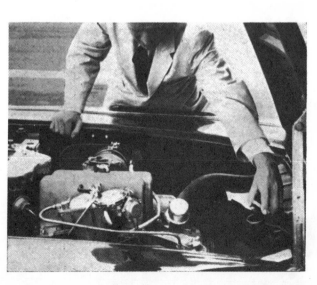

Our test-driver Mr. Rose, who was provided by GM to do the driving while Wilder did the timing, confessed that standing starts were not his speciality. As we have said before, they were not the Corvette's most polished manoeuvre either. It is a crying shame that the new parallel trailing arm rear suspension on the standard Chevrolet is not used in the Corvette, because its ability to completely eliminate axle wind-up would be most appreciated. Parenthetically, this major advance in rear suspension (for American cars, that is) comes about as an incidental result of the switch to air suspension and the attendant loss of a means of location provided formerly by the leaf springs.

Once under way, the limited slip differential really earns its keep and the acceleration is quite breath-taking. The gear ratios in the four-speed gearbox are well spaced—the ratio step between gears ranges from 1.265 to 1.325—and all gears are synchromesh (will wonders never cease?) It is at least the equal of any box we've ever tried, not only with respect to the suitability of the ratios to the engine performance, but the smoothness of the synchromesh brings to mind the old metaphor about a hot knife and butter.

One fault which did show up towards the end of our acceleration runs was a trace of clutch slip when rushing the change. When you consider that for the previous 10 days this same car had been subjected to the machinations of various and sundry road-testing "experts", this is perhaps understandable.

Because our tests were made on a working day at the Proving Grounds, the normal "traffic" on the high-speed straight (2½ miles of level, three-lane road in each direction with a banked turn-round at each end) prevented the Test Manager, Mr. Caswell, from allowing us to exceed 110 m.p.h. With the same final drive ratio and engine as last year's fuel injection test car, the top speed should be about the same, namely 125 m.p.h., as the frontal area is not changed all that much.

As before, the throttle linkage seems a bit quicker than we would prefer, and with the faster bends requiring careful feathering, it is necessary to brace the edge of your right foot to operate the throttle. The steering wheel, in typical Chevrolet fashion, is right under the driver's chin. Even so, the Corvette is easily controlled, the brake and clutch pedals are both well placed and smooth in operation, and there is plenty of room to stretch your left foot—or brace it, on sharp right turns. And brace it you must, because the Corvette's bucket-type seats are the best argument for seat belts we've met; one sits on them, not in them, and there is virtually no lateral support whatsoever. Seat belts will be standard equipment this year, which is admirable; but better contoured seats would be another big step forward, too.

The brakes were so good that we extended our punishing test for twelve stops instead of the usual ten, and it was only in the last two that a slight but definite weakening showed up. We are therefore quite disappointed to find that these were experimental linings only. Still, it's encouraging, as it shows that Chevrolet has been doing a lot of work to provide the average Joe with significantly better brakes, without him being subjected to the disadvantages of the Cerametallic brakes—and with a fair amount of success. ★

SPECIFICATION: 1958 Chevrolet Corvette with fuel injection

Engine: V8, overhead valves. Bore 98.4 mm. (3.875 in.), stroke 76.2 mm. (3 in.), capacity 4,638 c.c. (283 cu. in.). Compression ratio: 9.5 : 1 (10.5 : 1 optional). Output 250 b.h.p. at 5,000 r.p.m.

Chassis: Wheelbase 8 ft. 6 in., track (front) 4 ft. 9 in., (rear) 4 ft. 11 in., overall length 14 ft. 9 in., overall width 6 ft. 1 in., overall height 4 ft. 3 in. Kerb weight 2,912 lb. (26 cwt.). Distribution 52.5/47.5. Turning circle (right) 38 ft. 6 in., (left) 39 ft.

Performance:

o to 30 m.p.h.	3.3 sec.
o to 50 m.p.h.	5.8 sec.
o to 60 m.p.h.	7.6 sec.
o to 70 m.p.h.	9.5 sec.
o to 80 m.p.h.	12.2 sec.
o to 90 m.p.h.	15.7 sec.
o to 100 m.p.h.	21.4 sec.

Maximum speeds:

First gear 56 m.p.h., second gear 72 m.p.h., third gear 93 m.p.h., top gear 125 m.p.h.

Fuel consumption:

Touring speeds 22.6 m.p.g., high speeds 18.4 m.p.g.

Synchromesh on all four gears is offered on the 58 Corvette: will wonders never cease? Incidentally, the selectors for the box are of steering column type although the lever is the conventional type.

In the swim with dual headlights, the new model has grown too fussy.

1958 CORVETTE

Sportsmen and comfort-lovers can fit it to either personality, or both

That supposedly hard-to-sell commodity, elegant simplicity, is gone.

A beautiful wheel, crying for instruments and switches to match . . .

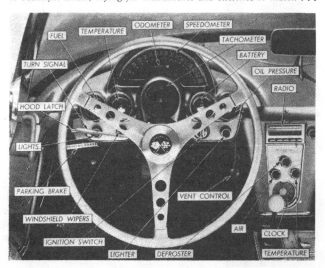

THEY SAY that the functions of the automotive press social season, now in full swing, fall into two major categories: those where the liquor is noteworthy but the car is not, and vice versa. Unfortunately, the same does not apply to the first flow of gilded rhetoric from the advertising agencies in regard to the latest products.

This month's cover car has been the subject of sundry improvements, as well as the corrosive influence of the "stylists." It can stand firmly on its still-15-inch wheels without the assistance of copywriters' ecstatic groans, from which we have gleaned the following facts:

Chevrolet has gone farther than ever before in attempting to please, via the option route, all potential Corvette buyers. Those who want a real sports car will lean toward the dual 4-barrel carburetors or the fuel-injected engine, with or without the special camshaft; compression ratios go up to 10.5:1, and an 8000-rpm tachometer comes with the top performance combination. A heavy-duty clutch and a non-slip differential (with either the standard close-ratio 3-speed gearbox or the all-synchronized 4-speed transmission; the latter was tested by Road & Track in the August issue) will also please the driving-minded buyer. So will optional heavy-duty suspension, with spring rates of 340 at front and 125 at rear instead of the standard 300 and 115; 1⅜-inch-diameter shocks instead of 1 inch; a 1³⁄₁₆-inch roll bar instead of ¹¹⁄₁₆; and an adapter for heavy-duty steering (also optional), whose 16.3:1 overall ratio replaces 21.0:1.

The cockpit, whose features are identified for the feeble-minded in the photo at left, is a highly satisfactory job of pleasing buyers with different tastes. The most glaring fault of previous models, the too-small tachometer placed low in the center, has been rectified. It is now in front of the driver, where it belongs, though it is still too small.

The first mass-production use of a central "control tower" is here haltingly pioneered. No true car controls are mounted in this spot, which has the advantage of their not being reachable, on purpose or accidentally, by a passenger. There are true gauges for oil pressure and generator charge. A broad, vinyl-covered grab bar takes up most of the right-hand side of the dash. Reflectors on the inside of the door warn oncoming drivers at night. A transistor radio and a new hard top (see cover) are extras, as is a power-operated soft top.

What does an Indianapolis
race driver look for when he
tries out a sports car?
Here's a candid report as,
for the first time...

SAM HANKS TESTS

EDITOR'S NOTE: When Sam Hanks announced his retirement from racing, having completed his most successful season yet, we asked him, "What next, Sam?"

"Don't know," Hanks replied. "Just sort of sitting tight to see what breaks. I'll be doing something in the car field, though, you can betcha."

"How about running some road tests for us?" we asked. "You could start with the Corvette. We'd like to get an opinion of the handling and overall impressions of this car from a real racing expert."

"Don't know why not," came the quick reply. So here's the report in Sam's own words.

I HAVEN'T HAD lots of experience with sports cars, but from what they tell me, the Corvette's doing a pretty good job of passing for one. That's what made me so interested when I was asked by MOTOR TREND to give my opinions of the Corvette—*four* of them, no less!

I won't try to describe all the details of the cars to you, for you're probably pretty familiar with them. I'll just tell you what I think of them, from the place that I know best, behind the wheel.

It might be good to first tell you what the four different versions were. One was a 230-horsepower job with a single four-barrel carb and three-speed box. The second had 245 horses, two four-barrels, a three-speed box and a limited-slip differential. The third was fuel-injected, with five more horsepower, but had a four-speed box. The last one was an all-out racing job, with special springs and shocks, heavy-

SAM HANKS (on left) confers with Walt Woron during tests at Riverside International Motor Raceway. Sam gave the Corvettes a thorough work-out and was frank in his opinions.

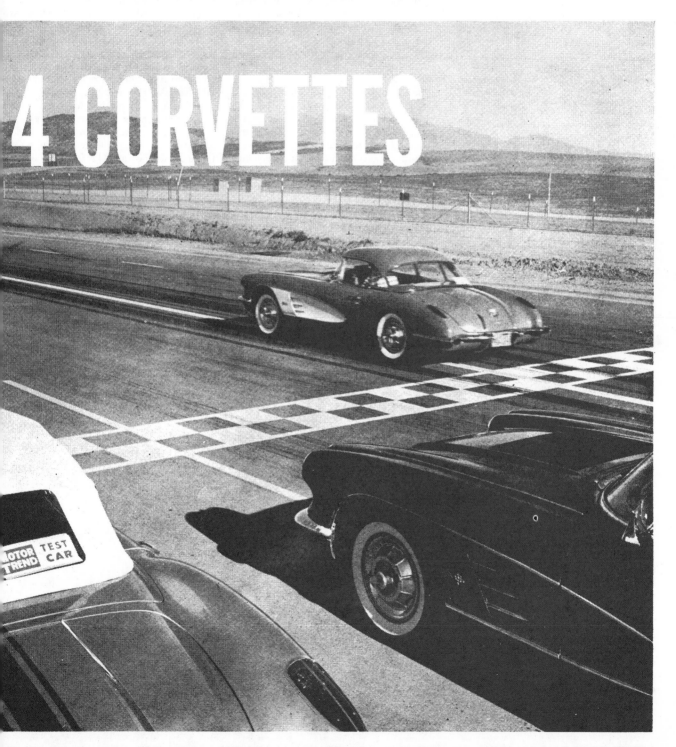

4 CORVETTES

duty brakes. It put out 290 horsepower from a fuel-injected engine, and used a four-speed box and limited-slip rear axle.

To get back behind the wheel—the first thing I noticed about all of them was that they had seat belts for driver and passenger. I don't know whether these were standard or not (*They're not. Editor*), but they should be. Anybody who's driving a car as hot as the Corvette ought to be glad to slip on a belt. I used them all the time, whether it was just driving around town or going full-bore around the course at Riverside Raceway. Several times that I took bad dips at high speeds, if I hadn't had my belt strapped on I would have stuck my head through the roof (*see photo at left*).

Being real critical, the first thing I objected to was the wheel position. To me it's too straight and too close to the driver. You don't get any leverage this way for fast cornering. It's like throwing close-in uppercuts instead of long-range jabs where you can get the weight of your body behind them. This may be the way they do it in sports cars, but I'd personally like the wheel further away and lying flatter like in the midgets and race cars I've driven. They could cut down the size

a bit, too, so your hand would clear the door release knob when you're steering. Seems to me this, and the armrest, would obstruct left arm movement and create a hazard at high speeds on a road course. Then again, it may be the sort of thing you get used to. Other people who drove the car didn't seem to complain about it.

The instruments are nicely grouped and because they have white needles and numbers against a black face they're easy to read—but only at night with light behind them. In the daytime, the convex glass that covers each instrument has a mirror effect, so instead of reading them quickly you see five reflections of yourself. I think if they made the glass flat it would be better. And while we're on instruments, I'd also like to see a bigger tach, even though this new location for the tach is a big improvement over where it was.

Two more things I think could stand improvement—then I'll get on to what I like about the car. The first one is the small sun ball you see reflected at eye level in the windshield. This is the result of the shiny paint on the cowl over the speedometer. If it was painted a dull color, or padded, or flocked, they could eliminate that annoying reflection.

FEAR NOT bad dips which may send you skyward in a Corvette. Good balance and stability will bring you safely back to earth.

POSITRACTION, limited-slip differential, shows its advantages here. Although right wheel is spinning in loose dirt, full traction is maintained as shown by the strip of rubber laid by the left tire. Car shown on the opposite page has a conventional differential and demonstrates almost complete loss of traction due to wheelspin in dirt.

PADDED ASSIST BAR that is fine for passengers to hold onto around turns can become a hazard in a sudden stop. In far right photo, bar is removed and shows steel channel covered by a small amount of foam rubber and plastic.

The second thing is a bit more serious, and that's the assist bar or hand grip across the curved-in area in front of the passenger. It's a good thing to hang on to, but it's not a good thing to bash your face or neck on. Even though it may feel soft on the outside because it's padded with some sponge rubber and is covered with leatherette, the main piece is channel iron that's 1/16-inch thick. It's tied in on each end to a heavy bar-plate that's bolted in place. This is the first thing Your Ole Dad would take off any Corvette he'd own. If I replaced it, it would be with a solid rubber bar, firm enough to hold you, but soft enough to give.

I like the position of the clutch, brake and throttle. They didn't take any getting used to and I never fumbled around with my feet trying to find the right pedal. This means a lot if you're doing any fast driving, particularly in a road race.

The gearshift levers on both the three-speed and four-speed transmissions are in a good position. The short stick is sitting right where you naturally drop your hand when you let go of the wheel to shift. I was particularly impressed with the four-speed unit because of its smooth operation and positive gear selector control. You can shift up or down just about anytime you want, providing you don't let the

continued

1 COMPETITION-EQUIPPED 290 (left) unlike other models has rear brake cooling air duct openings in front.

2 REAR BRAKE DUCTS lead from front opening and pass on underside of front fenders to ducts in the body.

FRONT BRAKES are also heavy-duty type with finned drums, airscoops.

engine over-rev. You can even downshift to low at speeds close to 50 mph!

The range between gears of the three-speed box seemed to be a bit greater, which allowed me to take the 245 Corvette around the Riverside course almost as fast as the two fuel-injected jobs. This was when the 245 wasn't running up to snuff, too. I didn't get a chance to take it around after it was broken in better and re-tuned, but if I had, I'm sure I could have equalled the time of the 250 easily. On another course it might be a different story.

One thing I'd do with any car as hot as the Corvette, and especially if I drove it hard, would be to adjust the clutch so the pedal would have about an inch of free travel after the clutch is fully engaged. This is a must if the car is to be used in competition on a dragstrip or road course. This proved out when I took the competition Corvette around Riverside. After running three laps and booming down the long straightaway at 6000 revs for the top speed check, the cockpit filled with smoke. It had that odd smell you

STEERING PIVOT ARM on non-competition models, combined with gear, linkage, gives 21 to 1 overall ratio.

FAST STEERING ADAPTER on competition model lengthens steering pivot arm, changes overall ratio to 16.3 to 1.

3 DISCHARGE ENDS of cooling ducts in body structure direct air toward finned, competition brake drums.

4 REAR BRAKES also have airscoop for cooling. Lining pads are sintered metal and ceramic composition.

get from a burning clutch, so I was pretty sure that was what caused it. It may also have been engine blow-by, but in our acceleration runs later we also got the same smell after a number of clutch-offs. A proper clutch adjustment might have corrected this.

On the way to Riverside during one day of the test I was following one of the other Corvettes. I noticed that its rear track was as wide as the front and this came as somewhat of a shock. How could such a car handle any good, I wondered.

It should be narrower in the rear if they really want a handling-bear, I thought. Yet I was surprised to see it go into corners and not get into any trouble. On the course later I found that it would break loose quite easily, yet the power slide was easy to correct. I soon found myself taking it around like I took my racing "stock" '57 Merc. Down the chute, brake hard, downshift, through the corner fast without going sideways, on the throttle coming out, snapshift to the next gear and wait—not too long—for the next corner.

Riverside is a tough test of transmissions and brakes. Outside of the trouble mentioned with the improperly-adjusted clutch, there was no transmission trouble. Some brake fade and hard pedal were noticed after two laps around at an average speed of 73.5 mph in the 250 Corvette. To show you what bigger brakes, finned drums, and airscoops front and rear will do for braking, I took the racing Corvette around for three laps at an average speed of 75.2 mph and didn't get a bit of brake fade at any time. This says a lot too for the stiffer

continued

FOUR-LEAF rear springs and standard shocks give the non-competition models softer ride, less stability.

COMPETITION MODEL has extra leaf in rear spring and heavy-duty shocks to improve handling characteristics.

Acceleration

	230	245	250	290
0-60	9.2 secs.	7.6 secs.	7.6 secs.	6.9 secs.
Quarter-mile	17.4 & 83.3 mph	15.9 & 91.6 mph	15.6 & 92.4 mph	15.6 & 95 mph
Half-mile	98.2 mph	109 mph	111.8 mph	114.9 mph
30-50	4.1 secs.	3.4 secs.	3.1 secs.	3.0 secs.
45-60	3.6	2.5	2.5	2.2
50-80	9.8	6.9	6.0	5.9

Top Speed

103.1 mph	112.0 mph	113.6 mph	118.7 mph

Handling

(Time around 3.3-mile Riverside Raceway road course)

3 min. 4.8 secs.	2 min. 45.0 secs.	2 min. 41.6 secs.	2 min. 37.9 secs.
Avg. 64.3 mph	Avg. 72.0 mph	Avg. 73.5 mph	Avg. 75.2 mph

Fuel Consumption

Stop-and-Go Driving	11.6 mpg	13.5 mpg	13.6 mpg	13.8 mpg
Highway Driving	14.0	12.4	15.5	14.0
Overall Average	12.9	12.9	14.9	13.9

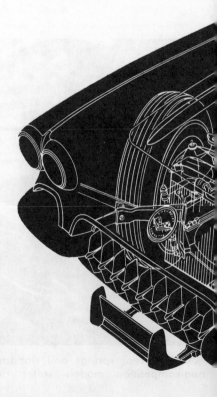

4 CORVETTES continued

springs and shocks and the limited-slip rear end. When your inside rear wheel lifts slightly enough to lose traction, you have the other one biting in. This should make a noticeable difference in lap times. It's handy in mud or on slick streets too.

There's one thing about the racing version of the Corvette. It's strictly not a street job. It's noisier, not only when you first start it, but all the time. It rides rougher, but is the kind I'd want to do any racing in. The brakes squeaked loudly in town, but that's because of the hard lining. If you're not interested in racing, you have a wide choice from among the other Corvettes—with or without fuel injection, four-speed, three-speed, or even Powerglide transmissions, hardtop with or without manual soft top, power-operated soft job, etc. I think my choice for an everyday job would be either the 250 with fuel injection or 230 with single quad carb and three-speed box. I'd also choose the

hardtop model because vision is better. When the soft top is up, there's a blank spot over on the right hind quarter.

You've got lots of power and good handling characteristics with all the Corvettes I drove. It's only natural that as you go up in horsepower, you go up in speed. The 290 had lots more zoom at the upper end than the 230 or 245, for example. It and the 250 also seemed to take the corners better too. Or maybe—in the case of the 250 versus the 245—it was because of the quicker response you get from fuel injection and the greater flexibility you get in four gears over three. Any way you look at it, I think the Chevrolet designers ought to be proud of the style of the Corvette, and their engineers should be proud of a fine sports car. It's real great to have an American-built production car that's available to the public as a combination cross-country, city traffic, competition sports car. I'm impressed. **/MT**

245  250 290

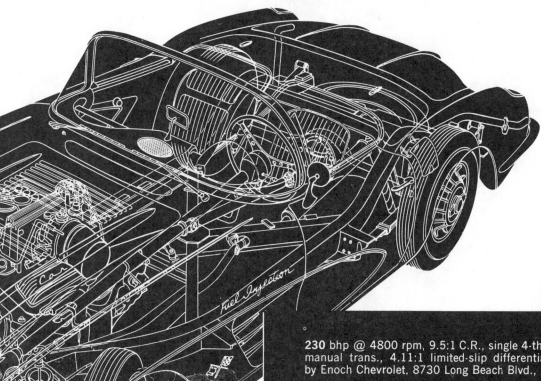

fuel injection

230 bhp @ 4800 rpm, 9.5:1 C.R., single 4-throat carb, 3-speed manual trans., 4.11:1 limited-slip differential. (Car furnished by Enoch Chevrolet, 8730 Long Beach Blvd., South Gate, Calif.)

245 bhp @ 5000 rpm, 9.5:1 C.R., two 4-throat carbs, 3-speed manual trans., 4.11:1 limited-slip differential. (Car furnished by Courtesy Chevrolet, 886 S. Western Ave., Los Angeles.)

250 bhp @ 5000 rpm, 9.5:1 C.R., fuel injection, 4-speed manual trans., 4.11:1 conventional differential. (Car furnished by Harry Mann Chevrolet, 5735 Crenshaw Blvd., Los Angeles.)

290 bhp @ 6200 rpm., 10.5:1 C.R., fuel injection, special cam, 4-speed manual trans., 4.11:1 limited-slip differential, racing brakes and suspension. (Car furnished by Courtesy Chevrolet.)

ROAD TEST 1959 CORVETTE

A pretty package with all the speed you need, and then some

CHEVROLET is now entering the sixth year of production on its famous and highly respected Corvette. Since its introduction as the 1954 model, the car has changed so much that it is hard to think of it as the same make.

Body configuration and general styling were the same for the 1954-55 models and for the 1956 and 57's. Now the 1959 version shares the body used on the 1958 Corvette.

The 1954 model was rather prosaic and had little to offer with the exception of being different from the other U.S.-built cars. Powered by a 6-cylinder engine that was essentially the same as the one introduced in the 1937 Chevrolet, the Corvette offered neither performance nor exceptional appearance. In 1955 the fiberglass-bodied car started to come alive when Chevrolet's new V-8 engine was offered as an option.

In 1957 the performance potential was given a real boost when fuel injection and a 4-speed, all-synchromesh transmission were made available. A heavy-duty suspension kit (developed at the request of competition-minded enthusiasts) included stiffer springs, dampers and improved brakes. These were all retained for 1958, and the commercial artists inflicted quad headlights and fake hood louvers on the only production sports car built in the U.S.

The new car will not necessarily make owners of the 1958 Corvette rush out to buy a new one, but a few worthwhile changes have been made.

Looks, while not the most important factor to consider, are certainly the first thing noticed about any car. The appearance of the 1959 Corvette has been improved by the simple expedient of removing the phony hood louvers and the two useless chrome bars from the deck lid.

Inside, the most significant change, and one of the only two that are noticeable, is in the seats. These have been redesigned and are among the most comfortable seats in any car, sports or otherwise. They quite adequately do the job of holding driver and passenger comfortably in place during all but the most violent action. We do feel, though, that safety belts would be desirable if much hard driving is to be done.

The second obvious change in the interior is the addition of a fiberglass package tray under the passenger's "grab rail." This tray serves in the usual glove compartment capacity as a catch-all for odd bits of useless detritus and

Cleaner hood lines (from simply eliminating the fake hood louvers) have made a slight improvement in looks for the 1959 Corvette. Trim on Corvettes, like all GM cars, is extremely well executed whether it is functional or mere decoration.

Even if the Corvette does carry more embellishment than most sports cars, it is still a sleek-looking package.

in this case (if the top is down), leaves, dust and possibly rain water.

This package tray is the first item that should be removed from a Corvette, as this badly placed receptacle also presents a safety hazard to the passenger's knees. The second item to be removed would be the grab rail itself: the thinly padded bar would probably do more harm than good in most cases.

We were fortunate, through the efforts of Steve Mason, to be able to use the facilities of Riverside Raceway to conduct the Corvette test. Frank Milne of Harry Mann Chevrolet (who furnished the test car) accompanied our test crew to the site and assisted in assembling the data on page 79

The first item on the check list, and one on which all results would hinge, was speedometer error. The mile-long straight at Riverside has a measured quarter and half mile which made this check simple and quick to perform. After taking the readings in 10-mile increments from 30 to 100 miles per hour we discovered the error to be about average for most cars tested, with the maximum error of 4 mph indicated at 100 mph.

Tapley readings, as can be seen in the data panel, were somewhat lower than those obtained with a similarly equipped 1957 Corvette (Road & Track, August 1957). The subsequent acceleration tests indicated the newer car to be somewhat slower getting off the starting line, but the figures improved as the upper speed ranges were reached. This could be explained by the additional weight of the 1959 model and by the newness of the car (it had less than 500 miles on the odometer) when we took it out for the test.

Starts were brisk but made with very little wheelspin, due to the efforts of the Positraction rear end, causing the engine to bog down just off the line. The first 20 yards were not very impressive as the engine struggled to overcome the lack of low-speed torque.

This is not to imply that the Corvette does not have torque. It does, but with a combination of peak torque at 4400 revolutions per minute and peak horsepower at 6200 rpm, it does have a lag before the engine really gets to work. This initial hesitation can be seen on the acceleration graph.

The 4-speed, all-synchromesh gearbox is still one of the smoothest-working units it has been our pleasure to use. (It is now optional on all Chevrolet V-8's.) The lever is placed at just the right location for driver convenience, and shifts, either up or down, can be made quickly and easily at any speed within engine limits. The main factor to consider in downshifting is the possibility of over-revving the engine in the process.

A new feature this year is a positive lock-out for reverse gear. This simple pull handle on the gearshift lever can be actuated by the first two fingers of the right hand as it rests on the shift knob.

Weight distribution of the car had shown 53% of the weight to be on the front wheels with one person in the car, but in spite of the nose-heavy attitude there was a marked tendency to oversteer. It was found with a little practice that a drift, once set up, could be maintained with little effort by dextrous manipulation of the throttle and steering wheel. The abundance of horsepower at the driver's command and adequately quick steering helped somewhat, too.

An extremely comfortable, though not very capacious, interior has new seat contours.

Heart of the Corvette is the fuel-injected, 290-horsepower, 283-cubic inch V-8 engine.

PHOTOGRAPHY: BATCHELOR

Panel lifts with top to disclose more luggage space.

The test car was equipped with the optional suspension (stiffer springs and dampers) which contributed to the ability to negotiate curves at maximum speed. Also installed on the car as part of the suspension kit was the racing brake set-up which includes Cerametalix lining, finned drums and air ducts for additional cooling. The brakes proved completely satisfactory during the test, with no fade being evident, and brought the car down from high speed in a straight line on every application.

The Cerametalix lining is not as effective when cold as it is when hot, and after the test was completed the lining squeaked when the brakes were applied. In spite of these minor annoyances, the brake kit is to be recommended for anyone contemplating fast driving with a Corvette and is an absolute necessity for competition work.

Driving this course at high speeds also confirmed our earlier opinion of one definite advantage of fuel injection. It is claimed by many Corvette enthusiasts that a Corvette equipped with dual 4-barrel carburetors will outperform the FI model at the upper end. This may or may not be true, but the fuel injection has it all over carburetors for throttle response and lack of sensitivity to motion. There is no flooding or starving on hard cornering with fuel injection.

Taking everything into consideration, the Corvette is a pretty good car. It probably has more performance per dollar than anything you could buy and parts are obtainable without sending to Italy, Germany or England.

The changes to the car in the last six model years are not so great as we think will come about in 1960. We predict that this will be the year of the big changes for Corvette, and most of them for the better. ⊙

Trunk space is larger than that of most sports cars but still requires owner to travel light.

1959 CHEVROLET CORVETTE

SPECIFICATIONS

List price	$4017
Curb weight	3020
Test weight	3370
distribution, %	53/47
Dimensions, length	178
width	72.8
height	51
Wheelbase	102
Tread, f and r	57/59
Tire size	6.70-15
Brake lining area	121.5
Steering, turns	3.2
turning circle	37
Engine type	V-8 cyl, ohv
Bore & stroke	3.875 x 3
Displacement, cu in	283
cc	4639
Compression ratio	10.5
Bhp @ rpm	290 @ 6200
equivalent mph	122
Torque, lb-ft	290 @ 4400
equivalent mph	86.5

GEAR RATIOS

O/d (n.a.), overall	
4th (1.00)	4.11
3rd (1.31)	5.38
2nd (1.66)	6.82
1st (2.20)	9.04

CALCULATED DATA

Lb/hp (test wt)	11.62
Cu ft/ton mile	148.6
Mph/1000 rpm (4th)	19.6
Engine revs/mile	3050
Piston travel, ft/mile	1525
Rpm @ 2500 ft/min	5000
equivalent mph	98.4
R&T wear index	46.5

PERFORMANCE

Top speed (6500), mph	128
best timed run	n.a.
3rd (6500)	98
2nd (6500)	77
1st (6500)	58

FUEL CONSUMPTION

Normal range, mpg	11/17

ACCELERATION

0-30 mph, sec	3.1
0-40 mph	4.2
0-50 mph	5.1
0-60 mph	6.6
0-70 mph	7.5
0-80 mph	10.0
0-90 mph	12.2
0-100 mph	15.5
Standing ¼ mile	14.5
speed at end, mph	96

TAPLEY DATA

4th, lb/ton @ mph	360 @ 75
3rd	475 @ 70
2nd	575 @ 55
1st	off scale
Total drag at 60 mph, lb	135

SPEEDOMETER ERROR

30 mph	actual 29.1
40 mph	38.3
50 mph	47.4
60 mph	57.0
70 mph	67.3
80 mph	76.5
90 mph	86.2
100 mph	96.0

Graph: MPH (corrected) vs ELAPSED TIME IN SECONDS — 1st, 2nd, 3rd, SS ¼

1959 CHEVROLET CORVETTE
ROAD & TRACK

'59 CORVETTE

Banked track hides considerable roll as Zora Arkus-Duntov places Corvette close in.

WITH EACH ANNUAL change, Zora Arkus-Duntov, the Corvette's godfather, has emphasized performance improvements. His theory is that to sell, the Corvette must first go. Styling has had its innings, too, but they have acted with more restraint than one expects from Detroit.

Perhaps in acknowledgement to the discriminatory taste of the sports car market, external changes for '59 were of a customizing nature only. The washboard-like, phony louvers on the hood and the Pontiac-like silver streaks on the trunk lid are now things of the past. Inside, there are recontoured seat cushions, a reverse lock on the four-speed's shift lever and an open-at-the-top catch-all which fills the opening in front of the "sissy-bar". Also the doorknob and arm-rest have been moved. Engineering changes at the rear include newly added longitudinal radius rods to prevent axle wind-up and re-arranged and recalibrated shock absorbers.

In discussing the new seats with Mr. Duntov, he pointed out that this is one of the most difficult compromises to make in a high-performance car. "In a racing car, the seat is 100% for working, just like a stool by a lathe. But in a passenger car, you're lucky if it's a 'work chair' more than 10% of the time. It must be easy to get in and out of, and comfortable for lounging in. The high sides of a real bucket seat are just right for holding you in place but they don't meet these other requirements."

Opening the trunk, later, we discovered an experimental seat cushion. We tried it and found it lets you sit a lot lower, accentuating the side support of the cushion edges and increasing headroom, too. The secret is foam rubber in place of the usual coil springs, the drawback is that it bottoms out too quickly on large bumps — sooner than the suspension. Oh, well, back to the drawing board.

Commenting on the door handles, Mr. Duntov pointed out that after driving Cor-

vettes for thousands of miles on the Proving Grounds, he decided to move them forward during a visit to Riverside, California when he had to borrow a raincoat (?). The one he got had cinch-straps on the sleeves and he kept opening the door when turning left!

The sissy bar is unfairly named, it's really quite the thing for hanging on when the driver is trying to prove something or other. The trash tray appeals to us, too, though others have condemned it as unsafe. We suspect that someone must have been road testing with their knees tucked under their chin because it just isn't that low.

The world's largest producer of automobiles, Chevrolet offers not just a wide range of models, but a staggering array of optional equipment on each model. As on the sedans, so on the Corvettes. Five variations on the 283 V8 theme are offered, three transmissions (two, three, and four speeds), four final-drive ratios, three brake lining choices and two suspensions, just to name the mechanical ones.

There is some interlocking involved, for instance, you can't order the Positraction limited slip differential with Powerglide; the latter must have the 3.55/1 rear end and cannot have the 290 hp version of the Fuel Injection engine. On the other hand, the stiff suspension is available only in combination with the latter engine and Positraction.

For this test, the editors of SCI checked through the list of equipment options, nominating those we thought would add up to the most desirable all-around Corvette that you can buy. We had in mind, not the all-out racing version sampled in the December issue but a happy compromise that would be suited to both serious traffic and casual racing.

Having carefully selected our list, we were pleasantly surprised to find that the Chevrolet Division could put such a sample at our disposal immediately. Seems a fellow

named Arkus-Duntov has a company car fitted out identically but for one exception. His car also has the quick-steering adaptor (3.25 instead of 3.7 turns lock to lock). Generally available only as part of the heavy-duty suspension kit, it's worthwhile on its own if you can stand the noticeably stiffer steering. And if you can get it.

Omitted from our list were the heavy-duty brake and suspension kits. For 1959, the heavy duty suspension features much stiffer springs than last year. In pounds-per-inch, the spring rate on the standard suspension, last year's HD kit and this year's are, respectively, 300, 340, and 550 at the front and 115, 125 and 145 at the rear. Though the kit's anti-roll bar diameter remains at 13/16-inches, the vast increase in spring stiffness contributes to both much flatter turns and much harsher bouncing. Nice for racing only, but not for the all-around usage we have in mind.

Corvette cornering has been the butt of many rude remarks by the anti-roll brigade. Duntov had interesting thoughts on this matter too. "For flat, smooth courses, such as Le Mans or Sebring," he said, "the heavy duty suspension option is very effective. But because it is so much stiffer, especially in roll, it would actually be a hindrance on a bumpy circuit such as the Nürburgring." An interesting thought, and interesting examples, too.

With so much power so freely available, rapid cornering necessarily becomes a maneuver requiring careful control of all the elements involved.

Though a stiffer anti-roll bar would reduce the independency of the front end, the reduction in roll would certainly promote more driver security. The experimental seats helped, so did the seat belts.

The steering, stiff for parking, was fine for controlling incipient slides, but as before, we found the throttle linkage much too sensitive. As a result, the car again appears to have two personalities. Either you motor sedately (though deceptively

Re-shaped seats increase lateral support.

Left, sintered linings; right, Cerametalix.

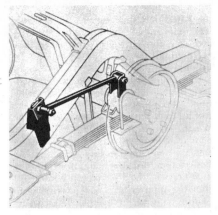

Axle wind-up prevented by radius rods.

quickly) through a corner, or pressing on somewhat, you're herding an untamed beast, one which responds more to the throttle than the wheel, and rather violently, at that.

In making up our list, the Cerametalix brake linings lost out as being entirely unsuited to highway use. When cold, they grab violently and erratically. Besides, they come only with the HD suspension.

Using regular drums, the sintered metallic brake linings at only $26.90 are so good and so cheap that they should be standard equipment. Though the 15° F. temperature during our test helped their heat dissipation, it gave us a chance to prove that they have no nasty habits when cold. Being inorganic, they don't soak up water either.

Flared drums, standard on all Chevies this year, have a bell rim-like flange which helps scoop air in from the inboard side. Between these and the linings, we repeatedly made stops from 90 and over without a trace of fade or increase in pedal travel. Pedal pressure, though, is higher than with organic (asbestos) linings. Running against a mild breeze, we managed zero to 100 mph and back to a standstill in 26.4 seconds, a figure that could be improved upon with experience.

Though it runs $484.20 more than the standard engine, we were anxious to see what the fuel-injected, hot cam V8's 290 horsepower felt like in a roadable Cor-

vette. To its great credit, it must be mentioned that cornering antics have no effect whatsoever on throttle response. This is in great contrast to quad-equipped cars, whether single or dual. They will just plain quit in the middle of a hard corner.

Racer Brown's chart (see Part II of his article in next month's issue) indicates that the all-out dual-quad version boasts better output than FI-cars at the top end. However, the ability of the latter to mix correct quantities of fuel and air, no matter what the car's gyrations or speed, assures it of better lap times on any circuit.

That one Corvette is not the same as another is evident from the variety of options. What comes as a considerable surprise is the dualistic personality of the particular car tested. In the twinkling of a throttle linkage, it turns from a submissive, sidewalk stalker to a fierce, roaring eater-upper of metallic monsters. Just as quickly, it reverts to silent smoothness, its exhaust murmuring, barely audibly, "Who, me?"

This high output engine enjoys such tractability that it will pull smoothly from its 750 rpm warm idle in fourth gear. No flat spots, no hesitation, and no matter how fast you mash the throttle. Just to rub it in, you can start from rest in any gear whatsoever without stalling and with hardly a thought of the clutch lining. Strangely, starts in first gear seem equally touchy. Seems the "fast" clutch linkage (you have your choice of 4.5 or 6.4 inches

of travel) has the unfortunate side characteristic that its mechanical advantage decreases quickly just as engagement occurs. For city traffic, we found that the combination of close ratios and the wide rev range made use of just first and fourth gears quite acceptable.

Despite this, the four speed gearbox ($188.30) was high on our list. For real get-up-and-go, it is well laid out. Shifting at 6500 rpm each time drops the revs only to 5000 or so, where the V8 is pulling strongly. To compare with the three speed box, all you do is skip second. Then coming out of first at 6500 drops revs to only 3900. Quite a difference when you're trying to make tracks.

Acceleration, while breaking no SCI records, is tops for pushrod equipment, and at the top end, quite similar to the 3.0 liter Ferrari 250 GT tested last year. Not so good off the line though, proving that smoothness at low revs is not synonymous with strength.

Duntov, in his kidding, quizzical way, said, "You know, the 3.70 axle gives better acceleration times than the 4.11." The operative word is "times", and specifically the times for zero to sixty, eighty and one hundred.

Assuming one is driving the car for best acceleration down a quarter-mile, (which is what we're after in our road test runs), this is quite true. With the 4:11 gears, shift points are 57, 75, and 95½. But with

Shapely body plays down large proportions of Corvette, derived from stock suspension.

the 3.70's, they change to 63, 83, and 106. The elimination of one shift and the necessary, though slight pause more than makes up for the lessened torque multiplication.

We thought our car went pretty good, even if it does cost twice as much as the Chev "315" tested in our January issue. But a recent letter from Don Gist of Lake Worth, Florida shows what can be done. Similar to this test car but without the weighty non-essentials and using the 4.56 Positraction rear end plus the following modifications, he has recently recorded a standing quarter in 12.57 seconds, completing it at over 109 mph! The changes he mentions are Traction Masters (his is a '58 model), open exhausts, an aluminum flywheel, Packard 440 wiring, 7.60 x 15

Bruce Slicks and the all-important flywheel shield. He adds, that the engine was "properly tuned." Uh-hunh.

If you want a particular kind of Corvette, pick out the options you want and GM'll make it. If they haven't the options you want, your local speed shop will.

If your interests lie in drag-racing, by all means pick the 4.56. If road-racing is more your style, then you'll probably want either the 3.70 or the 4.11, depending on which course you're running. Remember. 6500 in top corresponds to 139, 125, and 113 mph respectively with the 3.70, 4.11, 4.56 ratios.

For straight highway use, the 3.70, which we would now prefer, will provide the minimum of engine noise with plenty of acceleration. And if the chips are down,

you can always use the gearbox. The 3.70 might improve gas mileage, but a lighter foot would help more.

On the luxury side, we chose the station seeking push-button radio ($149.80), the heater-defroster ($102.25), windshield washers ($16.15) and, sybarites to the end, both the folding canvas top and the removable hardtop ($236.75). Added to the $3875.00 base price, the total climbs to $5127.80; transportation and state and local tax are extra.

It's not a low price car, and it's none too cheap to operate, but it goes well, it stops well, and with reservations, it corners well, too. For all around performance per dollar, the Corvette is hard to beat.

—*Stephen F. Wilder*

'59 CHEVROLET CORVETTE

PERFORMANCE

TOP SPEED:

Estimated .... 125 mph

ACCELERATION:

From zero to	seconds
30 mph	3.2
40 mph	4.2
50 mph	5.2
60 mph	6.6
70 mph	7.9
80 mph	10.1
90 mph	12.3
100 mph	15.6
Standing ¼ mile	14.9
Speed at end of quarter	98 mph

SPEED RANGE IN GEARS:

(700-6500 rpm, 7000 permissible)

I	0-57 mph
II	8-75
III	11-96
IV	14-125

SPEEDOMETER CORRECTION:

Indicated Speed	Timed Speed	Indicated Speed	Timed Speed
30	29½	70	65
40	38	80	74
50	47	90	83
60	56	100	92

FUEL CONSUMPTION:

Hard driving   10 mpg

SPECIFICATIONS

POWER UNIT:

Chevrolet 283-FI	Water-cooled V-8
Valve Operation	Pushrods and stamped rockers
Bore & Stroke	3.875 x 3.00 in. (98.4 x 76.2 mm)
Stroke/Bore Ratio	0.774/1
Displacement	283 cu. in. (4640 cc)
Compression Ratio	10.5/1
Carburetion by	Rochester fuel injection
Max. Power	290 bhp @ 6200 rpm
Max. Torque	290 lbs.-ft. @ 4400 rpm
Idle Speed	750 rpm

Chart: MILES PER HOUR vs SECONDS — STANDING 1/4 — gears I, II, III, IV — 1959 CORVETTE 290 H.P. FUEL INJECTION —S.C.I.—

DRIVE TRAIN:

Transmission ratios	test car	optional ratio
I	2.20	(2.21)
II	1.66	(1.32)
III	1.31	(1.00)
IV	1.00	
Final drive ratio	4.11	(3.70, 4.56)
Axle torque taken by	rear springs and radius rods	

CHASSIS:

Frame	Welded box section side members, I-beam X-member, box section front and rear cross members
Wheelbase	102 in.
Tread, front and rear	57, 59 in.
Front Suspension	Unitized, independent, coil springs and unequal wishbones, 13/16" dia. anti-roll bar.
Rear Suspension	Rigid rear axle housing, semi-elliptic leaf springs, upper radius rods
Shock absorbers	Delco telescopic, 1⅜ in. piston diameter
Steering type	Saginaw worm and ball bearing sector, 16.3/1 ratio
Steering wheel turns L to L	3.25
Turning diameter, curb to curb	37 ft.
Brakes	Sintered metallic linings in composite drums with cast iron rim, pressed steel web
Brake lining area	108 sq. in.
Tire size	6.70 x 15
Rim size	5.0 x 15

GENERAL:

Length	177 in.
Width	73 in.
Height	51½ in.
Weight, as tested	3400 lbs.
curb (factory figure)	3092 lbs.
Weight distribution, F/R as tested	53/47
Fuel capacity	16.4 U.S. gallons

RATING FACTORS:

Specific Power Output	1.02 bhp/cu. in.
Power to Weight Ratio, laden	11.7 lbs./hp
Piston speed @ 60 mph	1560 ft./min.
Braking Area per ton, laden	63.6 sq. in./ton
Speed @ 1000 rpm in top gear	19.2 mph

Remember the complaints a couple of years back that America had no real sports car . . . that this was a European monopoly?

Well, Corvette really shattered that legend, didn't it? And now the new four-speed gearbox* puts the lid on, but good!

This is the real McCoy—four speeds forward, and ALL Synchro-Mesh, even low gear. And the ratios are just what Herr Doktor ordered: 2.2 to 1 Low, 1.66 Second, 1.31 Third and 1 to 1 High. With these you ought to be able to find the top of the power curve in any situation.

Put this together with the new Positraction *limited-slip* rear axle,* the 4.6-litre fuel injection V8* and the rear axle ratios you want

(3.7, 4.11 or 4.56) — then buckle your chin-strap tight: You have just assembled the toughest, solidest, *goingest* machine that ever rolled down the American pike!

Right here we ought to mention that you can have a Corvette in just about any combination of performance you choose, from the 283-horsepower hot iron outlined above to the cream-smooth Powerglide* version with power-operated top* and all the extras. But, whatever you pick, you'll know one thing for sure: This is one of the genuinely great sports cars made in the world today—and the only one manufactured in America! . . . *Chevrolet Division of General Motors, Detroit 2, Mich.*

*Optional at extra cost.

CORVETTE
by Chevrolet

Here's what the hot pilots wanted for Corvette . . .

four speeds forward!

CORVETTE OR PORSCHE

"**Y**OU'VE REALLY STUCK YOUR FOOT IN IT NOW.**"** "How's that?" I asked. "It can't be done. You can't compare a Corvette with a Porsche. How unlike can two cars be?"

Briefly that was the feeling among some of the MT staff members when we decided to compare these two sportscars. On the surface they would seem to defy comparison. But dig a little and see how much alike they really are.

Both are in the $4000 price class. The Porsche Convertible D (replaces the Speedster) is slightly under—$3745 delivered on the West Coast. Our 250-hp soft-top Corvette rolls out in Los Angeles for $4375 including heater and four-speed gearbox.

Both are priced in the $4000 class. One is Europe's best sportscar in this category; the other America's best — and only — sportscar. How do they compare in handling, ride, performance?

by Wayne Thoms

Cost of fuel injection, $484, has not been included. (Although our test car carried an injection system, it does not materially affect overall performance. See "Sam Hanks Tests Four Corvettes," MT, March 1958.)

The obvious difference in the cars is power. No one denies that the Corvette has pure brute force available—power which makes the Porsche's 70-hp standard engine seem puny. But that force has to be transmitted to the ground, converted into forward motion, stopped, turned, controlled — sometimes by persons who don't fully realize the potential dangers involved. The result is that for all practical purposes a lot of that horse-

power becomes excess—an unusable excess. We're not knocking the Corvette. It's an exciting handful of performance which is not duplicated for the money, even from countries where labor is considerably cheaper than in the U.S.

Let's see how the two cars stack up, point by point, in areas where they are comparable.

How well are they put together?

We enter two schools of body building—steel vs. fiberglass. If you have definite feelings against fiberglass, consider revising

Corvette Convertible

your views. Corvette's 'glass work is smooth and every bit as functional as steel. During minor prangs it will come off unscathed, absorbing amounts of energy which would dent steel panels. Our only objection is to a certain amount of flexing around door jambs which means a few creaks and groans, apparently congenital in fiberglass construction. Panels match properly, doors close in a satisfying fashion; it is a carefully constructed automobile.

The Porsche is a masterpiece of precision fitting and close tolerances in its body construction. The wonder is that any coachbuilder can work so accurately. There aren't many cars in the world that are turned out free from visual defects, but the Porsche approaches perfection as nearly as can be.

After squeezing inside, what?

They're both sportscars and require a technique for entry and exit. It is really no problem and is, in truth, not as difficult as exiting from the rear door of some domestic '59s parked alongside a curb.

Visibility in both is perfect with tops down, limited in the rear quarter areas with tops erected. Designers of both cars kept the driver in mind when vital instruments were installed. Speedo, tach and the rest of the gauge layouts are clearly visible through the wheel.

Seating is a critical factor in sportscars. The consensus was that Porsche's well-upholstered, fully-reclining bucket seats are almost too good. They offer excellent support but tend to be overly soft, especially as compared to seating in previous year models. Individual seats in the Corvette are comfortable but could use added support under the knees. Both cars would benefit from adjustable steering columns. To obtain arms-out seating in the Corvette, for example, the seat must be run so far back that it is nearly impossible to fully depress the clutch.

How easily do they start?

Both engines turn over easily, starting quickly hot or cold. The Porsche has no choke, but a husky accelerator pump shoots big charges of raw gas through the carbs, giving a rich choke

Porsche Convertible D

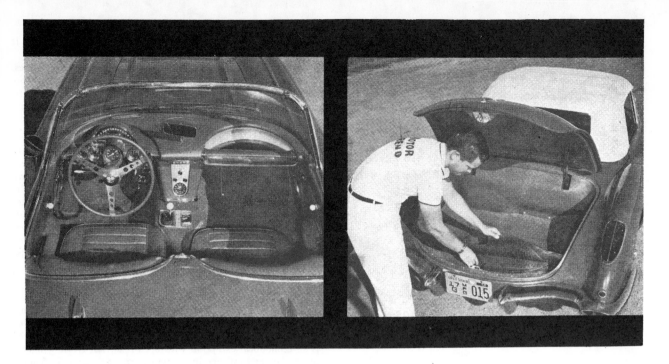

effect. Porsche carburetor heating is different. A pair of thermostatically controlled tubes blow hot air directly on the carburetors as the engine warms up.

How are they for city driving?

Both cars are good traffic machines requiring different driving techniques. We must give a slight edge to the Porsche here because quicker, lighter steering makes moving through tight traffic less of a chore. We found that most of the Porsche's city work was in second and third gear in order to avoid the overdrive fourth and to keep the revs in the "happy zone" above 2500 rpm. Torque from the Corvette is so fierce that the engine can loaf along in fourth, say at 20 mph, and pull away smoothly, although third is a more satisfactory traffic gear. Pushing the Corvette through town, the sensible driver will rarely exceed 2500 rpm.

How about open-country driving and high-speed handling?

Being forced to choose one of these cars in which to make a cross-country trip would be difficult. Both of them are capable of speeds far in excess of any legal speed limit. The Porsche will cruise all day long at 90 mph—comfortably; so will the Corvette—even faster. And make no mistake. This Corvette will handle. It corners flat and can be jockeyed through a hot turn with surprising ease.

Firmly suspended, as good handling sportscars should be, these two cars vary considerably in riding qualities. The Corvette rides harshly with a substantial amount of pitch and chop on rough roads. The same routes are gobbled up by the Porsche's four-wheel-independent suspension with a minimum amount of shock transmitted to driver and passenger.

Match the two cars on a tight mountain road where the Corvette's torque and acceleration can't be utilized and you'll probably get there quicker in the Porsche. It just hangs on better in the turns. If this mountain road should be downhill, the Porsche's brakes will outlast the Corvette's. The Germans have installed brakes that stop in a hurry and refuse to fade. Corvette's standard binders are more than adequate for normal use but for competition or extremely hard use, the optional

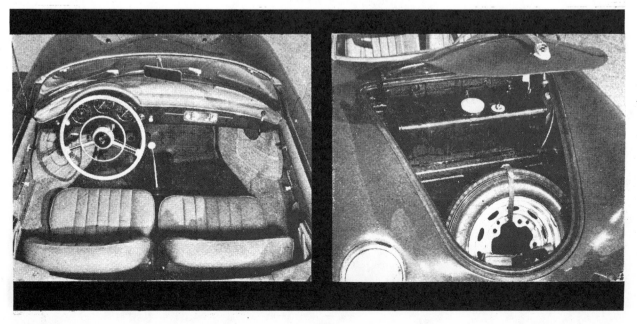

Acceleration

	Corvette	Porsche
0-60	7.8 secs.	15.2 secs.
Quarter-mile	15.7 & 90 mph	19.9 & 67.5 mph
30-50	4.2	5.9
45-60	3.2	6.1
50-80	6.8	19.6

Top Speed

(Test cars, estimated)	120 mph	105 mph

Handling

(Comparative times around 3.3-mile Riverside Raceway road course)

	2 min. 32 secs.	2 min. 47 secs.
	Avg. 78.5 mph	Avg. 71 mph

Fuel Consumption

Stop-and-Go Driving	14.3 mpg	24.5 mpg
Highway Driving	14.9	35.0
Overall Average	14.6	29.7

(Fuel Used: Mobilgas Special)

Cerametalix lining is a must. Because it works best when hot, it is not recommended for idling around the city.

Both cars are blessed with four-speed, all-synchro gearboxes. Porsche takes justifiable pride in theirs but we prefer the Corvette's. It's smoother, faster and has a shorter throw between gears—qualities which rank it with the best in the world.

How about fresh air, heating and defrosting?

Here is an area where Detroit engineers, attuned to the luxury requirements of their customers, have an edge on overseas sportscar designers. Porsche has a perfectly good hot air heating and defrosting system, better than most other sportscars. The Corvette has a flexible system of heating, ventilating and defrosting which will warm up sub-zero days or take the edge off a nippy Southern California night with equal ease. It has been designed with passenger comfort in mind rather than installed as something which works but which no true enthusiast will be using anyway.

Did someone mention fuel economy?

First of all, sportscars shouldn't be purchased for economy. The nature of their use—fast acceleration, high speeds, use of intermediate gears—precludes good mileage figures. The Porsche is an economical exception with open-road, fast cruising figures of 35 mpg and mileage in congested areas averaging 24.5 mpg. Combining the Corvette's city and open-road fuel consumption gave us 14.6 mpg—really not too bad for 283 cubic inches constantly begging to be opened up.

Where do I put the suitcases?

There is luggage space enough for two persons in both cars. The Porsche stows it behind the front seats, occupying the occasional rear seat. A conventional trunk in the Corvette will take about the same amount of material as the Porsche. There is a very limited amount of space under the Porsche front hood.

How about service?

The Corvette's obvious advantage is parts and service from thousands of Chevy dealers across the country. Porsche service, often combined with Volkswagen, is fairly good but the dealer distribution will never approach Chevrolet's. Corvette's high-

performance V8 gets expensive to maintain when the owner insists upon the ultimate in performance. On the other hand, the specialized nature of Porsche maintenance has kept repair prices high. It adds up to the fact that sportscars are luxury items with upkeep prices to match.

Which one is the best buy?

Depends on what you want in a sportscar. Both have a lot to offer. If getting a lot of performance from a precision-built, small-displacement engine is intriguing, then the Porsche is the answer. If you like the idea of having one of the world's fastest accelerating sportscars, then pick the Corvette.

MT staff members became extremely partisan—on both sides of the fence. Feelings were evenly divided except for one nameless male who refused to choose, insisting that he would be happy only with both cars.

The truth is that both are excellent buys. They're sturdy, reliable, comfortable and above all, fun to drive. What more can you ask of a sportscar? **/MT**

CORVETTE

ENGINE: Ohv V8 with rockers. Bore 3.88 in. Stroke 3.0 in. Stroke/bore ratio .78:1. Compression ratio 9.5:1. Displacement 283 cu. in. 1 4-bbl. carburetor. Dual exhaust. Advertised bhp 250 @ 5000 rpm. Bhp per cu. in. .88. Piston speed @ max. bhp 2500 ft. per min. Max. torque 305 lbs.-ft. @ 3800 rpm.

TRANSMISSION: Manual shift, 4-speed all-synchromesh. Ratios 2.20:1, 1.66:1, 1.31:1, 1.00:1.

CHASSIS: Welded box section frame with I-beam X-member. Front suspension—Independent ball joint, with long and short control arms, coil springs and tubular shock absorbers. Rear—Solid axle, with outrigger-mounted semi-elliptic leaf springs and tubular shock absorbers. Axle torque taken by radius rods. 6.70 x 15 tires. Steering—Saginaw semi-reversible worm and ball bearing, 3.7 turns lock-to-lock, ratio 21.0:1. Rear axle—conventional, ratio 3.70:1.

DIMENSIONS: Wheelbase 102 in., overall length 177.2, overall height 51.6, overall width 72.8, front tread 57, rear tread 59, rear overhang 42.4.

PRICE: Factory-suggested retail price of test car equipped with heater and four-speed gearbox—delivered Los Angeles, $4375 plus taxes.

PORSCHE

ENGINE: 4-cylinder opposed, air-cooled, ohv with rockers. Bore 3.25 in. Stroke 2.91 in. Stroke/bore ratio .9:1. Compression ratio 7.5:1. Displacement 96.5 cu. in. (1588cc). Advertised bhp 70 @ 4500 rpm. Bhp per cu. in. .73. Piston speed @ max. bhp 2180 ft. per min. Max. torque 81.2 lbs.-ft. @ 2800 rpm.

TRANSMISSION: Manual shift, 4-speed all-synchromesh. Ratios 3.09:1, 1.76:1, 1.22:1, 0.85:1.

CHASSIS: Pressed steel welded in box section, unit body-frame construction. Front suspension—Two transverse torsion bars and trailing arms, anti-roll bar, tubular shocks. Rear—Swing axle, transverse torsion bars and trailing arms, tubular shocks. 5.60 x 15 tires. Steering—ZF worm gear with hydraulic damper, 2¼ turns lock-to-lock, ratio 16.0:1. Standard rear-end gears 4.43:1.

DIMENSIONS: Wheelbase 82.7 in., overall length 155.8, overall height 51.5, overall width 65.6, front tread 51.4, rear tread 50.1.

PRICE: Suggested retail price of test car equipped with heater (standard) and four-speed gearbox (standard)—delivered Los Angeles, $3745, plus taxes.

PHOTOS BY BOB D'OLIVO

CORVETTE

THE sportiest U.S.-produced automobile is probably the best description of the '59 Corvette. No other mass produced domestic vehicle falls into a similar category or challenges the supremacy of Chevrolet's two-seater. Although compared by many, in past years, with Ford's two-seater Thunderbird, the Corvette cannot be considered the same type of automobile.

When a Corvette is acquired it bestows upon its owner a certain prestige status that accompanies the ownership of an expensive car with eye appeal. However, the features that make the car appealing go deeper than its clean streamlined exterior. It can be a sports car or a prestige car depending on the desires of its owner. All manner of options can be had to suit the broad tastes of the buying public.

The car tested might be criticized by the spartan sports car enthusiasts who disapprove of "frills" and feel that performance and better handling are more desirable. For those people, a large number of chassis and engine options are available that will considerably alter the results obtained by the test. The majority of the options can be obtained as factory installed features, thereby eliminating the necessity of speed-shop work.

The test car was not equipped as an all-out racing machine but rather as a moderate high performance town and highway car. Powered by a dual four-barrel-equipped 245-hp engine, performance was better than that of all Detroit machinery except one. A 0-to-60 time of eight seconds flat is a testimonial to its ability. In a quarter mile, from a standing start, a speed of 88 mph was reached with an elapsed time of 15.26 seconds.

A strong contributor to the quarter mile performance was the fine shifting four-speed gear box. After once winding the engine to its peak the close ratios of the transmission made it possible to maintain a high engine rpm after each shift. After the first shift engine rpm never dropped below 4300. After attaining a speed of 41 mph the engine rpm ranged between 4300 and 5500 for the rest of the course.

A top rpm limitation of 5500 was enforced by the hydraulic lifter cam. If the hottest optional solid lifter cam had been employed in the engine, it would have been possible to wind the engine 1,000 rpm tighter and the quarter-mile time would have been better.

Even though the rear end gear ratio was 4.11-to-1 the 2.2-to-1 first gear ratio made the car feel slightly sluggish initially. The small numerical ratios of the four-speed gear box produced a definite disadvantage in the 0-to-30 and 0-to-45 acceleration runs. A 4.56-to-1 rear end gear ratio would definitely be advisable if acceleration competition were anticipated.

The gear ratios of the four-speed transmission indicate that the selection was made with an eye toward closed course racing and not drag strip usage. A further indication of racing anticipation is the synchronizing of all forward gear sets. Downshifting into any lower gear, including first, can be accomplished without double clutching.

One of the most irritating frustrations that most drivers experience with four-speed transmissions is the shift into reverse and the confusion of reverse for some other gear while shifting forward speeds. This problem is completely eliminated in the design of the new Chevrolet transmission. A positive reverse gear lockout prevents any inadvertent clash with reverse when shifting the four forward gears. Knowing that a mistake is impossible, inspires a great deal more shifting confidence than existed in the past. The reverse position of the lever is forward and to the left of first gear, but a spring loaded trigger bar below the gear shift knob must be raised for this shift.

A further assist to the usually tedious procedure of shifting gears is the over-center spring used on the clutch pedal. This spring is so positioned when the clutch pedal is not depressed it helps slightly to keep the pedal up. After depressing the pedal a small amount, the spring's tension is shifted to the other side of the fulcrum and assists your leg to depress the pedal. This simple and effective system makes it possible to use a clutch pressure plate with sufficient pressure to transfer

DUAL FOUR-BARREL carburetion helps boost horsepower of Chevy's standard 283-cubic-inch engine to the 245 figure.

GOOD STORAGE space is an asset not even hoped for in a sports car, but the Corvette has it. The spare tire may be reached by lifting a hatch located in the trunk floor.

RICH INTERIOR is as comfortable as it is plush. Instrumentation (opposite page) is close and legible, and the four-speed stick-shift is right at hand to dish out more than ready passing power.

the engine's torque under all conditions without making the pedal pressure so great that it would be objectionable to frail drivers.

Although all floor mounted controls were easy to operate and appeared to be well placed, the same thing cannot be said for the all important steering wheel. A steering column adjustment similar to the types used on imports would add considerably to the comfort and safety of driving the Corvette. A tall person with the seat moved to the required rear extreme finds that the steering wheel interferes with brake application bcause it gets in the way of his right knee.

Seating positions give that "on-the-floor" feeling so prevalent in present day domestic cars. Although the seats were comfortably padded, they didn't display the positive positioning effect of the buckets in some of the competition imports.

One cannot be too enthusiastic in praising Chevrolet for equipping this car with a complete set of instruments. There is not a single red or green warning light on the panel. All instruments are well placed and easy to read, employing black faces with white numerals and letters. Most drivers prefer the large speedometer with the tachometer subordinated, but some competition enthusiasts would prefer the sizes reversed.

The test car didn't display outstanding handling characteristics as those expected from a sports car. In fact it is entirely possible that there are a couple of sporty production sedans that will corner better. Regular production chassis options, to improve roadability, listed as R. P. O.'s can be ordered installed at the factory when the car is being assembled. For the front suspension there is a heavy stabilizer bar, sriffer springs and stiffer valved shocks. The heavier stabilizer bar probably does more to improve cornering than any other option because it reduces body lean by utilizing tension from both front springs to support the side to which the car leans.

Rear suspension options include five leaf springs instead of the conventional four, heavy duty shocks and radius rods that anchor the top of the rear axle housing to the frame. The radius rods form a parallelogram with the forward half of each semi-elliptic rear spring, thereby more accurately maintaining rear axle position and preventing spring windup. Needless to say Positraction limited slip differentials are also available to improve rear end behavior.

The Corvette's light weight, only 2940 pounds, seemed to reduce the tendency toward brake fade to such a degree that considerably more brake abuse was possible than with a passenger car. Anyone wanting to use his Corvette for sports car racing can order the car with segmented ceramic-metallic linings and deep finned cast iron drums on all four wheels. The brake kit even contains ventilated backing plates with air scoops. Despite the obvious advantages of the special brakes for road racing, the person that buys a Corvette for normal use should pass them by. The cer-met linings give a much harder feel to the brake pedal and they squeal like the proverbial "stuck pig."

Steering ease and ratio seemed open to criticism by the test crew. Too many turns from lock to lock appeared to be the most objectionable feature coupled with the necessity for more than an average amount of muscle. These two complaints, unless remedied by the installation of power steering, are in complete opposition to each other since a faster steering will result in a stiffer action. The 1600-lb. weight supported by the front wheels is considerably more than one finds on the lightweight foreign sports cars. For those that don't mind the stiffer steering that is coincident with a faster ratio, a special long idler arm extension is available that changes the ratio from 21-to-1 down to 16.3-to-1. This arrangement could be used with power steering and you "could have your cake and eat it too."

TEST DATA

Test Car: Chevrolet
Body Type: Corvette
Basic Price: $3875
Engine: V-8
Carburetion: Dual 4-barrel
Displacement: 283 cubic inches
Bore & Stroke: 3.875 x 3.0
Compression Ratio: 9.5-to-1
Horsepower: 245
Horsepower per cubic inch: .87
Torque: 300 lb.-ft. @ 3800 rpm
Test Weight: 2940 lbs. without driver
Weight Distribution: 54 per cent on front wheels
Power-Weight Ratio: 12 lbs. per horsepower
Transmission: 4-Speed Synchromesh
Rear Axle Ratio: 4.11 to 1
Steering: 3½ turns lock-to-lock
Dimensions: overall length 177.2 inches, width 72.8, height
    51.6, wheelbase 102, tread 57 front, 59 rear
Springs: coil IFS, semielliptics rear
Gas Mileage: 14.3 mpg
Tires: 6.70 x 15
Speedometer Error: indicated 30, 45 and 60 mph are actual
    29, 43½ and 57 mph, respectively
Acceleration: 0-30 mph in 3.4 seconds, 0-45 mph in 5.4 and
    0-60 mph in 8.0 seconds
    RPM @ 60 mph—2800

EVOLUTION OF A DREAM CAR

CONTRARY to most cars built for prestige rather than profit, Chevrolet's Corvette has grown to a position of even greater respect today than it had at its birth as a most revolutionary infant. Proof of and reasons for this situation can be seen in this brief review of past MOTOR LIFE tests of the Corvette.

1954—Hurrah for a true American sports car. Chevrolet took up the European challenge and the result is proof that a "compromise" car can be built. We'd be much happier with a wider choice in transmissions (modified Powerglide) and engines (Chevy's reliable six which delivers 150 hp).

1955—The addition of two extra cylinders under the hood has made a tremendous difference. The V-8 engine makes this a far more interesting automobile.

1956—New, more graceful lines make the Corvette much racier looking. New three-speed stick-shift gear box is the best one Chevrolet has ever had.

1957—Driving the new fuel-injection Corvette left everyone in a high state of excitement. It will reach 100 mph in the length of time it formerly took to reach 60 mph.

1958—From the small changes that continue to be made to the Corvette there is proof that the car's designers have been listening to critics.

Thus the story of Corvette's sensible evolution continues. It has established a design philosophy that might well be copied by other manufacturers.

Collapsible cloth tops and fiberglass hardtops, made of the same material as the rest of the body, are both available either separately or together, if requested at the time the car is ordered.

The convertible top can be ordered as a power or manually operated unit. If a wife will be sharing the driving, the former is recommended.

One point where the various regular production options fail to fill a need is in the distributor. The ignition system's ability to produce a hot spark under full throttle at any rpm goes unchallenged. Hopped up Corvette engines have been known to turn 7500 rpm without missing a beat using the stock dual point distributor. When it comes to fuel consumption under cruise conditions, the distributor lacks the ability to squeeze the utmost mileage from a tank of gas. A diaphragm load control, similar to the one appearing on the single point ignition of the 230-hp Corvette engine, would have made possible better mileage than the 14.3 mpg average of the test car.

Instead of being stereotyped, the Corvette, with very few exceptions, can be whatever its owner wants it to be. Powered with five different engines, ranging from the conservative 230-hp model to the 290-hp fuel injected hot rod, it is one of the most versatile cars offered today. •

CORVETTE FAMILY of dream cars which was displayed in the 1955 GM Motorama was a real look at the future. Both the Corvette hardtop (top, center) and the glassed-in "Nomad" station wagon became reality. In the foreground is the first "Corvair" coupe.

'59 CORVETTE
by Chevrolet

ONCE AGAIN, THE REAL McCOY—WITH AN EVEN SWEETER, SOLIDER WAY OF GOING!

Here's the '59 version of America's only honest-to-Pete sports car. The changes are not earth-shaking when you read them—but wait until you drive this one. Try the new parallelogram rear suspension and see what it does to power hop—how it nails all that torque right down on the pavement, how it smoothes the rear-end steering effect, how it cuts axle wind-up under hard braking. Check the new form-fitting seats, the reverse lockout in the four-speed transmission*, the new "road" version of our metallic-lined brakes*, the subtle improvements in driving position, the easier-to-read instruments.

But you get the idea. The '59 has been honed and polished and refined. And we feel free to say now that this is not only a veritable sports car—but it will handle, go and hang on better than any other production sports car in the world. Bar none!

It is pure delight to drive. And if you haven't given Corvette a chance to talk to you yet, don't put it off any longer. This is the real thing, for real drivers.... Chevrolet Division of General Motors, Detroit 2, Michigan.

*extra-cost option

First Impressions

1960 CORVETTE

Below: Corvette cockpit and controls have not been changed for 1960. The body lines — as well as the fiberglass material — also remain the same. In consequence resale value of 1959 Corvettes will not plummet.

by Karl Ludvigsen

► 1960 will go down as the Year of Speculation for Corvette, SCI not being the only magazine that was caught well off base on predictions of radically changed styling and construction. New-type Corvettes along the lines theorized had actually been proposed, but the terrific engineering concentration on the Corvair project literally left no time for other developments. From the exterior and in all important respects, then, the 1960 Corvette is identical to last year's.

Major changes, and worthwhile ones, have however been made in the cylinder head design. On all Corvettes the valve chamber of the head has been widened to make room for a more efficient oil drainage system, incorporating a special drainage groove to lead oil away from the valve springs and guides. On fuel injection engines, moreover, the aluminum heads first developed for the SS Corvette have finally made an appearance, saving 53 pounds compared to the cast iron engine. This head has considerably different intake porting and intake valves enlarged from 1.72 to 1.94 inches in diameter. Correspondingly the plenum chamber of the injection unit has been enlarged to match the cylinder head improvements. With injection (available only with manual shift) also comes a special piston giving an as-yet-unspecified higher compression ratio.

If the Duntov camshaft is fitted, several other high-performance options can be applied. An all-aluminum cross-flow radiator can be installed, saving yet more weight, a cold-air tube adjacent to the radiator can be connected up, and the car in general converted to a raceable machine.

Optional within the standard sheme of things are asbestos-based or sintered iron brake linings, a third choice being the ceramic-metallic system available as a Regular Production Option (RPO). For 1960 there is no special handling kit,

First impressions

Right above: A major change for '60 is the use of aluminum heads on the fuel injected engines. Heads were first developed for the ill-famed SS Corvette. They save 53 pounds over the cast iron units. Right below: Also added for '60 is this light rear anti-roll bar.

Zora Duntov feeling that some further mods to the standard chassis have made its handling good enough to do away with heavy-duty springs, etc. In addition to increasing rear suspension rebound travel by one inch, he has increased the diameter of the front anti-roll bar to 0.70 inch and has added a light-weight anti-roll bar to the rear suspension as well.

In action, this realignment of the Corvette's suspension reacts just about the way you'd expect. The Corvette has always been known as a strong understeerer that was fine for fast courses but less sprightly on slow ones and a shade wearying to handle in town. By increasing the roll resistance at the rear Duntov has brought the car closer to neutral steer feel on fast bends, where the Corvette now seems "lighter" on its feet and a shade more sensitive—not necessarily a good feel for racing use. The car can now be tossed around tight corners much more easily, but it must also be admitted that the larger rear roll couple tends to lift the inside rear wheel sooner than was the case before. A tentative conclusion might be that the new setup will be good for all-round use and for slower courses, with Positraction differential installed, but that many owners might usefully remove the rear anti-roll bar when trying for best results on fast tracks. During our Proving Ground trial we made no attempt to evaluate the performance of a fuel-injected Corvette, which obviously had acceleration on a par with its ancestors. Slight gains might be expected from the horsepower increase, now to approximately 305 bhp, and the weight reduction made both by the aluminum heads and the aluminum clutch bell housings used on all manual transmission cars. As before, the Corvette for 1960 is a formidable performer.

—kl

CORVETTE FANS, who were thrilled by recent displays of the XP-700 as an indication of what might lie ahead for future models, can get all the excitement they need behind the wheel of today's 1960 model. We have in mind the Arctic white twin four-barreler with four-speed stick shift that we hated to part with after nearly a thousand miles of highway cruising and 30 "hot laps" on the Riverside International Raceways test course.

Similar "hot laps" on the same course nearly a year ago with the '59 Corvette were recalled as a day filled with fading brakes, the odor of smoke and pulverized rubber seeping into the cockpit, and wild spinning of the inside rear wheel as it left the ground on hard corners. There was also the little item of cracked hubcaps as the wheels flexed under abnormal body lean.

So, with the fifth wheel testing equipment removed and stowed after accelera-

Latest model has handling qualities to match potent power

CORVETTE '60

tion tests, and the removable fiberglass hard top safely resting against the timing shack, we donned crash helmet, fastened seat belt, and headed for the first turn. In a car with an engine whose torque can break the rear wheels loose in turns in about any gear, handling, or conventional response to wheel and throttle, is quite important in staying out of trouble when cornering at speed.

Chassis improvements claimed by the manufacturer for the '60 Corvette are certainly true and welcome. We noticed much less body roll due chiefly to a new stabilizer bar that has been added behind the rear axle. Further stability comes from a front bar of thicker material and shallower bends to reduce twist load concentrations. Ride is still comfortable and fairly soft as spring rates and shocks remain unchanged from last year, but rebound distance of rear suspension has been increased one inch. The inside rear wheel stays on the ground, side loading

New rear stabilizer bar and heavier front one keep Corvette flat in corners, prevent inside rear wheel from lifting and spinning. Positive steering and instant throttle response bring fun and safety back to the motoring sport.

Twin 4-bbl. carburetors are part of special power kit that includes Duntov cam. Single, large air cleaner (removed to show carbs) is polished, chrome plated.

Racing-type cockpit, with 3-spoked wheel, short-stroke, positive manual shift, and individual bucket-type seats, is functional for racing, comfortable for road touring.

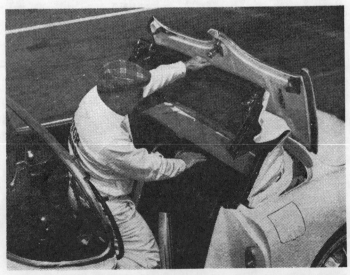

Well-fitting hatch covers storage space for heavy-duty canvas top that can be raised or lowered quickly by one person without tools. Roll-up windows fit snugly.

on wheels and tires is reduced (we didn't crack any hubcaps), and response to wheel and throttle is definite and predictable.

Brakes have been improved, but only slightly, by better leverage of pedal to reduce braking effort, and slightly larger diameter of front-wheel cylinders. The stock brakes are just not up to the potential of the car and unless it is driven by that "little old lady . . ." the optional ceramic-metallic or sintered iron options are certainly desirable for owners who like to drive Corvettes the way they were built to be driven.

It is not likely that the average person will ever wring his Corvette out on a road racing course, but with the power, speed and acceleration packaged into this sports machine, road racing conditions can unknowingly occur on any highway. That emergency stop from speed, an unmarked blind curve, the necessity of very short passing distances all occur in routine travel and require a car that can handle the job, without jarring your teeth out or torturing your aching back if the pavement is not smooth as glass.

Over the long haul, Corvette comfort for its maximum two-passenger load and minimum of luggage is adequate for average-sized persons. Six-footers and over will find their knees too close to the steering wheel if they do not have the seat adjusting tracks moved back. The roll-up windows and hard top add much to cross-country comfort and bad-weather driving, but Corvette provides a folding canvas top that actually gives more headroom than the hard top, and stows out of sight in its own compartment behind the seats.

Heating and ventilation are good, but the most tiring thing on long trips with hard top on and windows open is wind buffeting the side of the face. Windwings of some sort would certainly make the ride more comfortable.

While styling remains the same on the '60 models with a few more interior colors and deep pile rug offered, other changes, such as propeller shaft driveline angle, have done much to reduce vibration and noise in the driveline. As of this writing, the announced aluminum cylinder heads for fuel-injected models are not yet available, but all new Corvettes with three- and four-speed manual transmissions have aluminum clutch housings, which are 18 pounds lighter.

Further use of this light metal is in an aluminum cross-flow radiator that increases cooling capacity. It is offered as a regular production option only for special-camshaft engines. The MOTOR TREND test car was equipped with one of these options, and water temperature never went over 180° during maximum-throttle acceleration runs or "hot laps" during the heat of the day. This was especially noted as few stock American cars are able to go through this phase of road testing without a noticeable increase in water temperature.

Corvette's all-synchro four-speed manual transmission is a joy to use, and shifting is often overdone, due mainly to the ease and convenient location of the short, positive lever. Under ordinary driving conditions, unless it is desired to lay rubber for a block or kick up every traffic officer in the vicinity, engine torque is sufficient to lug out rapidly from 15 or 20 mph in 4th gear. While this is not acceptable to the true "sportscar clan," we never heard of anyone hurting a Corvette by lugging down in traffic occasionally. The twin four-barrel carburetors do not load up the engine under these conditions, nor is there any ping. True, shifting down is great, but the temptation to "stand on the throttle" is not always compatible with existing traffic flow.

Shifting also plays an important part in fuel economy, as evidenced by an interesting check made with this car and two entirely different drivers. Driver No. 1 was used to sportscars with comparatively small-displacement engines and manual four-speed transmissions. His average with the Corvette for a week under city traffic and freeway rush hour conditions was 11.4 mpg. Driver No. 2, familiar with large, powerful domestic cars and automatic transmissions, who knew how to handle manual gearboxes but didn't like to shift unless absolutely necessary, drove under practically the same city and freeway conditions during the same peak hours, and turned in a flat 16 mpg. It is a good bet that over the long haul, Driver No. 2 would get better tire mileage and less crankcase dilution than Driver No. 1.

This is a good example of the versatility of the Corvette—it can be enjoyed by speed-minded sportsmen or average daily drivers who like sporty-type cars, and still give service and satisfaction to both.

The public was slow in accepting fiberglass as body material for a production car, although the special builders of such components enjoyed great success. General Motors believed in this pliable, rugged material for car bodies and stayed with it in the face of some pretty rough opposition. As a result, they have continued to improve on their methods of manufacture, materials and assembly to a point where fit, finish and durability leave little to be desired. It is not unusual in Southern California to see the first 1953-'54 model Corvettes with six cylinders and triple side-draft carburetors, their fiberglass bodies still in "cherry" condition.

The Corvette has carved a definite niche in American motoring, and General Motors intends to widen that niche with continued development of this fine, fast two-seater sports machine.

Car At a Glance

THINGS WE LIKE	THINGS WE DON'T LIKE
Smooth, rapid acceleration	Short legroom for tall drivers
All-synchro four-speed gearbox	
Dual hard and soft top	Wind buffeting with windows open
Excellent handling	
Excellent finish, tight fit of doors, hood and trunk	Slow brake recovery after hard stop

Acceleration

0-45 mph 5.3 secs.   0-60 8.4
Quarter-mile   16.1 secs., 89 mph
30-50 3.0   45-60 3.1   50-80 6.9
Shift points: 6000 rpm

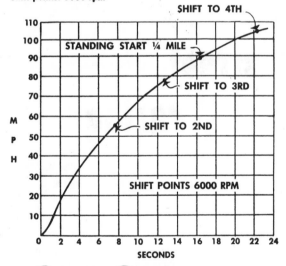

SHIFT TO 4TH

STANDING START ¼ MILE

SHIFT TO 3RD

SHIFT TO 2ND

SHIFT POINTS 6000 RPM

MPH vs SECONDS

Stopping Distance

From 60 mph to standstill 195 ft.
(In 4.8 secs., with maximum of 0.69-G deceleration)

Stop after maximum acceleration to end of ¼-mile 360 ft.
(In 6.9 secs. with maximum of 0.74-G deceleration)

Gas Mileage

	Mpg
City traffic and freeway	14.5
Highway, normal cruise	18.6
Highway, fast cruise	17.9

street racing strip

THE 1960 CORVETTE is an exciting, relatively expensive and somewhat incongruous automobile combining the "best of all possible worlds" within the confines of a stylish fiberglass shell —a fire-breathing monster with power windows—a gentle boulevard car with class that, as this report goes to press, has had one of its kind finish eighth overall in the grueling 24 Hours of Le Mans, fighting Ferraris and Aston Martins for the position. It's the kind of car that can smash an ET record at a drag strip and then deliver milady to a bridge tea, all with the same firm, precise response and cushioned ride.

You and your Chevrolet dealer can "build" a Corvette with a pencil, an order pad, an option book and money, tailoring it to motor gently down a freeway, hurtle across Bonneville's salt or drift through Turn Six at Riverside, with each separate and highly diverse task accomplished simply by selecting the proper item(s) from a voluminous list of options.

Like the fictional "Eve," the Corvette has three faces: tranquil, proud and fearsome—each face pretty, almost to a fault, and each exhibiting entirely different personalities within the same conformation. A progeny of Chevrolet's Svengali of Speed, Zora Arkus-Duntov, the 1960 version is the end product of seven years of breeding. The very fact that such a unit exists in the model line-up of an American constructor is an incongruity in itself in that it is, without a doubt, the most versatile sports/racing car manufactured anywhere in the world.

The Corvette has often been compared with the "XK" series Jaguar. Both cars have the same wheelbase (102 inches) and both the same overall length (177 inches). They also compare favorably in price, performance and seating arrangement. But, while the Jaguar offers two engine options (standard and "S"), the Corvette offers five such performance/horsepower packages and it is this wide range that we shall discuss first.

Corvettes to order

VERSATILITY of Corvette is widened by good selection of power and mechanical options, to suit the needs of tourist, dragster and road-racing competitor. A true American sports car, capable of holding its own with European counterparts, the Corvette has taken its share of trophies in all types of automotive events, equipped only with factory-built over-the-counter options.

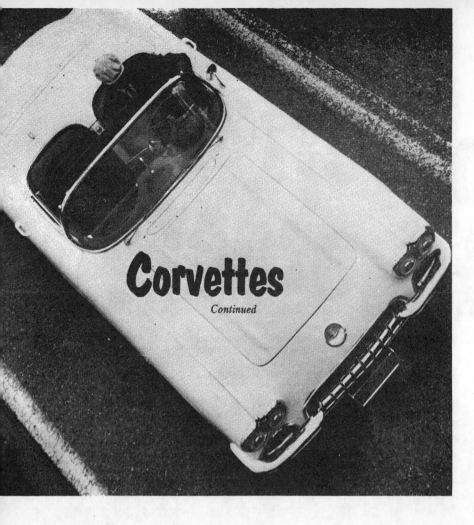

Corvettes
Continued

ENGINES

Because Duntov was the Corvette's creator, there is a very wide choice of engines offered within the line. On the surface such a statement doesn't mean much. Actually the explanation for so many different hp/torque combinations is simply that Duntov, a man who has devoted his life to motoring from place A to place B as quickly as possible, lives by the simple credo: "Go faster—if you can!"

On the other hand, the Chevrolet management and marketing people devote their collective waking hours to a less glamorous, though decidedly more lucrative code: "Sell cars—as many as you can!"

So, while the ex-motor racer, fighter pilot and dedicated engineer envisions "his" Corvette as an outright sports/racing car (which it most certainly is), the brass envision it as just another product—conceived, produced and marketed for profit. Therefore, there exist five variations of the 283-cubic-inch V-8, each integrated into the car's specifications to insure that each base is covered for each customer's particular choice of performance potential.

The engine itself is a classic. It's been wedged into Ferraris, bored, stroked and otherwise maligned for an infinite number of specials, dragsters and street machines and has served as the powerplant for hundreds of successful competition cars. Its proportions of 3.875-inch bore and 3-inch stroke appear ideal for high speed work. Three-ring pistons and drop-forged steel rods with steel-backed babbitt inserts (removable) are fitted to all units.

A forged steel crankshaft rides on five mains with an inertia-type vibration damper installed. Though there are two variations in cam grinds—standard and "Duntov"—both are cast iron and both ride on five steel bearings, both chain driven. The above items are standard on all five engine options. The normal

Corvette engine, the one you receive in the absolute "stock" version Corvette, is the 230-hp unit equipped with one 4-barrel carburetor, hydraulic lifters and a torque rating of 300 lbs. ft. at 3300 rpm. The 230 hp is developed at about 4800 rpm. Since we are concerning ourselves here with the equipping of three different types of Corvettes—a street machine, a dragster and a road racing car—the 230 engine becomes the first logical choice for consideration as a powerplant for the non-competition car.

The engine is a very mild one and quite pleasant to motor behind. It's ideal for installation with the automatic transmission unit. It is the basic engine and therefore is included in the basic suggested list price of $3872 (with either hard *or* soft top). It offers excellent idle characteristics and, because of its strong torque curve at low rpm, it pulls away briskly from the line.

Moving up a notch, we find the next "hairier" version, a 245-hp model that also develops 300 lbs. ft. of torque but at 3800 rpm. This option, too, is quite suitable for the street machine. Equipped with two 4-barrels, it also has a satisfactory idle for the Powerglide automatic. For the additional $150.65 that the 245-hp unit costs, one can expect a noticeable (though slight) improvement in performance, most evident in the higher rpm (and speed) range.

The next step up on the Corvette performance rail is the 250-hp engine option. Like the 230 and 245 units, this, too, is a hydraulic lifter unit with 9.5-to-1 compression. But, it costs a whopping $484.20 (and is an excellent example of "Americanized" sports car merchandising). This unit is the mild fuel injection plant, conceived for the sport who wants to impress his friends with FI but isn't really serious about competition motoring. The 250 hp arrives on tap at 5000 rpm, and the rated torque figure of 305 lbs. ft. comes into play when the tach reads 3800. This engine, too, is mild enough for the timid and gutty enough to shut down most stockers at stoplights. The instantaneous power that one associates with the Rochester FI is apparent in the lower rpm range, and the 250 therefore must be considered the "peppiest" of the three wet-stick powerplants. It is, however, the least desirable choice for a street Corvette.

All three of the above engines are applicable for street machine installation. If you're interested in "just motoring," the 230-hp is more than sufficient. If you have a spare hundred and fifty and you'd like to arrive at 60 mph from a dead stop a few seconds earlier, the 245-hp is an ideal choice. If you happen to be a *wealthy* pseudo-enthusiast, the 250-hp FI unit would be an obvious choice. Of course, the 270-hp and the 290-hp FI units that are about to be discussed are also possible choices for such a car but for general, all-around driving—without a thought to trophy hunting—the milder, hydraulic lifter powerplants are definitely a wiser buy.

Now if you're a serious drag strip enthusiast and you'd like to own a two-seater that "turns on" (and you're willing to sacrifice a percentage of smoothness and driving ease for a great deal more performance), chances are you would select the 270-hp engine option, parting with $182.95 for 270 hp at 6000 rpm and 285 lbs. ft. of torque at 4200 rpm. The 270-hp, like the 290-hp FI engine, is equipped with solid lifters and the "Duntov" cam (Chevy part number 3736098). The compression is 9.5-to-1 and the valves are the same as on *all* Corvette 283's (1.7-inch intake and 1.5-inch exhaust). Timing, however, differs greatly over the hydraulic lifter units. For the 270-hp (and 290-hp) the intake opens at 35(BTC) and closes at 72(ABC) with a duration of 287 degrees, as opposed to milder timing of 12, 57 and 250 for the other units. Exhaust timing is also quite extreme with openings at 76(BBC) and closings at 31(ATC) with the same 287 degrees of duration compared to the hydraulic's 54, 15 and 250.

As mentioned, with the 270-hp engine you must be prepared to give up some smoothness. It's also noisier and almost rough at idle. In fact, it's a handful for all but those drivers who really enjoy a strong car. It's not a wise choice for a woman driver (unless her name happens to be Denise McCluggage) and it should be considered only by those males who really like to move out. One definite point in the 270-hp's favor is the price. For less than $200 you are buying a truly fine racing engine that can turn in excess of 7000 rpm with a fair degree of reliability, and your chances of winning at the local drag strip are very good indeed. Corvettes, so equipped, are turning consistently in the low 12 seconds ET on many strips with terminal speeds well over 108 mph. Of course, a certain amount of "sweetening" (or what NASCAR-ite Smokey Yunick calls "legal cheatin' ") may be necessary to arrive at such performances but the 270-hp is the ideal base from which to begin such improvements.

The strongest engine in the line-up is the 290-hp FI unit, delivering 290 hp at 6200 rpm and 290 lbs. ft. at 4400 rpm. This unit requires an additional $484.20 of your cash just like the 250-hp FI unit does, but with the 290 installed there is a world of difference in performance. If you're really convinced that you, too, can be a motor racer and you foster fantasies of lapping Le Mans with the likes of Hill and Moss, or if you're sick and tired of seeing your neighbor walk off with all the silverplate at the local SCCA events, then this is the engine.

The Rochester fuel injection system is satisfactory. It's been damned by many an owner and some of the criticism has been valid. It does develop corrosion in the aluminum-housed unit, and deposits tend to clog the metering device after a few years. There is also the matter of servicing, a problem that a few years ago would have discouraged all but the really strong at heart. This problem, however, has been alleviated to some degree by more factory-trained mechanics. *continued*

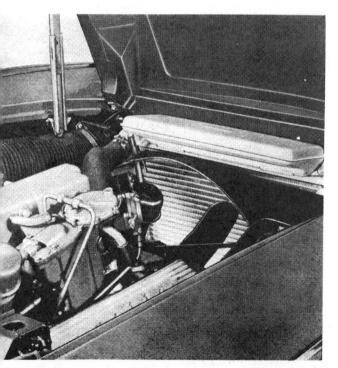

FUEL INJECTION option by Rochester has attracted a lot of attention from the competition-minded although it does give smooth and reliable performance for ordinary street use. A new cross-flow aluminum radiator (shown) is also available.

TWIN FOUR-BARREL CARBS have been a popular choice of both the tourist who likes to go and the drag strip participant who must go to win trophies. Like all of the Corvette options, the two 4-barrel carburetor setup can be ordered separately or with car.

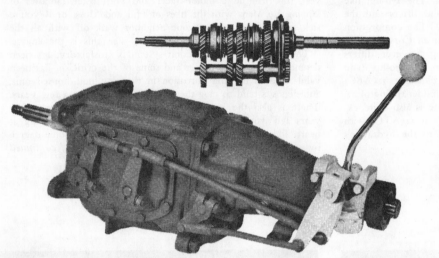

ALL-SYNCHROMESH 4-speed stick shift gearbox is one of the world's best. Close ratios cover road-racing needs and are quite adequate for use on highway.

OPTIONAL steering arm speeds up front-wheel reaction to steering-wheel turns, a must for the fast turns and switchbacks of the road-racing circuits.

Aside from these minor disadvantages, the 290-hp FI engine is one of the very few domestic powerplants that "comes on right now"—you step down and the tach needle rushes up and around the dial. As with the 270-hp engine, a Corvette equipped with the 290 isn't an ideal car for day-to-day driving. It requires a real strong hand and an educated foot, and in the wet it's all a good driver can do to keep from meeting his trunk lid when the tap is opened. The 270 appears to be, according to local Detroit drag enthusiasts, a quicker quarter-mile car but both are nearly equal in acceleration and the 290 gets the nod when the big end is sought as it is on the long straights in sports car racing.

The Cunningham team of Corvettes at Le Mans this year were equipped with such powerplants and their decisive eighth place finish is strong evidence that here is a real threat in the power department for all but the super-light, disguised Grand Prix sort of sports car. And so, we run the gamut from a mild little 230-hp plant to a screaming beast that will propel a Corvette into that magic 160-mph zone. Now let's continue along the driveline and investigate the transmission and rear axle options that team up with such broad engine choices.

TRANSMISSIONS AND REAR ENDS

Mating the proper transmission and rear end ratio to your engine choice requires a rather firm decision on your part as to what role you wish your Corvette to play. If you are only interested in moving from home to office and back, you have a number of choices, all of them satisfactory, some of them infinitely correct.

If you don't enjoy shifting gears (and lots of people don't) then you'd better consider the Powerglide option first. This is a beefier version of the normal Chevrolet passenger car unit without a heat exchanger (not needed because you aren't likely to ever overload such a car). It costs $199.10 more than the standard three-speed manual box that's fitted on the basic car. It's surprising how versatile this unit is. You can utilize Low gear a great deal in traffic and get out and around much the same way you would with a normal synchro Low. It's slightly paradoxical, though, to buy the Powerglide unit for two hundred dollars and then play the L-D game on the box, but for those drivers who like the convenience of automatic transmissions for most cases and also like to occasionally toy with Low gear, the Powerglide is a good choice.

The standard box, a three-speed with non-synchro Low, is fitted with a 2.21 first cog, a 1.32 second and direct third. This is a very satisfactory unit also and, when teamed with the hydraulic lifter engines, gives all the flexibility one would require for normal operation with a street machine.

Of course, if you're considering any sort of competition at all and/or you *do* like to shift gears a great deal, the four-speed, all-synchro box is your only choice. This $188.30 option is available with all engines from the 230 to the 290 and is probably one of the sweetest transmissions ever designed, most certainly the finest multi-gear manual changer ever offered from an American maker.

Close ratioed, with a first of 2.20, a second of 1.66, a third of 1.31 and direct fourth, this box allows the utmost flexibility. Reverse gear is locked out and can be engaged only when a two-pronged lever on the shift handle is pulled upwards. The gate is direct and each gear can be found simply and easily with only slight pre-loading evident. The four-speed is ideal for the street machine where it offers a new dimension to motoring behind, say, a 230-hp engine and is an absolute necessity when the 270-hp and the 290-hp plants are fitted.

Now that we've coupled the gearbox to the engine of your choice or requirement, we must select the proper rear end ratio to deliver the power to the rear wheels. Incidentally, the clutch in all manual-transmissioned Corvettes is the same—a 10-inch woven asbestos-faced component with 1620 pounds of pressure. There is no heavy-duty clutch available simply because Chevro-

let engineers insist that the 1620-pound unit is more than sufficient for any and all competition driving.

As for rear end ratios, if you are concerned with a Powerglide torque converter unit you have no choice of option—you receive a 3.55 ratio which, in the considered opinion of the factory people, is the proper ratio for general purpose touring with this sort of power transfer case. If you go the three-speed route (and don't specify otherwise), you'll receive a 3.7 rear end. If you do specify a ratio other than 3.7—i.e., a 4.11 or 4.56—you must also lay out $43.05 for RPO 675 which is the Positraction or limited-slip differential. The same is true of the gear choice for the four-speed unit. If you're concerned with general driving only and you go the manual route, the 3.7 is a fine compromise. If the drags and an NHRA trophy are in your sights, a 4.56 with Positraction is a real good choice (though it makes the 270-hp and 290-hp car a beast in traffic). If road courses are going to be assaulted in your car, either one of the three gears is good because chances are you'll end up buying a set of each for various track conditions. In any case, where any sort of competition is considered, the Positraction unit should definitely be fitted at time of delivery, no matter what rear axle ratio you decide upon. With it, the power transfer is of course more uniform and the small amount of initial expense will be amortized in the saving of rubber, if nothing more. *continued*

Corvettes

continued

SUSPENSION AND BRAKES

Until 1960, if you decided to buy a Corvette and race it you were required to lay out a healthy sum for what was known as RPO 684. This was the "competition package," so to speak, and no self-respecting young dragster or motor racer would be seen in a Corvette without this option. It included stiffer springs (front—550 lbs. deflection per inch, rear—145 lbs. vs. front—300 lbs. and rear—115 lbs. for the standard units), larger shocks (1⅜-inch vs. one-inch normal), a hefty stabilizer bar in front (.8-inch vs. .7-inch), finned drums and cera-metallic linings with air scoops on the backing plates, and the faster steering adaptor. This was the competition package that the street-type Corvette didn't require.

But for 1960, all is different underneath. Now, *every* Corvette enjoys the same type of competition chassis components with a superior degree of handling thrown in. The ride, however, is still as soft as it was last year with the normal unit because the same 300-pound and 115-pound spring rates and the smaller shocks are used. Confused? Well, it figures this way—Chevrolet engineers straightened out a few kinks in the standard front stabilizer bar putting more actual stress on the bar itself. Then Duntov fitted a rear stabilizer bar and the whole package ends up being a far better handling package and a much smoother one than the old RPO 684-equipped car. Thus, every Corvette for 1960 is sprung for road racing even if you never intend to move over the legal speed limit. The bigger and more efficient

brakes aren't included, however, nor is the faster steering adaptor. These are quite expensive items to machine and for 1960 come under the heading of RPO 687, a $333.60 option that is a must for anyone who plans to race his car on a road course, but is a decided luxury for the drag or street machine.

The cast drums and sintered iron linings (no more cera-metallic units—the sintered iron are far superior since they don't require "warm-up") are combined with vanes cast on the drums, air scoops on the backing plates and fans between the drum and wheel hub, to make up a very satisfactory anchor for all-out competition braking requirements. They might be said to be 60 per cent more efficient than the normal asbestos-lined, smooth drum units and are really a bargain even for $333.60. As mentioned, RPO 687 also includes the steering adaptor that converts the overall ratio from 21.1-to-1 to 16.3-to-1, another absolute necessity for road racing but not required for normal street or strip use.

There's another option, RPO 276, that should be considered by anyone who is going after silverplate but could easily be overlooked by the touring-type owner. This is the larger wheel that is a no-cost item but, like many things on any new car, must be ordered at the time of delivery. This option includes 5½-inch wheels in place of the normal five-inch units. If you should decide on RPO 276 for your Corvette you should know, too, that you won't receive those jazzy Corvette wheel covers that are standard on the five-inch wheels. Instead, you'll receive normal hubcaps.

Still on the wheel/brake subject, there's another option that

SEGMENTED sintered-iron liners mounted on ventilated backing plates offer the ultimate in braking for the Corvette for all-out competition. The complete unit has finned drums with centrifugal cooling fan fitted inside to speed air over hot areas. Unlike cera-metallic linings, sintered units need no warm-up.

Corvettes

CAR CLUBS, once exclusively dedicated to the imports, have accepted the Corvette as a respected and qualified member destined to preserve the breed. Agility, comfort make it popular for club events.

the drag strip enthusiast might be interested in and that's RPO 686—a segmented brake lining assembly that differs not in size of lining area from the normal asbestos units that are standard (both are 11-inch x 2-inch in the front and 11-inch x 1¾-inch in the rear for a total of 120 square inches), but does give increased brake life because of more lining material. For drag race deceleration techniques, such an option would be a wise choice.

There's also an FOA 121 item that can be ordered at the time of original purchase and this is one that should be fitted on both the drag racing and road racing types of Corvettes. This is the temperature-controlled fan option that costs $21.55 and saves some valuable horsepower in the upper rpm ranges. Above 3100 rpm the five-bladed, 17-inch fan shuts off by means of a transfer of viscous fluid from a coupling on the fan pulley. The fluid enters (and exits) thermostatically, uncoupling the fan (and returning it to use) as required.

Another option that applies to all three types of cars is the hard top, a fiberglass solid unit that bolts onto the Corvette. It costs $236.75 if you order it in addition to a soft top. At the time of original purchase you have a choice of either top. But the majority of owners select the soft unit since it cannot be installed later (without spending a great deal of money). For touring in colder climates it's an ideal option and for road racing on fast circuits (those with long straights where aerodynamics come to play a big part in top speed, such as Sebring and Le Mans), the solid top is a real necessity.

Then, for the touring type who dislikes stopping at gas stations on long runs or for the serious competition type who favors long-distance road events, there's LPO 1625, a 24-gallon gas tank that replaces the normal 16.4-gallon unit. One point must be brought out here—that the 24-gallon tank can be used only with hardtop models. The larger tank fits up into the well where the soft top is normally stored, and you cannot fold the soft top flat if the extra-gallons unit is fitted.

And that about ends the listing of factory options offered for the Corvette. Auto supply firms and speed shops that cater

to racing and drag strip enthusiasts pick up where Chevrolet leaves off and offer dozens of other big and little items that make competition an easier game. The factory options, however, are those that can be included at time of purchase from the dealer, thus making sure that your Corvette is as closely equipped as possible for the job you intend it to perform.

Just in case the vast maze of options have confused you a bit, I'll briefly run over them for each specific type of car—first the street or touring model. For normal driving you have the choice of any one of the five engines available though I'd recommend the 245-hp option with either Powerglide or three-speed transmission. The slight increase in power over the 230-hp engine is just enough to make the car "gutty" and not enough to make it a real handful for average drivers and average road conditions. If this is the kind of Corvette you have in mind, and you live in the eastern and northern part of the country, I'd also consider the hard top in addition to the soft.

If you decide that you want to try your hand at drag racing *and you want to win,* equip your Corvette with a 270-hp engine and a four-speed with a 4.56-to-1 rear end ratio. Forget the hard top but buy the segmented brake option (RPO 686 at $26.90) and the thermo fan unit (FOA 121 at $21.55).

And, if you want a Corvette for road racing, there can be only one choice—a 290-hp-engined car with fuel injection and four-speed close-ratio box. Buy the hard top option if you like but better still just order a hard top to begin with in place of the soft unit. Don't forget RPO 687 that includes the sintered iron linings and finned drums and faster steering and also the thermo fan and the 24-gallon tank. All three rear end ratios are necessary for different courses so which one you select initially is not too important. Positraction, of course, is a must and so, too, are the 5½-inch wheels that are included in RPO 276.

You'll also need things like roll bars and seat belts (and *not* the garden variety that come on each Corvette from the factory, either), plus several other items that individual tastes will dictate later as your competition work becomes more serious. ●

America's competition-proven sports car revisited

1961 CORVETTE

ONCE UPON A TIME, just a few years ago, owners of America's only sports car were on the receiving end of constant gibes from the "sporty car set," which held that the only thing the beast had to offer was drag strip performance. It would go like the wind (in a straight line, they said), but it wouldn't corner, it wouldn't stop, it had a boulevard ride, and a glass body. And it took 265 cu in. (4.5 liters) to get that performance.

Well, these derogatory remarks probably were true at one time. At least, some of them were. But Chevrolet engineers have now achieved an excellent package, combining acceleration, stopping power, a good ride and handling characteristics whose adequacy is indicated by the car's race-winning ways.

In our January 1959 test report of the 1959 Corvette we said that 1960 would be the year for big changes in the Corvette. We were wrong. The 1960 model wasn't too much different from, or too much better than, the 1959 version. Lacking any great changes in 1960, we might logically have predicted a major change in 1961, but luckily we didn't.

However, the few changes which have been made are for the better. Continual refinements since 1954 have made the Corvette into a sports car for which no owner need make excuses. It goes, it stops, and it corners.

The major change in the appearance is the rear end treatment, which was derived from the Sting Ray, GM racing Corvette, owned by Bill Mitchell. The stubbier look achieves a more crisp and a fleeter appearance than that of previous models, which looked "soft." The front end remains basically unchanged. New bumpers fore and aft blend nicely into the body design, and the exhaust tips are now under the body instead of through the bumper tips. This was a good move; there's no mistaking the Corvette for any other make and it is a better looking car now.

The finish of the fiberglass body is generally excellent, although we did find a few minor flaws on our test car, mostly in obscure places. Panel fit and fairing from one panel to another were good and showed Chevrolet's great attention to the Corvette molds.

Interior trim and design are similar to past models and well done, but have a little of the Motorama touch. The seats are excellently designed and are very comfortable. Our longest single excursion was of some 200 miles, but no sign of driver fatigue was evident and we honestly feel a day behind the wheel of a Corvette could be put in without undue strain.

The instruments are easy to read and include a speedometer, tach (reading to 7000 rpm—red-lined at 6200), gas gauge, temperature gauge, oil pressure gauge and ammeter. Indicator lights are used for the turn signals, high headlight beam and parking brake. The parking brake light on the panel lights up when the key is turned on (if, of course, the parking brake is on) and when the engine is started the light blinks its warning to the driver. The only fixture in the Corvette interior that's hard to use is the radio, which is mounted in a console deep under the instrument panel. This console also carries the clock, which is difficult to see and should be looked at only when the car is stopped.

The seats have 3 in. of fore and aft movement, which gave everyone on our staff adequate leg room, but the body panel between the seats interferes with the driver's elbow (when shifting) when the seat is at its rearmost position.

Vision in the Corvette is excellent when the car is equipped with the hardtop. Slim pillars and lots of glass area are responsible. We used two test cars, one white and one metallic blue. Reflections from the white rear deck into the rear window of the white car caused a hazy view when we looked out of the back window or used the rear view mirror. The darker colored car did not give us this trouble. Even in the white Corvette no haze was noticeable in the windshield, because the cowl was covered with red material to match the upholstery.

We noticed a considerable amount of wind noise with the windows rolled down, and if the windows are rolled up they have to be all the way up or the driver feels a bad draft. Some engine and wind noise was evident even with both windows up.

The car started with a flick of the key on cool morn-

when it corners in the opposite direction; and quite often they will flood under extreme deceleration, making it difficult for the driver to accelerate properly out of the turn.

Options for 1961 include five horsepower ratings: 230 (standard), with a single 4-barrel carburetor; 245, with twin 4-barrels; 270, with twin 4-barrels; 275, with fuel injection; and 315, with fuel injection. Three transmission options are available: 3-speed synchromesh; 4-speed synchromesh, and Powerglide. Five rear axle ratios are available: 4.56:1, 4.11:1, 3.70:1, 3.55:1 and 3.36:1.

Obviously, any buyer should find a combination to suit his needs. Performance of this Corvette was little different from the one we tested two years ago and only improved at the upper end. A similar car, owned by Alan Lockwood, race tuned, timed 107 mph at the end of a quarter mile at the LADS drag strip, Long Beach, Calif.

We've said many times that we think the Corvette 4-speed transmission is one of the best in the world and we have no reason to change our minds. In all, five different people on our staff drove the car and none was able to fault the synchromesh. The ratios are excellently spaced and, with synchromesh on all four gears, the driver always has the proper ratio at his disposal by a mere movement of the lever.

We were greatly impressed by the combination of a very good ride coupled with little roll on corners. Most cars with riding qualities approaching those of the Corvette can't match its sticking ability on curves. And those that match or beat its handling usually ride like the proverbial truck.

The Corvette is absolutely unmatched for performance per dollar in terms of transportation machinery (some of the newer Formula Junior cars will beat it for performance per dollar, but are, of course, single purpose cars).

The steering is accurate, though a little slower than we would like in a car with this much power and speed. The brakes proved up to every test we put them to and a sudden panic stop to avoid a day-dreaming motorist increased our admiration for the refinements and improvements made by Chevrolet engineers in the Corvette since its introduction. Once again we want to thank Harry Mann Chevrolet for furnishing the test car. The following weekend the Corvette was used as the pace car at the Riverside Sports Car GP.

ings but, oddly, it was difficult to start on several occasions after the car had been thoroughly warmed up. This is unusual and could most likely be cured by further tuning.

The clutch operation proved extremely smooth, whether we were plugging along in slow-moving traffic or getting off the line for a standing start acceleration run. We tried a stop and start on a hill of approximately 30% grade and found that by dextrous manipulation of the clutch and throttle it could be surmounted with ease and smoothness. We hadn't been worried about a lack of horsepower, but we had wondered about the flexibility of the engine until we tried the hill.

Once more we found the injector to be extremely flexible. The engine is able to pull smoothly from under 15 mph to top speed with no bucking or hesitation. In our test car, which had 4.11:1 rear axle gears, it was much easier, of course, than it would have been with the top ratio available. Flexibility, rather than actual increased power, is the main justification for the injectors and in road racing use they allow full power to be maintained under all conditions. Carburetors will almost invariably starve when the car turns one way and flood

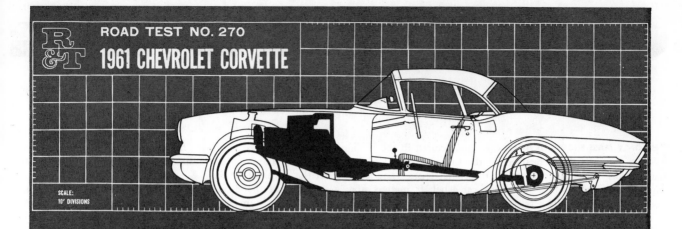

ROAD TEST NO. 270
1961 CHEVROLET CORVETTE

SCALE:
10" DIVISIONS

DIMENSIONS

Wheelbase, in	102
Tread, f and r	57/59
Over-all length, in	178
width	70.4
height	52.1
equivalent vol, cu ft	378
Frontal area, sq ft	20.4
Ground clearance, in	6.7
Steering ratio, o/a	21.1
turns, lock to lock	3.7
turning circle, ft	37
Hip room, front	49
Hip room, rear	
Pedal to seat back	38
Floor to ground	14

CALCULATED DATA

Lb/hp (test wt)	10.7
Cu ft/ton mile	148.3
Mph/1000 rpm (4th)	19.6
Engine revs/mile	3050
Piston travel, ft/mile	1525
Rpm @ 2500 ft/min	5000
equivalent mph	98.4
R&T wear index	46.5

SPECIFICATIONS

List price	$3872
Curb weight, lb	3080
Test weight	3390
distribution, %	53/47
Tire size	6.70–15
Brake lining area	157
Engine type	V-8 cyl, ohv
Bore & stroke	3.88 x 3.0
Displacement, cc	4639
cu in	283
Compression ratio	11.0
Bhp @ rpm	315 @ 6200
equivalent mph	122
Torque, lb-ft	295 @ 4700
equivalent mph	96.1

GEAR RATIOS

4th (1.00)	4.11
3rd (1.31)	5.38
2nd (1.66)	6.82
1st (2.20)	9.04

SPEEDOMETER ERROR

30 mph	actual, 26.4
60 mph	56.6

PERFORMANCE

Top speed (6500), mph	128
best timed run	n.a.
3rd (6500)	98
2nd (6500)	77
1st (6500)	58

FUEL CONSUMPTION

Normal range, mpg	11/17

ACCELERATION

0-30 mph, sec	3.1
0-40	4.2
0-50	5.1
0-60	6.6
0-70	7.5
0-80	9.6
0-100	14.5
Standing ¼ mile	14.2
speed at end	98

TAPLEY DATA

4th, lb/ton @ mph	360 @ 78
3rd	475 @ 72
2nd	580 @ 57
Total drag at 60 mph, lb	135

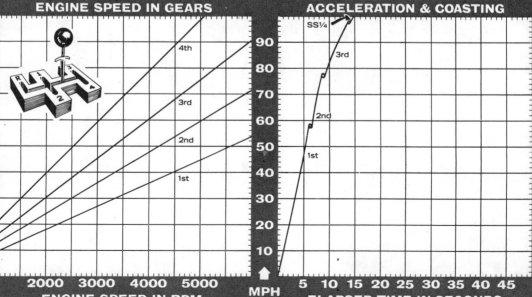

ENGINE SPEED IN GEARS

4th
3rd
2nd
1st

2000 3000 4000 5000
ENGINE SPEED IN RPM

ACCELERATION & COASTING

SS¼
3rd
2nd
1st

90 80 70 60 50 40 30 20 10
MPH

5 10 15 20 25 30 35 40 45
ELAPSED TIME IN SECONDS

CORVETTE

FULL RANGE ROAD TEST

THE ONLY MASS-PRODUCED sports car manufactured in the U. S. is the distinction still retained by the Corvette. In all of its many forms it definitely possesses the characteristics and personality necessary to bear the sports car label. It matters not whether someone wants a two-seater merely for transportation, or an all-out racing machine — there is a Corvette to fit his desires, no matter how extreme.

In order to sample at least a couple of Corvette variations, we tested two automobiles that were identical except for color and engine option. The more conservative of the two, ironically, was painted a bright red both inside and out — even the carpeting and upholstering matched the paint. Specifically, all that made it more conservative was the installation of the mild, 230-hp engine which is the lowest-powered unit available.

The more sedate-appearing white test car displayed an identical interior except for one important instrument panel feature, a tachometer red-lined at 6500 rpm instead of 5300. Even before the key is turned to start the engine, this sliver of red is a dead give-away that a 315-hp fuel-injection engine lies ahead of the four-speed gearbox.

This power and drive train package, though similar to previous years, received some important alterations in the 1961 version. Intake valves and ports were both enlarged to improve breathing and help raise the output from the previous maximum of 290 hp. The

Two variations of the Chevy sports car show some of the many faces of speed

superb four-speed gearbox, fitted to both cars, now has a completely aluminum case instead of just using the light metal in the tail-shaft housing.

An under-hood view reveals one other important area in which aluminum is now being used — the radiator and top tank. The tank is divorced from the radiator and is bracketed to the engine, allowing a more graceful hood slope. In this case the use of aluminum cut the radiator weight in half.

Seated in the cockpit, a 1961 underbody contour change becomes apparent — the transmission hump has been narrowed so that the driver's right leg and throttle foot don't appear to be as cramped.

The instrument panel is still one of the very few that contain a full complement of instruments. The only warning lights that appear are for the hand brake and high beam of the headlights. The brake light is a new addition for 1961; both lights spell out their purposes luminously, so that even an unfamiliar driver will understand their purposes. The centrally-located tachometer is in a very practical position, just ahead of the steering wheel hub. Forward and higher, the speedometer dominates the center of the panel proper. In certain types of competition events it would be nice if the tach and speedo could trade places, so that the rev counter could be bigger.

Driving both Corvettes definitely demon-

A look inside the engine compartment of the fuel-injected Corvette reveals a new use of aluminum. Both radiator and top tank are of the lighter metal.

Familiar interior of the sports car has all necessary instruments arranged in a near-ideal manner. Gearbox is one of the best. Note lockout latch for reverse.

ACCELERATION TESTS OF THE TWO CORVETTES SHOWED MOST DIFFERENCE EXISTS NOT AT LOW AND MID SPEEDS, BUT AT TOP END.

strated that their character is very much the sports variety, even though they are very plush vehicles. Tufted carpeting and considerable use of chrome trim, including pattern chromed teardrop-shaped panels attached to the doors and kick pads, create an air of luxury. When you grasp the steering wheel and negotiate a turn at high speed, and when you shift the four-speed gearbox, you completely lose sight of your luxurious environment and realize that you are driving a true sports car.

Both test cars were not fitted with power steering, so they inspired a feeling of confidence when cornering. The fast steering ratio, which required a little better than 3½ turns of the steering wheel from lock-to-lock, might be too stiff for some of the more delicate members of the fair sex, but any driver that appreciates the security of having maximum feel of the car will be very happy with it. For those that don't wish to flex their muscles, power steering is available.

No matter what you pay for a sports car, whether it be in the four-figure or five-figure bracket, there is none that shifts more easily and more consistently than the Corvette four-speed box. Being synchromesh in all forward speeds, all gears can be selected in any sequence of up- or down-shifting without gear clash. The best feature of all is the reverse gear lockout, which is controlled by lifting a couple of prongs on the side of the shift lever about two inches below the knob. It is impossible to shift into reverse unless these prongs are raised, so one need never fear hitting reverse when shifting into first. Without the

lockout, many drivers have a tendency to move the lever too far to the right in their avoidance of reverse, with the net result that the lever gets hung up between first and third, so we can't offer enough praise for this device.

The Corvette's cornering ability is definitely in the superior category, and for many reasons. The car has a fairly low center of gravity, moderately stiff suspension and a stiff front stabilizer bar. Engineering wisely sacrificed softness of ride for safety in this machine. The body appears to lean a minimum amount during fast cornering, probably because of the heavy torsional stabilizer bar and lighter unit of the same type on the rear suspension. Though this rear bar doubtless contributes to flat cornering, it has a detrimental effect on rear wheel adhesion. In a hard corner it has a tendency to take weight off the inside rear wheel, causing the outside rear wheel to be called upon to offer the majority of the resistance to side thrust. This is not good racing practice for power-on cornering. In actual driving, though the back end wasn't uncontrollable, it did start drifting earlier than the other characteristics of the car would indicate.

One of the pleasantest things about cornering a Corvette with the 315-hp engine is the behavior of the fuel-injection system. Since it is not dependent on its float bowl level for fuel metering as in a four-barrel carburetor, it acts completely insensitive to motion. In maneuvers that would cause a four-barrel-equipped engine to lose power or die completely,

MOTOR TREND TEST DATA

TEST CAR:	Corvette
BODY TYPE:	Two-door convertible
BASE PRICE:	$4636
ENGINE TYPE:	V-8
DISPLACEMENT:	283 cubic inches
COMPRESSION RATIO:	11.0-to-1
CARBURETION:	Fuel injection
HORSEPOWER:	315 @ 6200 rpm
TRANSMISSION:	4-speed manual
REAR AXLE RATIO:	3.70-to-1
GAS MILEAGE:	10 to 14 miles per gallon
ACCELERATION:	0-30 mph in 3.5 seconds, 0-45 mph in 5.4 seconds and 0-60 mph in 7.4 seconds
SPEEDOMETER ERROR:	Indicated 30, 45 and 60 mph are actual 29, 43½ and 58 mph, respectively
ODOMETER ERROR:	Indicated 100 miles is actual 95 miles
WEIGHT-POWER RATIO:	9.6 lbs. per horsepower
HORSEPOWER PER CUBIC INCH:	1.1

the fuel-injected engine purrs like nothing was happening. Due to the fact that injector nozzles spray the fuel into the ports, much larger throttle openings can be tolerated at low rpm than with carburetion. One simple butterfly is all that is necessary to control the system instead of a complex of progressive linkage and many throttles. Port distribution also eliminates the necessity for a heat riser, thereby improving volumetric efficiency by allowing a cooler, more dense charge to enter the cylinder.

When comparing the performance of the two engine options tested, we should not lose sight of the fact that the difference goes far beyond the single area of carburetion. Though all Corvette engines have a displacement of 283 cubic inches, there

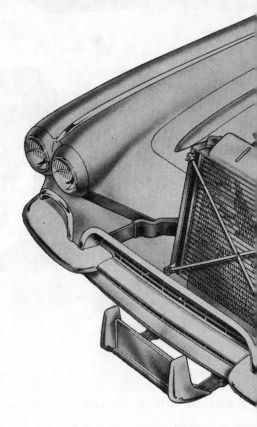

MOTOR TREND TEST DATA

TEST CAR:	Corvette
BODY TYPE:	Two-door convertible
BASE PRICE:	$4109
ENGINE TYPE:	V-8
DISPLACEMENT:	283 cubic inches
COMPRESSION RATIO:	9.5-to-1
CARBURETION:	Single 4-barrel
HORSEPOWER:	230 @ 4800 rpm
TRANSMISSION:	4-speed manual
REAR AXLE RATIO:	3.70-to-1
GAS MILEAGE:	11 to 15 miles per gallon
ACCELERATION:	0-30 mph in 3.8 seconds, 0-45 mph in 5.7 seconds and 0-60 mph in 8.3 seconds
SPEEDOMETER ERROR:	Indicated 30, 45 and 60 mph are actual 30, 45 and 60 mph, respectively
ODOMETER ERROR:	Indicated 100 miles is actual 95 miles
WEIGHT-POWER RATIO:	13 lbs. per horsepower
HORSEPOWER PER CUBIC INCH:	.81

is much that is done in the way of altering breathing ability to produce variations in output. The mildest engine is fitted with a hydraulic-lifter cam that limits rpm to the passenger-car range and provides only 250 degrees of valve-opening duration on both the intake and exhaust valves. An overlap duration of 28 degrees in conjunction with the use of a four-barrel carburetor makes the 230-hp engine behave like the best-mannered passenger car.

The 315-hp engine absolutely won't idle under 700 rpm and is most consistent in the 800-to-900-rpm range because of the combined effects of 66 degrees of valve overlap and the inability of the fuel-injection system to maintain pressure within its lines at low rpm. The overall duration of this engine's cam provides both valves with 287 degrees of opening.

Due to the 72-degree late closing of intake valves in the hotter engine, plus more accurate fuel distribution from the injection system, an 11-to-1 compression ratio requires no special concessions whatsoever. The short timing and carburetion system of the mildest engine limits its compression to a 9.5-to-1 ratio.

A good comparison of the performance potential of the two cars cannot be gained by merely comparing their low-speed and mid-range performance figures, because there really

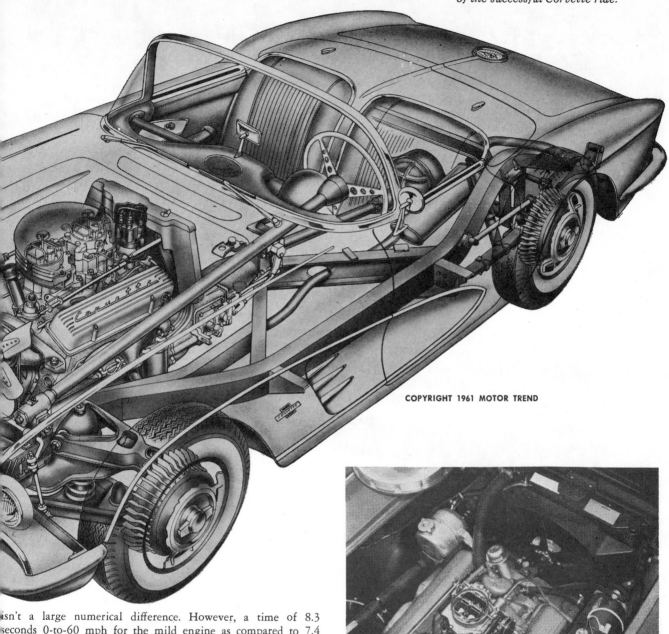

Cutaway drawing by MT'S Robert Temple shows the real inside story of the successful Corvette ride.

A single four-barrel provides carburetion for the mildest of the Corvettes. With 230-hp, it is designed for best performance at normal passenger-car ranges.

isn't a large numerical difference. However, a time of 8.3 seconds 0-to-60 mph for the mild engine as compared to 7.4 seconds for the hot version will impress those that have experience in the field of acceleration testing. A quarter-mile run would show a very large difference between the two.

In all ranges of acceleration, both cars would make more impressive showings if they had special tires and rear end gears more favorable than 3.70-to-1. This is actually the smallest ratio available in a Corvette, equipped as the test cars were, with a four-speed transmission and limited-slip differential combination.

Though our road test dealt only with the mildest and hottest engines available, there are three other optional powerplant choices possible: a 245-hp, 270-hp and a 275-hp. The most conservative of the three is the same as the 230-hp engine, except that it is fitted with dual-four-barrel carburetion. The 270-hp engine follows the same trend, but in addition to the carburetion a longer-duration mechanical-lifter cam replaces the hydraulic assembly of the two milder engines. At the other end of the list, the 275-hp option is the same as the hottest fuel-injection job. It shares the same 11-to-1 compression but uses a mild hydraulic-lifter cam.

Three transmissions are available with the two mildest engines: a three-speed, four-speed and Powerglide. The three hottest engines can be ordered only with three-speed or four-speed boxes because of their fast idle speeds.

Mechanical options aren't the only ones available, nor have we listed all of them — convenience items like power assists, convertible tops and removable hard tops make it possible to order a Corvette to fit any individual preference. /MT

3 Corvettes

0 to 100 to 0 in 22 seconds!

Which Corvette to buy? Here Car Life reports on 3 versions of this popular car: 315 vs. 270 vs. 230 bhp.

Today, CHEVROLET offers so many combinations and options in its complete line of cars that one year's production could be built with no two cars exactly alike. One of the more interesting Chevrolet "options" is America's only true sports car, the Corvette. The Corvette, too, is offered with a host of options and these will be dealt with later in this article.

The Corvette enjoys many distinctions, not the least being that it is a two-passenger-only vehicle. Its very high performance and general character have established it firmly as an exceptional prestige automobile, the car chosen by the true connoisseur, driven by those who know and appreciate the finer points of automotive engineering.

For this road test report, we decided to test not one, but several Corvette models. With so many options we couldn't possibly test every combination but we did manage to get 3 cars; the very top performer (315 bhp), a middle-range car (270 bhp) and the "bottom" of the line (performance-wise) in a 230-bhp job with Powerglide automatic 2-speed transmission.

Before dealing with each car in detail, a word about acceleration times. Many readers put great emphasis on the 0-60 time, or the e.t., and speed for the standing

start ¼ mile test. This is fine, but the Corvette models are rather special cases. In making an acceleration run with any of the engines (230 to 315 bhp) we have found that the 0 to 60 mph runs in particular and the ¼ mile to some extent do not vary a great deal, so long as a stick-shift transmission is used. Acceleration from a standstill to 50 mph is primarily a matter of getting the best tire

bite with just the right amount of wheelspin.

We believe, on the basis of the tests we have made, that any stick-shift Corvette, regardless of the engine or axle ratio choice, will accelerate from 0 to 50 in an almost identical space of time. The 0-60 time may vary a little because of the effect of axle ratio on the 1st to 2nd gear shift-point. For example, a 3.70 axle with 4-speed transmission can hit 60 mph in 1st gear (provided that the engine has mechanical lifters) but a 3-speed car with the same 3.70 axle will be slower to 60 because a 6500 rpm limit would put the 1-2 shift at 57 mph and lose a few tenths in time to 60 mph. At the same time a standard 3-speed car has a 3.36 axle and 6200 rpm would give 62 mph in 1st gear. Such a car would do 0 to 60 in the same time as a 4-speed job because the limiting factor is wheelspin.

Dealing first with the tame version of the Corvette, our figures show it to be a very lively performer despite its modest (?) 230 bhp and automatic slush-pump. In this connection we would like to point out that Power-glide may be correctly termed a "2-speed unit," but actually the converter provides an additional torque multiplication factor of 2.1:1, giving the effect of an extra low gear. Thus while the transmission ratio of 1.82:1 is roughly equivalent to a normal intermediate or 2nd gear, the initial start is effected by a ratio of 2.1 times 1.82 or 3.82:1, an excellent low gear type ratio which gives what the engineers call a good "breakaway." However, the Powerglide transmission is designed for smooth, jerk-free driving and a Corvette so equipped loses exactly one full second on the 0 to 30 mph test. This particular model also loses time by virtue of two other factors; the standard axle ratio is 3.55 and the automatic shift point (for low to high) is set at only 4500 rpm or 56 mph.

In summary, the 230-bhp Corvette with Powerglide is a very relaxing, comfortable car to drive, particularly in heavy traffic. And it romps from a standstill to 100 honest mph in 24.0 sec, a very respectable time. A 230-bhp, 3-speed, stick-shift model is the lowest-priced, basic Corvette and, though we did not test such a model, it should be able to out-perform the P-G car despite the fact that its standard axle ratio is 3.36:1.

Our next test Corvette had a 4-speed transmission, the standard (for 4-speed jobs) 3.70 axle ratio and a more exotic 270-bhp engine. This engine has two 4-barrel carburetors, a 9.5 compression ratio and, except for those items, it is essentially identical to the top-rated 315-bhp fuel-injection unit. Thus it has the special camshaft, mechanical lifters, lightweight valve gear, heavy duty bearings, positraction, etc.

We chose this model for test No. 2 in order to see what carburetors lose over the more expensive fuel injection. Unfortunately, the fuel-injection car had a 4.10 axle ratio, but even so we can conclude that the carburetors show no loss in low speed performance and very little depreciation at the top end. In fact our crew, after driving the cars and studying the mass of accumulated data, began to wonder "why fuel injection?" The 2x4 carburetor job was smooth, flexible and free from carburetion flat-spots. Side by side, the carburetor job would consistently edge out the f.i. car by a few feet in the 0 to 60 mph 1st-gear burst. Our conclusions were that the carburetors give more real torque in a usable speed range than fuel injection, and are almost as good as f.i. up to around 100 mph. Above that speed the extra power makes itself felt and the only real advantage of fuel injection is for competition and, in particular,

Corvette Power Teams

	ENGINE					TRANSMISSION	REAR AXLE	
Maximum Horsepower	Maximum Torque	Induction System	Compression Ratio	Camshaft, Lifters	Distributor Points, Advance	Type Available	Ratio	Positraction**
230 Std. @ 4800 rpm	300 lb. ft. @ 3000 rpm	Single 4-Barrel	9.5:1	Regular, Hydraulic	Single, Vacuum & Centrifugal	3-Speed Synchro-Mesh 4-Speed Synchro-Mesh* Powerglide*	3.36:1 3.70:1 3.55:1	Yes Yes No
245* @ 5000 rpm	300 lb. ft. @ 3800 rpm	Twin 4-Barrel	9.5:1	Regular, Hydraulic	Dual, Full Centrifugal	3-Speed Synchro-Mesh 4-Speed Synchro-Mesh* Powerglide*	3.36:1 3.70:1 3.55:1	Yes Yes No
270* @ 6000 rpm	285 lb. ft. @ 4200 rpm	Twin 4-Barrel	9.5:1	Special, Mechanical	Dual, Full Centrifugal	3-Speed Synchro-Mesh 4-Speed Synchro-Mesh*	3.36:1 3.70:1	Yes Yes
275* @ 5200 rpm	305 lb. ft. @ 4400 rpm	Ramjet Fuel Injection	11.0:1	Regular, Hydraulic	Single, Vacuum & Centrifugal	3-Speed Synchro-Mesh 4-Speed Synchro-Mesh*	3.36:1 3.70:1	Yes Yes
315* @ 6200 rpm	295 lb. ft. @ 4700-5100 rpm	Ramjet Fuel Injection	11.0:1	Special, Mechanical	Dual, Full Centrifugal	3-Speed Synchro-Mesh 4-Speed Synchro-Mesh*	3.36:1 3.70:1	Yes Yes

*Optional at extra cost.   **Choice of Positraction rear axle ratios: With 3-Speed Synchro-Mesh—3.36:1, 4.11:1, 4.56:1
With 4-Speed Synchro-Mesh—3.70:1, 4.11:1, 4.56:1

Rochester fuel injection helps boost horsepower to 315 maximum.

Wide, flat cleaner covers up single carburetor . . .

freedom from c.s.c. (carburetor starvation on corners).

The third test car was the "super" Corvette, often erroneously referred to as the "big" engine job. (All Corvette engines are of identical size, 283 cu in.) With fuel injection this sensational engine develops well over one horsepower per cubic inch. While the advertised figure is 315 bhp at 6200 rpm, a showroom stock model as tested and as installed with all accessories operating actually develops a net bhp of about 270 (our estimate; Chevrolet published 245 net bhp at 5600 for the 290-

Corvette Special Performance Options

Engine

All optional engines are valve-in-head short-stroke V-8, 283-cubic-inch displacement, 3.88 in. bore x 3.0 in. stroke, basically similar to the standard engine. The engine options are:

RPO 469 (245 bhp)—9.5:1 compression ratio. Hydraulic valve lifters. Finned aluminum rocker covers. Single oil-wetted air cleaner. Twin 4-barrel carburetors. Available with all transmissions.

RPO 468 (270-bhp)—9.5:1 compression ratio. Special camshaft, and heavy-duty main and connecting rod bearings. High-speed valve system with special valves and mechanical lifters. Finned aluminum rocker covers. Single oil-wetted air cleaner. Tachometer mechanically driven by distributor. This engine is designed primarily for high rpm operation and special events. Available with 3-speed or optional 4-speed synchromesh transmission.

RPO 353 (275-bhp)—11.0:1 compression ratio. Special cylinder heads and pistons. Hydraulic valve lifters. Finned aluminum rocker covers. Special paper element air cleaner. Ramjet fuel injection. Available with 3-speed or optional 4-speed synchromesh.

RPO 354 (315-bhp)—Maximum performance engine, 11.0:1 compression ratio. Special cylinder heads, pistons, camshaft and main and connecting rod bearings. High-speed valve system with special valves and mechanical lifters. Finned aluminum rocker covers. Special paper element air cleaner and outside air intake. Tachometer mechanically driven by distributor. This highly responsive engine suited for both pleasure driving and special events. Available with 3-speed or 4-speed synchromesh.

Transmission

RPO 685 (4-speed synchromesh)—All forward speeds fully synchronized. Close gear ratios take full advantage of high engine power. Ratios: 2.20:1 (1st), 1.66:1 (2nd), 1.31:1 (3rd), 1:1 (4th), 2.26:1 (reverse). Available with all engines and either standard conventional rear axle (3.70:1 ratio) or Positraction axle option.

RPO 313 (Powerglide automatic)—Hydraulic torque converter plus automatically engaged planetary gears. Available with standard 230 and optional 245-horsepower engines and rear axle with 3.55:1 ratio. Not available with Positraction axle.

Chassis

RPO 687 (Heavy-duty brakes and special steering)—Special brakes feature sintered-metallic brake facings, finned cast iron brake drums with built-in cooling fan, and vented brake flange plates with air scoops. Fast steering adapter gives 16.3:1 over-all ratio. This equipment suggested for special sports car events. Available only with 3-speed or 4-speed synchromesh and 270 or 315-horsepower engine with special camshaft. Positraction rear axle option must also be ordered.

RPO 686 (Special brake linings)—Special segmented sintered-metallic linings offer exceptional fade resistance and are not affected by water. These linings are designed for very hard use; however, the special brakes in RPO 687 are recommended for high performance sports car events. Available with 3- or 4-speed synchromesh.

RPO 675 (Positraction rear axle)—Positraction means positive power at the rear wheels, even if one wheel loses traction. Choice of 3.36:1, 4.11:1, or 4.56:1 axle ratio with 3-speed; 3.70:1, 4.11:1, or 4.56:1 axle ratio with 4-speed.

RPO 276 (15 - 5.50K wheels)—Includes 5 wheels with 5.5 in. rims required for special 7.10/7.60-15 tires which are available from tire suppliers. Can also be used with standard 6.70-15 4-ply tires. Hub caps replace wheel covers.

LPO 1625A (24-gallon gasoline tank)—Extends cruising range. Not available with RPO 473 (hardtop).

Body

RPO 419 (Removable hardtop)—Order at extra cost as a second top or at no extra charge in place of standard folding top.

RPO 473 (Power operation for folding top)—Electric-hydraulic mechanism to raise or lower the folding top.

RPO 426 (Power window controls)—Door windows operated electrically by switches on the doors.

FOA 102 (Radio and antenna)—Signal-seeking type; transistorized circuit, push-buttons.

or twin 4-barrels of the 270-hp Corvette.

bhp fuel injection engine in the 1959 models).

Some people claim that this true-competition Corvette is too hot for street driving. We do not agree at all. It is extremely easy to drive under any condition of traffic and the engine is so flexible that it doesn't seem to make any difference which of the 4 gears you happen to choose. It will start easily from a stop in either 1st or 2nd gear. It will even start in 3rd with a little clutch manipulation. When driving around in a 25 mph zone you can be in any one of the 4-gears and only a slight change in engine noise denotes the difference. If traffic allows an increase in speed, a nudge of the pedal puts you there, suddenly. Only when under full throttle do the differences in ratios become apparent. Then the slap-in-the-back acceleration is literally unbelievable and the fuel-injected engine propels you from 0 to 100 mph (104 mph on this particular speedometer) in 14.5 seconds or just over a ¼ mile in

distance. Top speeds given in the data panel represent a reasonable rpm, but not the absolute limit.

This engine makes a little more noise than the 230-bhp job—around town. The mechanical tappets can be heard and the exhaust note rumbles. When you really get on it, the noise increases considerably and at 6500 rpm it literally shrieks. But all this performance and crescendo is completely driver-controlled—you can have it if you want it, or not.

The interior of the 1961 Corvette has an inch or two more room here and there but is still not too roomy for oversize drivers. The ride is somewhat firm by sedan standards, soft as sports cars go. (Stiffer suspension is no longer optional, or needed, by the way.) The standard steering ratio is an excellent choice for all-around driving. Our second test car had the quicker steering option and with one half turn less lock to lock (3.2 vs. 3.7) it was noticeably stiff around town and very hard to park. The cornering powers and high speed roadability of a Corvette would be a revelation to drivers who have never tried a sports car and the Corvette rates very high as a good handling dual-purpose sports car. While Carroll Shelby admiringly calls it a "hawg" (*Car Life,* July), we must remember that such a tremendous surplus of power and speed would make any car on 4 wheels a bit of an adhesion problem under full throttle on a road-racing course.

Brakes on the standard Powerglide car showed a tendency to pull when used very hard from 90 mph 2 times in succession and took 4 to 5 min. to return back to normal. We definitely recommend ordering RPO 686, special metallic brake linings, and if you want the best, RPO 687 which is metallic linings and finned brake drums with special cooling vents.

The choice of engine is pretty much up to each individual's needs (and purse) and the same applies to the transmission. The new-this-year 3-speed is a heavy-duty unit (ratios 2.47 in 1st, 1.53 in 2nd) and though not as desirable as the 4-speed it will, nevertheless, give excellent results.

Unless you intend to enter your Corvette in competition we believe non-standard ratios should be specified

Powerglide utilizes floor shift . . .

so does 4-speed, all-synchromesh transmission.

Windshield dogleg hinders entry to comfortable seats.

Spare tire, tools are recessed into trunk floor.

and would be more satisfactory to more people. For example the clash-proof, all-synchromesh 4-speed transmission would permit a 3.36 ratio to be specified to give quieter running, less wear and tear, better economy, etc. Of course you would have to use 3rd gear all the time in town, but the overdrive effect of 4th gear would be pleasant. The positraction differential option is primarily a safety factor for low gear lead-foots; it eliminates snaking and makes control of wheelspin much easier.

In conclusion, we will readily admit that we would like very much to own an all-out fuel-injected Corvette with all the options. At the same time, it costs a lot more (well over $5000) and it seems to us that this tab is scaring off a lot of prospects. Our choice for a really fun-type Corvette at the lowest price would be as follows:
Engine: Standard 230 bhp with one 4-barrel carburetor.
But, with mechanical lifters, etc., to allow a 6500-rpm rev limit. (As this combination is not available,

the only alternative is the 270-bhp engine.)
Transmission: Standard 3-speed, but with 3.54 axle (instead of 3.36) so that 60 mph would be attainable in 1st gear, at 6500 rpm.
Brakes: Option RPO 686, metallic linings only, to save on costs, see chart, page 10.
Body: Removable hardtop (without the extra soft, folding top which again keeps the cost down) which effectively turns the Corvette into an all-weather coupe yet is convertible back to a roadster; radio and heater, both of which work excellently and provide added comfort for the driver.

With the rest of the car "standard" the above car should deliver for very close to $4200 and while this is still expensive, it is actually quite modest for a sports car in terms of performance per dollar. And depreciation, which is a definite part of the "cost," is very reasonable on a Corvette. ∎

3 CORVETTES

SPECIFICATIONS	315	270	230
List price	$3934	$3934	$3934
Price, as tested	5068	4667	4551
Curb weight, lb	3040	2950	3030
Test weight	3340	3290	3370
distribution, %	53/47	53/47	53/47
Tire size	6.70-15	6.70-15	6.70-15
Tire capacity, lb	3680	3680	3680
Brake lining area	157	157	157
Engine type	V-8, ohv	V-8, ohv	V-8, ohv
Bore & stroke	3.88x3.0	3.88x3.0	3.88x3.0
Displacement, cc	4639	4639	4639
cu in	283	283	283
Compression ratio	11.0	11.0	9.5
Bhp @ rpm	315 @ 6200	270 @ 6000	230 @ 4800
equivalent mph	122	131.7	109.4
Torque, lb-ft	295 @ 4700	285 @ 4200	300 @ 3000
equivalent mph	96.1	92.0	68.4

GEAR RATIOS

	315	270	230
4th (1.00), overall	4.11	3.70	
3rd (1.31)	5.38	4.85	2nd 3.55
2nd (1.66)	6.82	6.14	1st 6.45
1st (2.20)	9.04	8.14	1st 13.6

DIMENSIONS

	315	270	230
Wheelbase, in	102.0	102.0	102.0
Tread, f and r	57.0/59.0	57.0/59.0	57.0/59.0
Over-all length, in	178	178	178
width	70.4	70.4	70.4
height	51.6	51.6	51.6
equivalent vol, cu ft	374	374	374
Frontal area, sq ft	20.2	20.2	20.2
Ground clearance, in	6.7	6.7	6.7
Steering ratio, o/a	21.1	16.3	21.1
turns, lock to lock	3.7	3.2	3.7
turning circle, ft	37	37	37
Hip room	49	49	49
Pedal to seat back	39	39	39
Floor to ground	14	14	14
Luggage vol, cu ft	12.1	12.1	12.1

PERFORMANCE	315	270	230
Top speed (see text), mph	128	131	109
best timed run			
3rd (see text)	97 @ 6450	105 @ 6300	
2nd (see text)	77 @ 6500	85 @ 6450	
1st (see text)	58 @ 6500	64 @ 6450	65 @ 5500

FUEL CONSUMPTION

	315	270	230
Normal range, mpg	11/17	13/19	14/18

ACCELERATION

	315	270	230
0-30 mph, sec	3.0	3.0	4.0
0-40	3.6	3.6	5.2
0-50	4.5	4.5	6.6
0-60	5.5	5.9	7.7
0-70	6.5	8.0	11.1
0-80	8.9	10.3	15.1
0-100	14.5	16.5	24.0
Standing ¼ mile	14.2	14.6	16.5
speed at end	99	93	83

PULLING POWER

	315	270	230
4th, lb/ton @ mph	360 @ 78	370 @ 68	
3rd	475 @ 72	480 @ 62	2nd 465 @ 40
2nd	580 @ 57	590 @ 47	1st off scale
Total drag at 60 mph, lb	135	140	135

SPEEDOMETER ERROR

	315	270	230
30 mph, actual	28.2	29.2	29.7
60 mph	56.8	57.0	57.0
90 mph	86.0	86.2	85.0

CALCULATED DATA

	315	270	230
Lb/hp (test wt)	10.9	12.2	14.7
Cu ft/ton mile	151	136.7	128.5
Mph/1000 rpm	19.5	21.9	22.8
Engine revs/mile	3080	2740	2640
Piston travel, ft/mile	1540	1370	1320
Car Life wear index	47.5	37.6	34.8

ENGINE SPEED IN GEARS

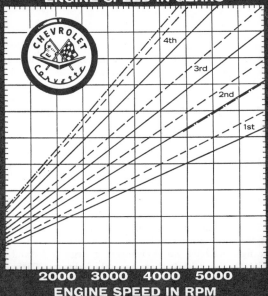

ENGINE SPEED IN RPM

ACCELERATION & COASTING

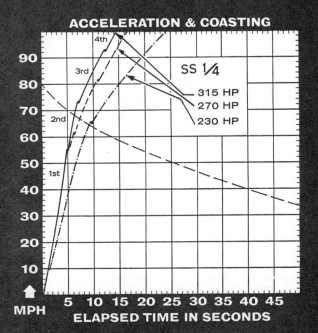

SS ¼
315 HP
270 HP
230 HP

ELAPSED TIME IN SECONDS

BIG 'VETTE

Once again that old adage, "There's no substitute for cubic inches," holds true as the '62 Corvette adds 44 and produces a maximum of 360 horsepower

by Ray Brock

Is that a '62? Does it have fuel injection? The big engine? Four-speed box?" Those were the questions we were asked every time we drove into a service station to fill up the Corvette we tested for this article. After we answered yes to each of the questions, the comment we then heard was, "Boy, what a car!" This didn't happen just a couple of times but every time we stopped for gas.

"Is it a '62," was always asked first because the new Corvette has minor exterior stlying changes when compared to the '61 and with only a few '62 models on the road in early November, service station attendants were not sure. We were usually asked to point out the exterior differences while the tank was being filled and the windshield washed. They are: The side cove is not outlined with chrome as it was in '61; the cove grille has many small chrome "teeth" instead of the three large ones last year; hood and cove emblems of crossed flags are changed; wide chrome rocker panels have been added beneath the doors; and the aluminum grille screen is black anodized.

After we had explained the styling changes, the next request was to explain the big new engine they'd heard about. "Was it a bored and stroked version of the 283?" *Yes.* "How much power with the hot cam and fuel injection?" *360 horsepower.* "Does it go?" *You bet. Those extra 44 cubic inches can really be felt, especially in low speed operation.* By this time, the tank was usually filled and we would pay the tab, crawl behind the wheel, nonchalantly buckle the seat belt, start the engine and pull away from the station smoothly while fighting back an overpowering urge to "stand on it" and let the boys back there see this baby go. Through the rear view mirror, we could watch the attendants and they never turned to the next customer until they heard our shift into fourth.

We borrowed the '62 Corvette for this test from our

RIGHT — Exterior dimensions of '62 Corvette engine are unchanged from '61 but displacement has been jumped to 327 cubic inches. Top engine option uses fuel injection, develops 360 hp. Shielding over all secondary ignition wiring is to prevent radio interference.

LEFT — With limited-slip differential and 4.10 axle, HRM's test Corvette was real tiger on steep dirt mountain trails, equally rapid on paved streets.

BELOW — On sharp corners, sporty 'Vette (that's what owners call 'em) stays level but can be "drifted" with good control despite 3000 lb. weight.

friends at Harry Mann Chevrolet again this year. This agency specializes in Corvettes and always has several hot models in stock. Excluding some optional chassis extras, the car we borrowed was the hottest version of America's only sports car. It was a hardtop model with the 360 horsepower fuel-injected engine, close-ratio four-speed transmission, limited-slip differential and 4.11 rear axle ratio.

Chassis and body specifications for the '62 Corvette are identical to those of the '61 Corvette with wheelbase 102 inches; tread 57 inches, front, 59 inches, rear; overall length, 14 feet, nine inches; width, 70½ inches; and height, 52 inches. The frame is unchanged from '61, consisting of fully boxed side rails with an I-beam X-member beneath the passenger compartment to resist frame twist.

A single change has been made in the suspension department for 1962; the front spring rates have been increased from 110 to 115 pounds per inch at the wheel to compensate for the slight increase in engine weight which accompanied the increased displacement. The unequal length front A-arms anchor to the front crossmember which in turn bolts to the frame side rails. Caster adjustment for the front wheels is by means of shims between the front crossmember

and the frame. Rear spring rates are unchanged for '62. Semi-elliptical leaf springs mounted outboard of the frame rails give excellent stability to the car, and radius rods above the rear axle housing bracket to the frame on each side to resist torque and braking forces.

Big news for the '62 Corvette is mainly concentrated in the engine compartment. The engine has been enlarged from 283 to 327 cubic inches but for reasons that are not commonly known. The extra 44 cubic inches for the Corvette came about because of an economy move by the larger Chevrolet passenger cars.

In 1961, Chevrolet passenger cars had V8 engines with three different displacements; 283, 348 and 409. The 283 engine was the economy version for passenger cars and because of its light weight and small physical dimensions, the standard engine for all Corvettes. The 348 option filled the needs for a more powerful engine than the 283 but one that would still be docile enough for an automatic transmission. The 409, which has reached national fame in less than a year thanks to its drag strip prowess, was strictly a high performance version for the speed enthusiast.

The medium-sized 348-inch V8 never was the "natural" that the smaller 283 had been when it came to performance in relation to size and it cost quite a bit more to make than the 283. The very fact that the 348 engine outweighed the 283 by approximately 115 pounds represented a higher cost for materials alone. Machining and other costs were also higher. Experimentation with the 283-inch V8 disclosed that an increase in bore of ⅛-inch and ¼-inch increase in stroke would give an engine of 327 inches displacement which had more power than the standard 348 engine, was cheaper to build, was lighter in weight and with smaller displacement produced better mileage than the 348. So, the 348-inch engine was dropped from the '62 Chevrolet line and a 327-incher announced to fit between the economy model 283 and the high performance 409.

Naturally, with this extra 44 cubic inches available in the same size package as before, the engineers were quick to drop it in the Corvette chassis so that America's answer to the Ferraris, E-Jaguars and Mercedes 300's would have even better performance than before.

Block patterns were reworked to accept the larger bore and longer stroke but to the unsuspecting eye, the 327's appear pretty much the same as the 283 blocks. Recoring of water jackets gives cylinder wall thickness to take the extra ⅛-inch bore. Although crankshaft journal spacing and sizes remain the same for the 327 as for the 283, extra strength was added to the main bearing web regions in the bottom of the block to resist the higher pressures of increased displacement. Extra material was added to the main webs and then the bottom of the block machined for crankshaft counterweight clearance. A slight bit of beefing was also done in the floor of the tappet chamber to increase upper block rigidity. Everything about the 327 block looks the same as the 283 and except for the larger bore, you'd expect everything from the 283 engine to bolt right in place. Not so!

The crankshaft for the 327 engine is new and many changes were made to compensate for the extra ¼-inch stroke. Crankshafts are forged steel and larger, reshaped counterweights were designed to take care of the new 3¼-inch stroke, heavier pistons and heavier rods. Journal sizes and lengths for both main and rod bearings are the same as the 283, 2.3 and 2 inches respectively. In 1961, premium grade steel-backed aluminum bearing inserts were used only on the high performance Corvette engines but for 1962, aluminum bearings are standard for all passenger car and Corvette 327-inch engines.

Connecting rods for the 327 are the same length and have the same bores as the 283 rods but extra material has been added to the beam section of the forged steel rod to give added strength. This extra material increases the weight of each rod by slightly less than one ounce. Incidentally, for those readers who are using 265 or 283 Chevy engines in competition machines, especially with blowers, the stronger 327 rods would be a valuable and thrifty addition next time the engine is apart. Chevrolet still favors an interference fit between rod and piston pin. Engineers from Chevrolet as well as other companies tell us the pressed-in pin is best for high performance engines although somewhat awkward for the average home mechanic to take apart or assemble.

Pistons for the 327 are new to take care of the larger bore and higher pin location. For the 250 and 300 horsepower Corvette engine, a flattop cast aluminum piston with machined reliefs for valve clearance gives a compression ratio of 10.5 to 1. The 340 and 360 hp engines use a pop-up type piston which gives a compression ratio of 11.25:1 and these pistons are aluminum forgings for increased strength. The forged pistons also have valve reliefs machined in the top. To compensate for the longer stroke, pin hole height in both pistons is ⅛-inch nearer the top than on the 283 pistons and skirts are shorter to clear the crankshaft counterweights at the bottom of travel. Cast 327 pistons are 1.6 ounces heavier than the 283's; the forged pistons 1.5 ounces.

For those of you who own 283 engines and have already started wondering which of the 327 parts will fit your block, here's the answer. Only the rods. The pistons won't work with the 283

360 HP CORVETTE V-8

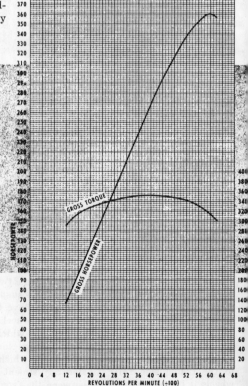

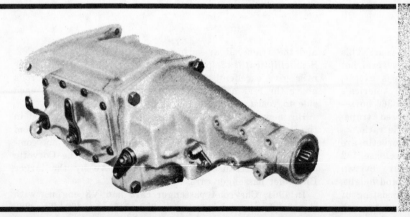

ABOVE — Optional four-speed transmission for the Corvette has all aluminum case and two selections of ratios. For lower horsepower engines, forward ratios are 2.54, 1.92, 1.51 and 1:1. Higher horsepower engines use a four-speed with ratios of 2.20, 1.66, 1.31 and 1:1. Clutch used is same for all transmissions. RIGHT — 1962's hottest engine option gains 45 horsepower from '61 with extra 44 inches displacement and the flat torque curve shows broad effective range.

stroke because of higher pin location. The 327 crank has larger counterweights which strike the bottom of 283 blocks. Grinding the block for clearance would be tough because the counterweights interfere by almost ¼-inch. A better solution would be to turn counterweights down and add steel plates to balance. The best solution would be to buy a 327 short block assembly with all needed pieces. They list for less than $300.

Two types of cylinder heads are used on '62 Corvette engines but neither is new for this year. The base Corvette engine rated at 250 horsepower is identical to the 250 hp 327-inch engine used in '62 passenger cars and the cylinder heads used are a carry-over from last year's four-barrel carbureted 283 engine. These heads are fitted with 1.719-inch intake valves and 1.50-inch exhaust valves. The three optional Corvette engines for '62 are rated 300, 340, and 360 horsepower and use the cylinder head carried over from 1961's 315 hp performance Corvette engine. These heads have larger ports and use 1.938-inch exhausts.

Valve timing and actuation is also a carry-over from last year with the 250 and 300 hp engines for both the passenger cars and Corvettes equipped with the same camshaft, hydraulic lifters, pushrods, 1.5:1 stamped rocker arms and valve springs as last year's 283-inch engine. The 340 and 360 hp engines which use a high performance camshaft and mechanical lifters are fitted with components from 1961's 315 horsepower V8. The hot cam has durations of 287° for both intake and exhaust with valve lift of .400-inch. Valve lash

is .008 intake and .018 exhaust, hot.

The intake manifold used on the 250 and 300 horsepower engines has a new part number for '62 although the only real change was to enlarge the riser tubes to match larger throttle bores in a pair of new four-barrel carburetors. Both carburetors are made by Carter and the one used for the 250 hp base Corvette engine has 1.438-inch throttle bores for both primary and secondary barrels. The 300 and 340 horsepower engines are fitted with a carburetor that has a much higher air flow capacity through 1.5625-inch primary and 1.6875-inch secondary barrels. Automatic chokes are used on each carburetor with oil-wetted polyurethane air cleaners.

Rochester's fuel injection unit which has been successfully used on high performance Corvettes for several years is again fitted to the top engine option in the line rated at 360 horsepower. Minor changes have been made for the '62 injection unit, mostly to improve cold-weather starting and warmup. The cast

celeration. For '62, all Corvette engines will use distributor tachometer drives. The 360 hp model also has an additional distributor drive to turn the high pressure fuel injection pump.

Advance curves have been completely retailored to fit the larger engines for '62. The two milder engines with hydraulic camshafts and 10.5:1 compression use a distributor with maximum centrifugal advance of 24° @ 4600 rpm and also are fitted with vacuum advance which gives a maximum of 15° @ 15½ inches of manifold vacuum. Initial lead is recommended at 8°. For operation above 4600 rpm and with low manifold vacuum so that vacuum advance does not function, maximum spark advance would be 32° crankshaft before top dead center. Single points are used for the distributors on 250 and 300 hp engines.

The two higher horsepower engines use dual-point distributors and have no vacuum advance mechanism. They also have 24° centrifugal advance at 4600

1962 CORVETTE ENGINES

ENGINES	HORSEPOWER (@ rpm)	GROSS TORQUE lbs/ft @ rpm)	COMPRESSION RATIO	EQUIPMENT
Standard	250 @ 4400	350 @ 2800	10.5:1	Four-barrel carburetor Hydraulic camshaft
RPO 583	300 @ 5000	360 @ 3200	10.5:1	Large four-barrel Hydraulic camshaft
RPO 396	340 @ 6000	344 @ 4000	11.25:1	Large four-barrel Special camshaft
RPO 582	360 @ 6000	352 @ 4000	11.25:1	Fuel injection Special camshaft

All engines have 4" bore, 3¼" stroke and 327 cubic inches displacement.

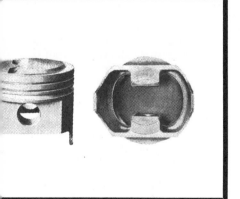

Pistons for the 340 and 360 horsepower engines with 11.25 compression have a raised top and milled reliefs for valve clearance. They are forged from aluminum extrusions. Pistons for 10.5 compression engines are cast, have flat tops.

aluminum intake manifold has a high box-like exterior appearance but inside, eight tuned ram passages feed a cylinder each. These cast tubes form passages 12 inches long from their top end to the center of the cylinder and are slightly larger in area at the top than the bottom to aid air flow. With a constant flow nozzle in each tube just above the intake valve, fuel metering is very equal and even with the hot camshaft, low speed operation is smooth.

There has been a distributor change for all of the '62 Corvette engines. First of all, in previous years, only the high performance fuel-injected engines were equipped with a tachometer drive on the distributor housing. Other engines picked up their tach drive from the rear of the generator. A slightly loose fan belt meant slippage and incorrect tach readings, especially on rapid engine ac-

rpm but use 10° initial lead for a total of 34° crankshaft advance above 4600 rpm. Last year's 315 engine used a total of 40° @ 6000 rpm. Evidently the new larger bore size and piston configuration combine to create more combustion chamber turbulence and permit later firing than in 1961.

AC 44 spark plugs with ⅜-inch reach are used in the 250 and 300 hp engines and their equivalent in Champion is J7, A5 for Autolite. The high performance 340 and 360 hp engines are factory equipped with AC 44FF which is equal to L7, L10S or L85 Champions and AE4 Autolites. These plugs have ½-inch reach.

The viscous coupling five-bladed fan used in '61 for high performance engines only is standard for all '62 Cor-

Corvette interior is beautifully styled and well-fitted. Seat belts are standard and each of the bucket seats is adjustable. Steering wheel is nearly vertical and feels awkward at first. Shift lever for the 4-speed is conveniently placed.

BIG 'VETTE continued

vettes. This fan is controlled by engine temperature so that it free-wheels when the engine is cold but operates in a progressively more direct hookup as the engine temperature rises. The fan will not exceed 3100 rpm even though the engine speed might be 6000, so high speed fan losses are reduced. The aluminum cross-flow radiator is retained for '62 but changed slightly in core thickness to increase cooling ability. The radiator is also painted black to conform with the black anodized grille.

Transmission selection is the same as in previous years with a three-speed manual transmission standard equipment for all engines and either automatic or four-speed optional. A new lightweight Powerglide is offered this year for use with either the 250 or 300 hp engines. The unit is "beefed" to take the increased horsepower and is air cooled. Lining with increased wear-resistance is used on the clutches, high temperature resistant seals are used and the governor pressure is higher to increase shift points. The low and reverse ratios are 1.76:1 and drive is direct with a stall ratio of 2.10:1 in the torque converter.

Three-speed manual ratios are the same as for '61 with a low gear ratio of 2.47, 1.53 in second, 1:1 in third and 2.80 in reverse. The four-speed selection is double what it was last year as two sets of ratios are available. For the 250 and 300 hp engines, four-speed ratios of 2.54 first, 1.92 second, 1.51 third, 1:1 fourth and 2.61 reverse are used. The four-speed used with high performance 340 and 360 hp engines has ratios of 2.20 first, 1.66 second, 1.31 third, 1:1 fourth and 2.26 reverse. On special order, either of the four-speeds can be specified despite engine rating. Four-speed transmission cases are aluminum for all models.

The clutch used for all standard transmission models is a Borg and Beck unit with coil springs in the pressure plate and a 10-inch disc. Despite spring pressure of 2000 pounds, the action is smooth and pedal pressure required is nominal. The bell housing for all models is aluminum.

Standard rear axle ratios vary according to engine and transmission. For the three-speed transmission, an axle ratio of 3.36:1 is standard with all engines. With four-speed, the stand-

ard ratio is 3.36:1 for the 250 and 300 engines using the low ratio transmission, 3.70:1 for the high performance 340 and 360 engines using the high ratio transmission. The Powerglide ratio is 3.36:1 for both the 250 and 300 engines. A 3.08 optional ratio is available for the 250 or 300 engines with four-speed. Another option for use with all engines and transmissions is a limited-slip differential, Positraction. Ratios available with Positraction are: 3.08, 3.36, 3.55, 3.70, 4.11, 4.88, 5.14, and 5.43.

Brakes for the '62 Corvette are unchanged from last year. Standard service brakes use 11-inch drums 2 inches wide at the front and 1.75 inches at the rear. Conventional organic lining material is used with a total area of 157 square inches for the four wheels. These brakes are adequate for average operation but for severe use, two heavy-duty options are available. Regular Production Option 686 uses the regular 11-inch drums 2 inches wide front and rear and a sintered iron lining replaces the organic material. This lining is composed of tiny granules of cast iron and graphite which is unaffected by heat or water. Instead of strips of lining the full length of the shoes, small blocks of sintered iron are welded to the shoes. These blocks, six for each primary shoe and secondary shoe, give a total effective area of 114 square inches. Brake fade is virtually eliminated with this lining and repeated stops can be made from high speeds safely.

A second brake option, RPO 687, also uses sintered iron lining material but has more total lining area, 124 square inches and the cast iron brake drums are finned for maximum heat dissipation. Stamped steel fans fasten between the drum and wheel to aid air circulation and each backing plate is equipped with an air scoop and vents to promote rapid cooling. This option is for Corvette which might be raced in sports car events and RPO 687 also includes heavy-duty shock absorbers for all four wheels and a fast steering adaptor which quickens the ratio from a standard 21:1 to 16.3:1. For highway or drag strip use, the RPO 687 option is not recommended.

The first thing we noticed when driving the '62 360 horsepower Corvette was the increased low speed torque that accompanied the increased displacement. Last year's hottest engine was rated 295 pounds feet of torque at 4700 rpm while the big engine for '62 has a torque rating of 352 lbs/ft at 4000 rpm. Note that the 327-inch engine not only has almost 20% more torque but it reaches its maximum at 700 rpm lower engine speed. An even higher torque rating of 360 lbs/ft is given the 300 hp engine that uses a hydraulic camshaft.

We went through the same familiarization period that seems to be needed when driving a Corvette for the first time in several months. The vertical steering wheel close to the driver and little room between lap and wheel always gives us fits for the first few days. We asked several people to slip behind the wheel of our test car and they too had the same compliants. One fellow who measures less than 5'6" really had problems. By the time he got the seat far enough forward to reach the pedals, he was in danger of getting his nose caught in the spokes of the steering wheel. Although thousands of Corvettes are being driven on the roads every day without undue difficulty by the drivers, we would guess that there might be even more Corvettes sold if the first impression behind the wheel weren't so awkward. It would appear that the best solution to the problem would be to restyle the instrument cluster into a flat panel so that the wheel could be pushed forward a couple of inches and then perhaps a slightly smaller diameter wheel used.

The vinyl-covered bucket seats are very comfortable and seat adjustment is ample for even the driver with very long legs. Clutch, brake and throttle action is smooth and the shift lever for the four-speed transmission in our test car was in a perfect position. On tight, narrow mountain roads, one of the differences we noted was that not as much gear changing was needed to maintain a fast pace in the '62 as it had been in the '61. With the larger engine, corners that required a downshift to second last year could be taken in third with smoother handling also resulting.

The '62 Corvette does not lean on corners but maintains very good balance up to the point where the wheels start to slide. With the limited-slip differential, medium speeds through tight corners produced heavy steering and the front end "pushed" but if enough power was used to get the rear wheels "loose," front wheels tracked much better and the car could be directed through a corner by the throttle. Acceleration off the corners was a real thrill and plenty of speed could be attained in a short stretch before braking and downshifting for the next corner.

When we borrowed the Corvette from Harry Mann, less than 500 miles had been registered on the odometer but we were assured that everything was in good shape and to drive it as we wished. Standard 6.70 x 15 tires were fitted to the car and although these were not ideal for traction in drag strip operation, we decided to try the car out anyway. We learned that Mickey Thompson planned to do some mid-week tests with a dragster at the Lion's strip in

Long Beach so we made arrangements to run the Corvette at the same time.

We made no special preparations but ran the car exactly as it had come from the dealer. Tire pressures were standard 24 pounds front and rear, spare tire was in place, fan belt was tight and the fuel tank was more than half full. The first start immediately confirmed our suspicions; the stock tires had very poor traction. Our first run registered 102.97 mph and an elasped time of 14.22 seconds. A half dozen runs later, we had only managed to raise the speed to 103.98 mph and lower the e.t. to 14.12. We asked Mickey what the average '62 Corvette had been turning during recent weeks at the Long Beach strip and he told us that 104 was about tops for cars right off the showroom floor.

We then asked Mickey to try his luck and after a trial run, he turned in a speed of 105.14 mph in 13.89 seconds. The difference between our times and Mickey's was his shifting speed. Mickey used full throttle "power shifts" while we released the throttle slightly between shifts. Power shifts give better results but unless you are experienced, you'd better stay away from them. Mickey confessed that he had scattered a few transmissions before getting the knack. We were reluctant to try.

At the time we made our drag strip runs, there was a steady head wind of approximately 15 mph so chances are both speed and elapsed time would be slightly better on a calm day. We did notice however, that the 327-inch engine did not seem to accelerate as rapidly from 5500 to 6000 rpm as the smaller 283 engine in last year's test Corvette. Perhaps a bit of super-tuning in timing and mixture departments could improve performance.

As the only sports car manufactured in volume in this country, the Corvette is a tremendous package. It costs much less than foreign cars of comparable performance, is a snap to service, and is not temperamental in traffic. If you wish, you can order options to go racing or if you are a little old lady from Pasadena, you can order one with Powerglide to get you to and from the knitting shop. If you want to have fun while driving, take a look at the Corvette, there just might be a model for you.

Photos by Chevrolet, Eric Rickman

TOP — Most of the '62 changes can be seen here. Recessed cove in body has a new grille design, new emblems behind front wheel cutout and a broad strip of chrome has been added beneath doors.

RIGHT — Fast downhill tests on twisting roads taxed the standard brakes but did not cause excessive fade. Metallic heavy-duty linings can be ordered extra.

TECHNICAL REPORT BY PETE BIRO:

A Very Special
CORVETTE SPECIAL

Many people have had the same thoughts: If only the Corvette weighed a thousand or so pounds less . . .

WATCHING DAVE MacDONALD cross the finish line at Cotati in First place, ahead of some of the finest imported and home-built machinery running on the West Coast, was his sponsor and car owner, Jim Simpson. Simpson was having a ball. "There goes my house!" said Simpson, "I was all set to build a house, but instead I decided to go racing and build a car. If I had the decision to make again, it would be the same — the car, instead of a house."

Pretty enthusiastic words, wouldn't you say? Simpson has reason to be enthusiastic. Take the hottest American engine in racing today, the new 327-inch 1962 Corvette, put it into a chassis by Max Balchowsky, drape it with a body out of Detroit styling studios and you'd be feeling pretty good, too. Simpson has been sponsoring MacDonald throughout his meteoric career, first helping him with his ride in

Hot . . . with both wrench and right foot, Dave MacDonald handles mechanical and driving chores of Jim Simpson's car.

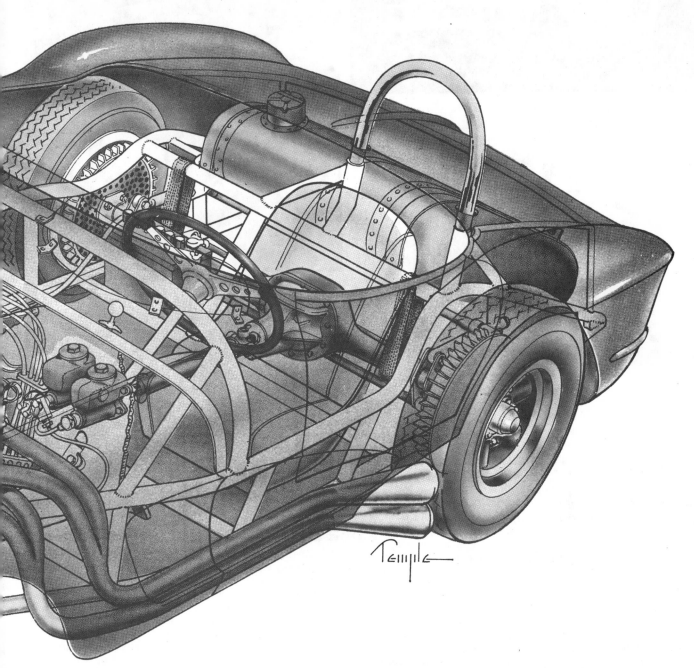

CORVETTE SPECIAL

1.—The special, sponsored by Sorenson Chevy, blasts through turn at Cotati — first finish, first win.

2.—Fiberglass body was made from mold lifted off a '61 Corvette but is many pounds lighter than stock.

3.—Based on an Old Yaller Mk IV frame, the car has torsion-bar suspension with Jaguar and Morris parts.

4.—"Loosened-up" Chevy engine carries original fuel-injection. Crew feels the brute has power to spare.

CORVETTE SPECIAL (continued)

consecutive wins. After a phenomenal domination of production car racing, they initially decided to race the Corvette in the modified contests to see how they could do against all-out racing machinery. Dave feels a Corvette is just as fast through the turns as the modified cars but the stock Corvette's big drawback, its weight of 3000 pounds, makes it tough to out-brake the lighter modifieds.

Their very next idea was what you see on these pages — a car that looks like a Corvette, a car with Corvette power, a car that outruns, out-stops and outperforms a real Corvette in every department.

From chalk marks on Balchowsky's floor to the win at Cotati took just two and one-half months. The chassis is basically the same as the Old Yaller Mk IV, as pictured in the July 1961 issue of SCG, but from that point on there is little resemblance.

The engine is the very latest 327 cubic inch Corvette powerplant out of Detroit. MacDonald modifications are minor, practically non-existent. Dave, from experience, found the Corvette performs better, and is far more reliable, if you leave it stock — stock valves, pistons, rods, crank, etc. All Dave has done, aside from having everything balanced, is to polish the combustion chambers.

One of the tricks in aiding reliability is in the way Dave sets up the piston clearance — he calls it "no clearance." What he does is knurl the pistons (stockers) and practically pound them into the bore with a hammer. "After a couple of laps the knurl wears off, they run right in, making their own clearance."

When asked why he doesn't go farther with the engine, he stated, "We've actually got more power than we need right now. Engine response couldn't be better . . . and traction is great."

One modification, though, not directly to the engine but a great aid to performance, is an experimental set of reverse cones at the exhaust ends. It was Dave's idea to use them on a car and he had them made up in a motorcycle shop. Completing the exhaust system are Jardine Headers, which, with their cross-over design (see accompanying photos), offer the least restriction to a good exhaust flow, by alternating exhaust pulses.

For safety reasons an aluminum Weber flywheel, weighing 14 pounds, is used. The gearbox is a standard four-speed Corvette, which originally transferred the 360 (plus) horsepower to a Studebaker rear-end.

Body lines are a direct descendant from the Corvette. Only the size and weight has been changed. With brackets, mounts and hardware the entire body tips the scales at 85 pounds. The glass-fiber material is 1/16th of an inch thick. The overall length has been reduced from 176.7 inches to 160 inches, width is five inches narrower, at 65.4 inches, and height has been reduced four inches, from 52.2 to 48.2. The body itself was taken from a mold of Jim Simpson's

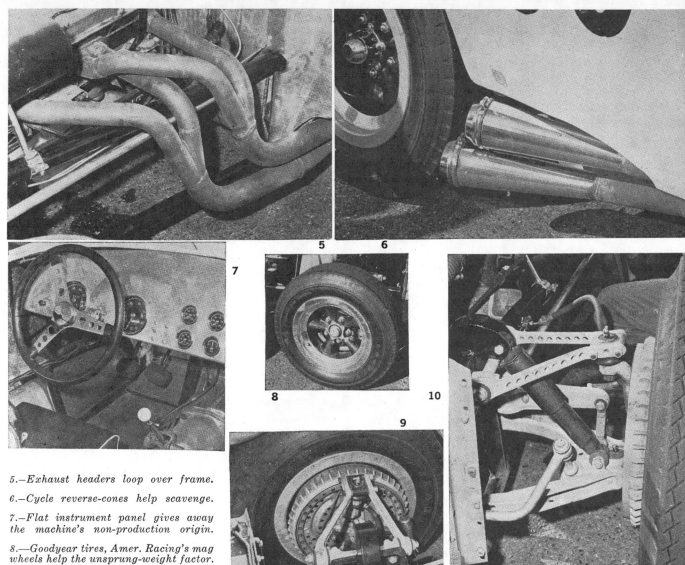

5.—*Exhaust headers loop over frame.*

6.—*Cycle reverse-cones help scavenge.*

7.—*Flat instrument panel gives away the machine's non-production origin.*

8.—*Goodyear tires, Amer. Racing's mag wheels help the unsprung-weight factor.*

9.—*Buick finned-aluminum brake drums.*

10.—*Pontiac, Jag, & Morris parts shown.*

Corvette and the glass-work was done by Jim and Dave, along with much help by Jim Burrel.

Front suspension, like previous Balchowsky work, comprises many stock items. It has unequal length wishbones, the upper members being Jaguar, well-lightened, the lowers are stamped Pontiac units. Springing is by Morris-Minor torsion bar. Shocks are Gabriel adjustables. The torsion bars run parallel to the frame rails and are fully adjustable. Unlike Max's Jaguar disc-braked Mk IV, the front brakes are 11-inch Pontiac drums, with aluminum fins. Twelve-inch Buick Alfins supply the stopping power at the rear. The backing plates, front and rear, are liberally drilled to reduce unsprung weight and to aid cooling.

An inch longer than the Mk IV, the Corvette-powered charger has a 92-inch wheelbase. Formerly the live rear axle was Studebaker, with rear stabilization by leading arms. These were connected to Morris torsion bars, mounted transversely, providing rear springing. Tubular Gabriel shocks were mounted at as near vertical as possible. Lateral location was by Panhard bar.

The Studebaker-rear-end has recently been swapped for a similar unit of Chevy II derivation, that has the advantage of being both lighter and stronger. Load-leveler springs have been adapted up front to stiffen this section. Aside from considerable shake-down problems, such as re-welding brackets, etc., the crew has found it necessary to change Max's "set 'em up loose" method of anchoring his

suspension components. The car's tendency to wallow, especially in the tighter corners, has found MacDonald in some ticklish situations already. Both Simpson and Dave feel that considerably more development can and will be accomplished in the near future, but meanwhile they have a basically potent machine to compete with, and the refinements can be made as they go along. The frame is rugged and its weight of 95 pounds is far from a handicap.

Getting back to performance — at Riverside, first time in the car, Dave got his lap times down to about 2:07. "I only pushed it on the straight. Until I really get the feel of it I don't want to go hard through the turns. We were running 3:30 x 15's, taching 6700 to 6800 on the straight."

At Cotati, Dave reached 116 mph from the starting line to the timing lights, a distance of about 1000 feet.

"Should do about 130 in the quarter, with the right gears," stated Dave.

During the race at Cotati, Dave went through the traps at better than 140 mph.

"I was just getting on the brakes for Turn One, when I went through the timing lights."

The next time you see what you think is a Corvette outhauling the latest from Modena, you'd better take a closer look. And if you see the number "00" you'll know what you're looking at — Dave MacDonald's "beauty-is-only-skin-deep" Corvette. It weighs 1750 pounds wet, on the grid; it goes like a tiger, and it should be able to run all day. It has. Fast.

FUEL-INJECTED

Road Test

BY JIM WRIGHT
TECHNICAL EDITOR

AMERICA'S only *true* production sports car is still going strong after eight years on the market and shows no signs of letting up. True, every year one hears the rumor that the factory is going to drop the beast because they don't make a profit on them. But don't you believe it — the profit on this one is measured in prestige, and Chevrolet loves it. In fact, as long as Chevy continues to build it strictly from the prestige angle, it'll probably remain a great car — built on a straight dollar-profit basis they'd probably ruin it.

Exterior changes are minor this year: the grille is painted black, a wide piece of chrome trim covers the rocker panel, and the three horizontal bars in the cove have been replaced with a multi-bar grille configuration. The only real change for '62 is in the engine compartment.

The old 283-incher has been bored ⅛-inch and stroked ¼-inch to give 327 cubic inches. This is the only engine size available for the 'Vette, but it comes in various stages of tune.

The basic engine uses a single four-barrel, 10.5-to-1 compression ratio, and

a mild cam with hydraulic lifters to put out 250 hp. The addition of a larger four-barrel (RPO 583) ups this figure to 300 hp. RPO 396 consists of the large four-barrel, a wilder cam with mechanical lifters and relieved dome pistons, giving a compression ratio of 11.25 to 1. This one is rated at 340 hp.

The real bear of the line is known as RPO 582 and uses the RPO 396 goodies plus fuel injection to pump out 360 horses at 6000 rpm! This represents 1.1 hp per cubic inch, which is not bad at all — Ferrari 250 GT's put out only two-

CORVETTE

Chevrolet's sporting thoroughbred still sets the pace for performance with a Yankee accent

tenths more horsepower per cubic inch, and they cost almost four times as much.

A wide variety of power trains is available, and with a little thought, a prospective owner can order just about any combination to meet any condition imaginable.

The three-speed manual transmission is the standard offering with any engine option. The Warner four-speed box is available with either the 2.54 or close-ratio 2.20 low gear, but the factory recommends the 2.54 version with the 250- and

300-hp models. Powerglide can also be had with both of these models.

The standard rear axle for Powerglide and three-speed models is 3.36. The four-speed with 2.54 low also uses the 3.36 ratio, but the 3.08 axle is optional. Close-ratio boxes take a 3.70 axle. Positraction axle ratios are the same for all models, with the exception of the 340- and 360-hp close-ratio combos. With these two, the choice is expanded to include ratios of 3.08, 3.55, 3.70, 4.11 and 4.56.

The MOTOR TREND test car was equipped with the 360-hp engine, close-ratio transmission and 3.70 Positraction rear axle. This car also happened to be the work horse of the local Chevrolet zone office and had over 5000 miles logged on it by everybody from their janitor to such visiting firemen as Astronaut Allan B. Shepard, who had it just before MT. We didn't get a chance to ask him how the car compared to his space capsule, but we'll bet the 'Vette had a better e.t. for the first quarter-mile.

The car felt and sounded healthy when we picked it up, so we didn't do anything to it in the way of tuning. While our times aren't the best you've seen, they are at least the most honest. With the usual load — full gas tank, instrumentation and two up — we racked up 0-to-30, 0-to-45 and 0-to-60 mph in 2.4, 3.9 and 5.9 seconds. Through the quarter-mile trap our fifth-wheel-connected electric speedo recorded a top time of 102.5 mph with a 14.9 e.t.

This goes to show that the stock 6.70 x 15 boots aren't the answer for traction. No amount of experimenting off the line could keep the tires from smoking, clear to second gear. Several top-end runs produced an honest 132 mph long before the end of the Riverside straight.

The stock brakes worked well, but after

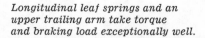

Longitudinal leaf springs and an upper trailing arm take torque and braking load exceptionally well.

SOME MAY CALL THE STOCK SUSPENSION A BIT STIFF, BUT WE WOULDN'T HAVE IT OTHERWISE. THE CAR REALLY HANDLES IN THE BENDS.

At the top of the Corvette power line, the 360-hp fuel-injected version of the stock 327-cubic-inch 'Vette engine pumps out 1.1 hp per cubic inch! The Rochester fuel injection unit was responsive and smooth at any speed or gear.

the high-speed runs they needed a ten-minute break because they were all through. After the binders had their rest we were able to run the regular braking tests, and these were carried off with no apparent fade, grab or swerve. Stopping distances from 30 and 60 mph were 34 and 167 feet.

If you can stand a little squealing and don't mind the heavier pedal pressures, RPO 686 gives more stopping power with sintered iron brake linings. For all-out competition, choose RPO 687. This option includes sintered iron linings with special cooling provisions at each wheel, also heavy-duty shocks and fast steering adaptor.

We had the car long enough to put over 1000 miles on the odometer, and one trip to the high desert exposed the car to temperatures that ranged from a low of 35° to a high of 93, and the Rochester fuel injection unit worked perfectly. It was very responsive at any rpm in any gear. Even when idling along at 1500 rpm in fourth cog, the throttle can be floored and the car will take off strongly without missing a beat. In fact, around town we seldom used any gears except first and fourth.

It is perfectly docile in city traffic as long as the rpm's are kept above 1500 in the top two gears. The characteristic "lope" of a hot engine isn't felt until the mill is lugged down below 1000 rpm in either first or second. We never had to use any gear but fourth to pass *any-thing* on the highway above 50 mph. This is like second, or passing gear, in most other cars.

Fuel consumption wasn't too bad. Overall average, for 1000 miles of all types of driving, was 13.8 mpg. This included a low 9.8-mpg figure recorded during acceleration tests and a high 16.4 mpg for open road (65-90 mph) cruising.

The stock suspension feels just about right — a trifle on the hard side, but we, personally, wouldn't want it any softer. We had it up on our favorite mountain road and found we had no trouble negotiating the curves 20 to 25 mph faster than we've been taking them in sedans. The 'Vette is rock-steady and dead-flat in the corners.

Understeer is slight, with the front end pushing only on the tightest corners. At high speeds through sweeping turns the feeling is definitely towards understeer. If the rear end starts to come around, one has to apply corrective steering wheel lock and throttle lightly because the Positraction axle has a tendency to grab a bite and send the car in whichever way the wheels happen to be pointing.

At high speeds (100 to 130 mph) the ride is completely smooth, and the Corvette displays a directional stability and solid road feel that can be matched only by a few high-priced Grand Tourers from Europe.

The interior is unchanged from last year. The vinyl-covered bucket seats are contoured in the right places and give excellent support to the back and upper legs. There is enough fore-and-aft adjustment to satisfy just about any size driver.

The steering wheel is a beautiful thing, with its three drilled, engine-turned spokes, but its location leaves much to be desired. It is mounted in a vertical position and most drivers will find it too close. It also leaves very little room between the driver's lap and the bottom of the rim. This and the miserably mounted throttle pedal (it kept falling off) are the only real beefs we have with this otherwise completely satisfying car. All-around visibility is good with the soft top in place, and better with the hard top.

The trunk offers a surprising amount of usable space and should be big enough for two people for a weekend. The engine compartment is crowded and it is pure hell to change the plugs, but carburetion and ignition components are in the open.

This is an exciting high-performance automobile with real hair on its chest — the type of car that only the true enthusiasts will appreciate. /MT

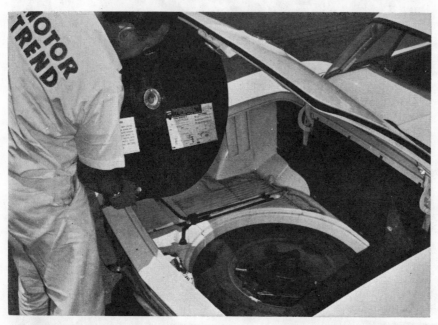

For a pure sports machine, the Corvette has a surprising amount of usable trunk space. With spare in its well, there's room for most normal luggage needs.

Instrumentation is fine and well placed. Only complaint is with beautiful steertng wheel, which is mounted a bit too close for the comfort of some.

THE BRAKES GRAB WITH POWER BUT NEED SOME REST AFTER HIGH-SPEED RUNS. OPTIONAL SINTERED IRON LININGS ARE A GOOD THOUGHT.

CORVETTE
2-passenger

OPTIONS ON CAR TESTED: 360-hp fuel injection engine, 4-speed, close-ratio gearbox, Positraction rear axle, radio, heater, whitewall tires

ODOMETER READING AT START OF TEST: 5610 miles

RECOMMENDED ENGINE RED LINE: 6300 rpm

PERFORMANCE

ACCELERATION

0-30 mph	2.4 secs.
0-45 mph	3.9
0-60 mph	5.9

Standing start ¼-mile 14.9 secs. and 102.5 mph

Speeds in gears @ 6300 rpm

1st	60 mph	3rd	94 mph
2nd	80 mph	4th	132 (observed)

Speedometer Error on Test Car

Car's speedometer reading	31	47	53	64	75	85
Weston electric speedometer	30	45	50	60	70	80

Observed miles per hour per 1000 rpm in top gear . . . . 21 mph

Stopping Distances — from 30 mph, 34 ft.; from 60 mph, 167 ft.

SPECIFICATIONS FROM MANUFACTURER

Engine
Ohv V-8
Bore: 4.00 ins.
Stroke: 3.25 ins.
Displacement: 327 cubic inches
Compression ratio: 11.25:1
Horsepower: 360 @ 6000 rpm
Torque: 352 lbs.-ft. @ 4000 rpm
Horsepower per cubic inch: 1.1
Ignition: 12-volt coil

Gearbox
4-speed manual, all-synchro; floor-mounted shift lever

Driveshaft
One-piece; open tube

Differential
Semi-floating Positraction
Standard ratio: 3.70:1

Suspension
Front: Coil springs, unequal control arms, direct-acting telescopic shocks and anti-roll bar
Rear: Rigid axle, 4-leaf longitudinal semi-elliptic springs with radius rods, limit straps, anti-roll bar and direct-acting telescopic shocks

Steering
Worm and ball bearing sector
Turning diameter: 37 ft.
Turns: 3.7 lock-to-lock

Wheels and Tires
Steel disc—5 lugs
6.70 x 15 4-ply
whitewall tires

Brakes
Hydraulic; 11-inch, cast-iron drums; bonded linings
Front: 9.29-in. dia x 2.0 in. wide
Rear: 9.29-in. dia. x 1.75 in. wide
Effective lining area: 157 sq. ins.

Body and Frame
Box section rails with I-beam cross member; fiberglass body
Wheelbase: 102.0 ins.
Track: front, 57 ins.; rear, 59 ins.
Overall length: 176.7 ins.
Curb weight: 3137 lbs.

RECAPPING THE ROAD TESTS

LOOKING AT BARE FIGURES AND 25 YEARS

On the following 13 pages are specifications for the first quarter-century of Corvette production, 1953-1978. We have tried to be as authoritative as possible, using construction and optional equipment data straight from the Motor Vehicle Manufacturers Association forms as provided by the Chevrolet Engineering Center, while road test figures came from Motor Trend files and the PPC research library.

The bare figures tell the story of the Corvette's remarkable progress through these 25 years. From a spartan little ragtop roadster that could be ordered with only a 6-cylinder engine, Powerglide transmission, and one axle ratio, Chevy's fiberglass image car soon blossomed forth with a fire-breathing fuel-injected V-8, the slickest 4-speed manual transmission in all the world, and a raft of competition options that turned it into a racetrack terror. Yet Chevrolet made sure that the Corvette would also appeal to those who did not

necessarily aspire to become the next A.J. Foyt or Dan Gurney by offering such amenities as an automatic transmission, air conditioning, power steering, power brakes, electric windows, a removable hardtop, leather upholstery, fine radios, and in the more recent models, a tilt-telescope steering wheel and removable roof panels. Because of this long list of options in the best time-honored American tradition, the Corvette is easily the most versatile sports car the world has ever seen.

It is also one of the most popular, a fact not generally realized. Take a look at those production figures, especially the ones for the

last few years. From a humble beginning of only 300 cars in its initial year, followed by overproduction the following year and a sharp dropoff in 1955, sales have grown steadily to 50,000 per year. That's an enormous production number for a 2-seat sports car; there is no sports car with a higher price which outsells the Corvette, remarkable considering that almost all Corvettes are sold in the U.S., while all other sports car manufacturers have a substantial market outside the U.S. as well. In America, Corvette sales are about the same as MG sales, and of course an MG is a considerably less expensive car than a Corvette.

Though the Corvette has changed so drastically through the years that the only resemblance between a '53 and a '78 is that they both bear the same name and both have fiberglass bodies, there is yet one other thing they share—the determination by Chevrolet that this model shall succeed,

and that it shall be the best sports car possible for the money. Undoubtedly this is the single greatest reason for the Corvette's continued success and continued excellence, and there were times when it was not at all easy to keep faith in the fiberglass sports car. Back when the Corvette was new, it was often compared to two similar cars, Ford's slick Thunderbird and the Jaguar XK-120. The little Chevrolet came off badly in these comparisons, for it didn't have the Thunderbird's V-8 and long list of comfort options, and it also wasn't as fast around a racetrack as the Jaguar. But after only three years Ford changed the 'Bird into a large and heavy four-place tourer—in which form it survives to this day—while Jaguar doesn't even make sports cars anymore. The Corvette has not only survived, it has thrived, while its one-time competitors have abandoned the sports car field. The reward for Chevrolet's persistence is not only the excellence of the Corvette itself, but the fact that its excellence is now being recognized and desired to the tune of 50,000 sales per year.

Another point which shows clearly from these specifications is the gradual change in preference of the closed car over the open car. The Corvette began as a roadster only, became a true convertible with wind-up windows in 1956, added a coupe to the line for 1963, and then became a coupe only for 1975. The demise of the convertible Corvette was not perverse-ness on the part of Chevrolet designers, it was merely a natural response to the clear-cut preference among customers for the coupe; in 1974, the last year for the convertible, only 12.4% of Corvette buyers opted for the ragtop. Thus the open Corvette suffered the same fate as all other American converti-

In the specification charts which follow, road test figures are presented for only one engine/drivetrain combination in each year; all others available. that particular year are listed separately. An effort was made to include representative cars, and not concentrate solely upon the most powerful optional engines, although they are well represented during the years of the big-block engine option.

Some clarification of terms might help. For "turning circle," Chevrolet lists both wall-to-wall and curb-to-curb distances, both left and right. The number we include is the maximum wall-to-wall distance, as we believe this is the minimum safe distance actually needed in which to turn the car around.

It should be realized that "curb weight" and "weight distribution" figures listed here apply only to the particular car tested, and should not be construed as being representative of all Corvettes of that year. Choice of optional equipment, especially engine, transmission, and air conditioning, considerably affects the Corvette's weight and its distribution. During the decade of the big-block engine option (1965-74), it was common for a small-block Corvette to be tail-heavy while a big-block version of the same year to be nose-heavy.

The base list price is FOB St. Louis. We have not included individual prices for each option as these prices proved difficult to obtain for all years.

The "steering ratio" listed is the overall ratio between steering wheel and front wheels, not the gear ratio in the steering gearbox.

Wherever Chevrolet listed an RPO (Regular Production Option) number for a particular engine option, that number is used in our tables when referring to that engine. In early Corvettes and with most base engines, a designation such as "195/265" is used, indicating rated horsepower and displacement.

All power and torque ratings are labeled either "gross" or "net," as the entire American auto industry shifted to net ratings beginning with the 1972 model year.

The type of emission control is not specified for early Corvettes as they had none.

"Delco HEI" listed for the ignition of late Corvettes is GM's exclusive "High Energy Ignition," a pointless electronic ignition system which utilizes a coil mounted integrally with the distributor cap.

Braking distances are included whenever they were recorded during the road test, but they should not be regarded as definitive. Too many variables enter into a maximum braking effort for the distances recorded to be regarded as absolutes. ♛

DISTINGUISHING 1953 FROM 1954

The early development of any car is one of on-going changes, particularly in the case of the Corvette with its many innovations and fiberglass body. While by Chevrolet's standards the '53 models and the '54's were the same, some alterations were made for the '54 changeover that will help the purist determine a given car's model year. Complicating this, however, are running changes made during production due to the use of different supplier's products, assembly line requirements, etc. Here are some of the more noteworthy differences between the '53 and '54, with running changes also indicated.

1. Vehicle Identification Number (VIN) plates located on upper cowl support inside driver door opening. The numbers E53F001001 through E53F001300 ("F" for Flint plant) means 300 cars were produced before manufacturing was switched to St. Louis in early December, 1953. Either 14 or 15 (it is not known which) additional cars were built during December at St. Louis but as these reflect certain component differences that were carried through for the '54 run, these calendar December cars are termed '54 models.
2. For 1954 cars, the VIN plate location was the same as '53 but the digits include the letter "S" indicating St. Louis assembly. The numbers started with E54S001001 and ran through E54S004640 (including the December '53 cars), indicating that 3640 were made.
3. All 1953 and early 1954 models have the VIN stamped on top of the left frame rail at the beginning of the axle "kick-up." The area must be scrubbed with steelwool to read the VIN, but it is visible (see page 17) without removing the body. Later '54 cars require that the body be removed to read the frame VIN.
4. The 1953 engine block casting number is 8701481. The '54 casting number is 3835911. The number is located on the right side just forward of the fuel pump.
5. The 1953 cylinder head casting number is 3836066. The 1954 head casting number is 3836241; it is located on the left front top.
6. The 1953 valve cover has the oil fill cap located just behind the top center, and the cover is attached by means of two acorn nuts. The 1954 valve cover has the filler cap near the front, and the cover is retained by four cap screws on the bottom flange.
7. The engine identification prefix stamping for 1953 is LAY. The number for '54 is prefixed F54YG. These numbers are found on a boss just behind the distributor.
8. The fuel pump lines for 1953 run at a 30° angle to the block with an "AC" fuel filter located forward of the number one carburetor. The '54 fuel pump lines run parallel to the block on the right side, with the filter attached directly to the pump.
9. The top of the engine crankcase breather for '53 is "smooth." The '54 engine breathers (and a small number of late '53's are known) have an "X" stamped on them.
10. There are variations between the '53 and '54 carb links.
11. The 1953 and very early '54 fuel and brake lines to the rear and on the right side run along the outside of the frame rail. The greater majority of '54's have the lines inside of the frame rail.
12. The 1953 top canvas is black as is the top bow irons' color. The 1954 top canvas is beige, and the irons are painted to match.
13. The 1953 parking brake bracket assembly is red, '54 is black.
14. The 1953 trunk mat (red only) molding number is 4636966. The '54 trunk mat, when red has molding number 4645541.
15. The window storage bag for '53 is black oil cloth and is irregularly shaped like the windows. It lies loose in the trunk. The '54 bag is red vinyl, rectangular in shape, and attaches to the trunk partition panel with two turnbuckles. Blue-painted '54's had beige bags.
16. Some fogging of the rear license plate cover was discovered with the '53's, so for '54 two dessicate bags were attached.
17. The trunk lip weather seal for '53 and '54 is the same, but it is installed in an opposite manner between the years.
18. The forward rear leaf spring perches on '54 cars have the addition of a welded-on triangular reinforcement on the top surface.
19. Although the exact number is not known, approximately the first 25 1953 cars had '53 Bel Air passenger car wheel covers.
20. Early '53's to about serial number 83 had a crude hinge at the gas-filler door made from the '53 passenger car hinge. Gas cap removal proved difficult so a swing-out hinge was designed.
21. Early '53's had a foot-operated windshield washer pump. Late '53's used a pushbutton coordinator.
22. Approximately the first ten '53 cars had no rubber seal attached to the back lip of the hood panel. In service it was discovered blowby oil seeped onto the windshield, so a seal was added.
23. A carburetor change occured in mid-1953, from Carter YH-2066S to a Carter YH-2066SA. They are identified by their brass tabs.
24. Early '53's have a chrome auxiliary coolant tank with a 90° bend in the overflow tube. Later '53 tubes have no bend.
25. Very early '53's have a chromed upper grille speaker. Later cars have a black one to more closely match the speedometer.
26. The '53 and '54 cars both had 11 body bolts, but on early '53's the four located just behind the seats were run up through the frame and into caged nuts. On late '53's and all '54's, bolts ran down from the top with lock washers and nuts on the bottom.

1953-54

GENERAL

Curb Weight: 2900 lbs.
Weight Distribution: 53/47
Turning Circle: 39 ft.
Body Styles: roadster
ID Location: left upper door pillar
Base List Price: $3250 (FOB Flint)
Options on test car: none
Price as tested: $3250 (FOB Flint)
Total manufactured: 300

CHASSIS

Wheelbase: 102 ins.
Length: 167 ins.
Width: 72.2 ins.
Height: 52.2 ins.
Track, front: 57 ins.
     rear: 59 ins.
Suspension, front: independent, A-arms, coil springs
     rear: rigid axle, semi-elliptic leaf springs
Brakes, front: hydraulic, 11-in. drums
     rear: hydraulic, 11-in. drums
Steering ratio: 16:1
Wheel rim size: 15 x 5K
Std. tire size: 6.70 x 15
Tire pressures: 22/22 psi

DRIVETRAIN

Transmission in test car: 2-speed automatic
Gear ratios-
Second: 1:1
First: 1.82:1
Reverse: 1.82:1
Other transmissions offered: none
Axle ratio in test car: 3.55:1
Other axle ratios offered: none

ENGINE

Test car engine designation: 150/235.5
Type: OHV inline 6
Bore x stroke: 3.5625 x 3.9375 ins.
Displacement: 235.5 cu. ins.
Compression ratio: 8:1
Carburetion: three sidedraft 1-bbl. Carter
Ignition: coil and distributor
Maximum power: 150 gross bhp @ 4200 rpm
Maximum torque: 223 gross lbs.-ft. @ 2400 rpm
Other engines offered: none

PERFORMANCE

Acceleration-
0-30 mph: 3.6 secs.
0-40 mph: 5.4 secs.
0-50 mph: 7.8 secs.
0-60 mph: 11.1 secs.
0-70 mph: 14.7 secs.
0-80 mph: 19.6 secs.
0-90 mph: 27.5 secs.
0-100 mph: 39.0 secs.
Standing quarter mile: 17.9 secs.
Speed at end: 77 mph
Top speed: 108 mph
Braking-
30-0 mph: N/A
60-0 mph: N/A

1955

GENERAL

Curb Weight: 2910 lbs.
Weight Distribution: 53/47
Turning Circle: 39 ft.
Body Styles: roadster
ID Location: left upper door pillar
Base List Price: $2901
Options on test car: 195-hp engine
Price as tested: N/A
Total manufactured: 700

CHASSIS

Wheelbase: 102 ins.
Length: 167 ins.
Width: 72.2 ins.
Height: 52.2 ins.
Track, front: 56.7 ins.
rear: 58.8 ins.
Suspension, front: independent, A-arms, coil springs
rear: rigid axle, semi-elliptic leaf springs
Brakes, front: hydraulic, 11-in. drum
rear: hydraulic, 11-in. drum
Steering ratio: 16:1
Wheel rim size: 15 x 5K
Std. tire size: 6.70 x 15
Tire pressures: 24/24 psi

DRIVETRAIN

Transmission in test car: 2-speed automatic
Gear ratios-
Second: 1:1
First: 1.82:1
Reverse: 1.82:1
Other transmissions offered: none
Axle ratio in test car: 3.55
Other axle ratios offered: none

ENGINE

Test car engine designation: 195/265
Type: OHV V-8
Bore x stroke: 3.75 x 3.00 ins.
Displacement: 265 cu. ins.
Compression ratio: 8.00:1
Carburetion: 1 4-bbl. Carter
Ignition: coil & distributor
Maximum power: 195 gross bhp @ 5000 rpm
Maximum torque: 260 gross lbs.-ft. @ 3000 rpm
Other engines offered: 155/235.5 inline 6

PERFORMANCE

Acceleration-
0-30 mph: 3.3 secs.
0-40 mph: 4.6 secs.
0-50 mph: 6.6 secs.
0-60 mph: 8.8 secs.
0-70 mph: 11.7 secs.
0-80 mph: 15.0 secs.
0-90 mph: 19.4 secs.
0-100 mph: 25.5 secs.
Standing quarter mile: 16.7 secs.
Speed at end: 83 mph
Top speed: 118 mph
Braking-
30-0 mph: N/A
60-0 mph: N/A

1956

GENERAL

Curb Weight: 3020 lbs.
Weight Distribution: 52/48
Turning Circle: 37 ft.
Body Styles: convertible
ID Location: left front body hinge pillar
Base List Price: $3145
Options on test car: 225-hp engine
Price as tested: N/A
Total manufactured: 3467

CHASSIS

Wheelbase: 102 ins.
Length: 168 ins.
Width: 70.5 ins.
Height: 52 ins.
Track, front: 56.7 ins.
rear: 58.8 ins.
Suspension, front: independent, A-arms, coil springs
rear: rigid axle, semi-elliptic leaf springs
Brakes, front: hydraulic, 11-in. drum
rear: hydraulic, 11-in. drum
Steering ratio: 16.0:1
Wheel rim size: 15 x 5K
Std. tire size: 6.70 x 15
Tire pressures: 24/24 psi

DRIVETRAIN

Transmission in test car: 3-speed manual
Gear ratios-
Third: 1:1
Second: 1.32:1
First: 2.21:1
Reverse: 2.21:1
Other transmissions offered: 2-speed automatic
Axle ratio in test car: 3.55
Other axle ratios offered: 3.27, 3.70, 4.11

ENGINE

Test car engine designation: 225/265
Type: OHV-V-8
Bore x stroke: 3.75 x 3.00 ins.
Displacement: 265 cu. ins.
Compression ratio: 9.25:1
Carburetion: 2 4-bbl. Carter
Ignition: coil & distributor
Maximum power: 225 gross bhp @ 5200 rpm
Maximum torque: 270 gross lbs.-ft. @ 3600 rpm
Other engines offered: 210/265

PERFORMANCE

Acceleration-
0-30 mph: 2.9 secs.
0-40 mph: 4.0 secs.
0-50 mph: 5.5 secs.
0-60 mph: 7.4 secs.
0-70 mph: 10.0 secs.
0-80 mph: 12.5 secs.
0-90 mph: 16.3 secs.
0-100 mph: 20.8 secs.
Standing quarter mile: 15.9 secs.
Speed at end: 88 mph
Top speed: 129 mph
Braking-
30-0 mph: N/A
60-0 mph: N/A

1957

GENERAL

Curb Weight: 2985 lbs.
Weight Distribution: 52/48
Turning Circle: 39 ft.
Body Styles: convertible
ID Location: left front body hinge pillar
Base List Price: $3427
Options on test car: 283/283 fuel-injected engine, 4-speed manual
transmission, limited-slip differential, radio, heater
Price as tested: $4112
Total manufactured: 3467

CHASSIS

Wheelbase: 102 ins.
Length: 168 ins.
Width: 70.5 ins.
Height: 52 ins.
Track, front: 57 ins.
      rear: 59 ins.
Suspension, front: independent, A-arms, coil springs
         rear: rigid axle, semi-elliptic springs
Brakes, front: hydraulic, 11-in. drums
      rear: hydraulic, 11-in. drums
Steering ratio: 16:1
Wheel rim size: 15 x 5K
Std. tire size: 6.70 x 15
Tire pressures: 24/24 psi

DRIVETRAIN

Transmission in test car: 4-speed manual
Gear ratios-
Fourth: 1:1
Third: 1.31:1
Second: 1.66:1
First: 2.20:1
Reverse: 2.26:1
Other transmissions offered: 3-speed manual, 2-speed automatic
Axle ratio in test car: 4.11:1
Other axle ratios offered: 3.55, 3.70, 4.56

ENGINE

Test car engine designation: 283/283
Type: OHV V-8
Bore x stroke: 3.875 x 3.00 ins.
Displacement: 283 cu. ins.
Compression ratio: 10.5:1
Carburetion: fuel injection
Emission control: none
Ignition: coil and distributor
Maximum power: 283 gross bhp @ 6200 rpm
Maximum torque: 290 gross lbs.-ft. @ 4400 rpm
Other engines offered: 245/283, 250/283, 270/283

PERFORMANCE

Acceleration-
0-30 mph: 2.9 secs.
0-40 mph: 3.9 secs.
0-50 mph: 4.8 secs.
0-60 mph: 5.8 secs.
0-70 mph: 7.6 secs.
0-80 mph: 10.2 secs.
0-90 mph: 13.5 secs.
0-100 mph: 17.0 secs.
Standing quarter mile: 14.3 secs.
Speed at end: 94 mph
Top speed: 133 mph
Braking-
30-0 mph: N/A
60-0 mph: N/A

1958

GENERAL

Curb Weight: 3050 lbs.
Weight Distribution: 53/47
Turning Circle: 39 ft.
Body Styles: convertible
ID Location: left front body hinge pillar
Base List Price: $3928
Options on test car: 250-hp engine, 4-speed manual transmission
Price as tested: N/A
Total manufactured: 9168

CHASSIS

Wheelbase: 102 ins.
Length: 177.2 ins.
Width: 72.8 ins.
Height: 52 ins.
Track, front: 57 ins.
      rear: 59 ins.
Suspension, front: independent, A-arms, coil springs
         rear: rigid axle, semi-elliptic leaf springs
Brakes, front: hydraulic, 11-in. drum
      rear: hydraulic, 11-in. drum
Steering ratio: 21:1 std.; 16.3:1 opt.
Wheel rim size: 15 x 5K
Std. tire size: 6.70 x 15
Tire pressures: 24/24 psi

DRIVETRAIN

Transmission in test car: 4-speed manual
Gear ratios-
Fourth: 1:1
Third: 1.31:1
Second: 1.66:1
First: 2.20:1
Reverse: 2.25:1
Other transmissions offered: 3-speed manual, 2-speed automatic
Axle ratio in test car: 4.11:1
Other axle ratios offered: 3.55, 3.70, 4.56

ENGINE

Test car engine designation: 250/283
Type: OHV V-8
Bore x stroke: 3.875 x 3.00 ins.
Displacement: 283 cu. ins.
Compression ratio: 9.5:1
Carburetion: fuel injection
Ignition: coil & distributor
Maximum power: 250 gross bhp @ 5000 rpm
Maximum torque: 305 gross lbs.-ft. @ 3800 rpm
Other engines offered: 230/283, 245/283, 270/283, 290/283

PERFORMANCE

Acceleration-
0-30 mph: 3.2 secs.
0-40 mph: 4.4 secs.
0-50 mph: 6.3 secs.
0-60 mph: 7.6 secs.
0-70 mph: 9.8 secs.
0-80 mph: 12.3 secs.
0-90 mph: 15.2 secs.
0-100 mph: 18.5 secs.
Standing quarter mile: 15.6 secs.
Speed at end: 92.4 mph
Top speed: 115 mph
Braking-
30-0 mph: N/A
60-0 mph: N/A

1959

GENERAL
Curb Weight: 3080 lbs.
Weight Distribution: 53/47
Turning Circle: 39 ft.
Body Styles: convertible
ID Location: left front body hinge pillar
Base List Price: $3745
Options on test car: 4-speed manual transmission, 290-hp engine, limited-slip differential
Price as tested: N/A
Total manufactured: 9670

CHASSIS
Wheelbase: 102 ins.
Length: 177.2 ins.
Width: 72.8 ins.
Height: 52.4 ins.
Track, front: 57 ins.
       rear: 59 ins.
Suspension, front: independent, A-arms, coil springs
            rear: rigid axle, semi-elliptic leaf springs
Brakes, front: hydraulic, 11-in. drums
        rear: hydraulic, 11-in. drums
Steering ratio: 21:1 std.; 16.3:1 optional
Wheel rim size: 15 x 5K std.; 15 x 5.5K opt.
Std. tire size: 6.70 x 15
Tire pressures: 24/24 psi

DRIVETRAIN
Transmission in test car: 4-speed manual
Gear ratios -
Fourth: 1:1
Third: 1.31:1
Second: 1.66:1
First: 2.20:1
Reverse: 2.26:1
Other transmissions offered: 3-speed manual, 2-speed automatic
Axle ratio in test car: 4.11:1
Other axle ratios offered: 3.55, 3.70, 4.56

ENGINE
Test car engine designation: 290/283
Type: OHV V-8
Bore x stroke: 3.875 x 3.00 ins.
Displacement: 283 cu. ins.
Compression ratio: 10.5:1
Carburetion: fuel injection
Ignition: coil & distributor
Maximum power: 290 gross bhp @ 6200 rpm
Maximum torque: 290 gross lbs.-ft. @ 4400 rpm
Other engines offered: 230/283, 245/283, 250/283, 270/283

PERFORMANCE
Acceleration -
0 - 30 mph: 3.1 secs.
0 - 40 mph: 4.1 secs.
0 - 50 mph: 5.2 secs.
0 - 60 mph: 6.7 secs.
0 - 70 mph: 7.6 secs.
0 - 80 mph: 10.2 secs.
0 - 90 mph: 12.2 secs.
0 - 100 mph: 15.6 secs.
Standing quarter mile: 14.6 secs.
Speed at end: 95 mph
Top speed: 130 mph
Braking -
30 - 0 mph: N/A
60 - 0 mph: N/A

1960

GENERAL
Curb Weight: 3104 lbs.
Weight Distribution: 53/47
Turning Circle: 39 ft.
Body Styles: convertible
ID Location: left front body hinge pillar
Base List Price: N/A
Options on test car: 270-hp engine, 4-speed manual transmission, radio, heater, hard top
Price as tested: N/A
Total manufactured: 10,261

CHASSIS
Wheelbase: 102 ins.
Length: 177.2 ins.
Width: 72.8 ins.
Height: 52.3 ins.
Track, front: 57 ins.
       rear: 59 ins.
Suspension, front: independent, A-arms, coil springs
            rear: rigid axle, semi-elliptic leaf springs
Brakes, front: hydraulic, 11-in. drums
        rear: hydraulic, 11-in. drums
Steering ratio: 21:1 std.; 16.3:1 opt.
Wheel rim size: 15 x 5K std.; 15 x 5.5K opt.
Std. tire size: 6.70 x 15
Tire pressures: 24/24 psi

DRIVETRAIN
Transmission in test car: 4-speed manual
Gear ratios -
Fourth: 1:1
Third: 1.31:1
Second: 1.66:1
First: 2.20:1
Reverse: 2.26:1
Other transmissions offered: 3-speed manual, 2-speed automatic
Axle ratio in test car: 3.70
Other axle ratios offered: 3.55, 4.11, 4.56

ENGINE
Test car engine designation: 270/283
Type: OHV V-8
Bore x stroke: 3.875 x 3.00 ins.
Displacement: 283 cu. ins.
Compression ratio: 11:1
Carburetion: two 4-bbl. Carter
Emission control: none
Ignition: coil and distributor
Maximum power: 270 gross bhp @ 6000 rpm
Maximum torque: 285 gross lbs.-ft. @ 4200 rpm
Other engines offered: 230/283, 245/283, 275/283, 315/283

PERFORMANCE
Acceleration -
0 - 30 mph: 3.3 secs.
0 - 40 mph: 4.8 secs.
0 - 50 mph: 6.7 secs.
0 - 60 mph: 8.4 secs.
0 - 70 mph: 10.5 secs.
0 - 80 mph: 13.4 secs.
0 - 90 mph: 16.8 secs.
0 - 100 mph: 20.2 secs.
Standing quarter mile: 16.1 secs.
Speed at end: 89 mph
Top speed: 124 mph
Braking -
30 - 0 mph: N/A
60 - 0 mph: 195 ft.

1961

GENERAL

Curb Weight: 3108 lbs.
Weight Distribution: 53/47
Turning Circle: 39 ft.
Body Styles: convertible
ID Location: left front body hinge pillar
Base List Price: $4109
Options on test car: 315/283 fuel-injected engine, 4-speed manual
transmission, limited-slip differential
Price as tested: $4636
Total manufactured: 10939

CHASSIS

Wheelbase: 102 ins.
Length: 176.7 ins.
Width: 70.4 ins.
Height: 52.9 ins.
Track, front: 57 ins.
        rear: 59 ins.
Suspension, front: independent, A-arms, coil springs
            rear: rigid axle, semi-elliptic leaf springs
Brakes, front: hydraulic, 11-in. drums
        rear: hydraulic, 11-in. drums
Steering ratio: 21:1 std.; 16.3:1 opt.
Wheel rim size: 15 x 5K std.; 15 x 5.5K opt.
Std. tire size: 6.70 x 15
Tire pressures: 24/24 psi

DRIVETRAIN

Transmission in test car: 4-speed manual
Gear ratios-
Fourth: 1:1
Third: 1.31:1
Second: 1.66:1
First: 2.20:1
Reverse: 2.26:1
Other transmissions offered: 3-speed manual, 2-speed automatic
Axle ratio in test car: 3.70:1
Other axle ratios offered: 3.36, 3.55, 4.11, 4.56

ENGINE

Test car engine designation: 315/283
Type: OHV V-8
Bore x stroke: 3.875 x 3.00 ins.
Displacement: 283 cu. ins.
Compression ratio: 11:1
Carburetion: fuel injection
Emission control: none
Ignition: coil and distributor
Maximum power: 315 gross bhp @ 6200 rpm
Maximum torque: 295 gross lbs.-ft. @ 5100 rpm
Other engines offered: 230/283, 245/283, 270/283, 275/283

PERFORMANCE

Acceleration-
0-30 mph: 3.5 secs.
0-40 mph: 4.7 secs.
0-50 mph: 6.0 secs.
0-60 mph: 7.4 secs.
0-70 mph: 9.1 secs.
0-80 mph: 11.3 secs.
0-90 mph: 13.8 secs.
0-100 mph: 17.5 secs.
Standing quarter mile: 15.4 secs.
Speed at end: 94 mph
Top speed: 130 mph
Braking-
30-0 mph: N/A
60-0 mph: N/A

1962

GENERAL

Curb Weight: 3137 lbs.
Weight Distribution: 53/47
Turning Circle: 39 ft.
Body Styles: convertible
ID Location: left front body hinge pillar
Base List Price: $4227
Options on test car: 360/327 fuel-injected engine, 4-speed manual
transmission, limited-slip differential, AM radio
Price as tested: N/A
Total manufactured: 14,531

CHASSIS

Wheelbase: 102 ins.
Length: 176.7 ins.
Width: 70.4 ins.
Height: 52.9 ins.
Track, front: 57 ins.
        rear: 59 ins.
Suspension, front: independent, A-arms, coil springs
            rear: rigid axle, semi-elliptic leaf springs
Brakes, front: hydraulic, 11-in. drums
        rear: hydraulic, 11-in. drums
Steering ratio: 21:1 std.; 16.3:1 opt.
Wheel rim size: 15 x 5K std.; 15 x 5.5K opt.
Std. tire size: 6.70 x 15
Tire pressures: 24/24 psi

DRIVETRAIN

Transmission in test car: 4-speed manual
Gear ratios -
Fourth: 1:1
Third: 1.31:1
Second: 1.66:1
First: 2.20:1
Reverse: 2.26:1
Other transmissions offered: 3-speed manual, 4-speed manual with
                wider gear ratios, 2-speed automatic
Axle ratio in test car: 3.70:1
Other axle ratios offered: 3.08, 3.36, 3.55, 4.11, 4.56

ENGINE

Test car engine designation: RPO 582 360/327
Type: OHV V-8
Bore x stroke: 4.00 x 3.25 ins.
Displacement: 327 cu. ins.
Compression ratio: 11.25:1
Carburetion: fuel injection
Emission control: none
Ignition: coil and distributor
Maximum power: 360 gross bhp @ 6000 rpm
Maximum torque: 352 gross lbs.-ft. @ 4000 rpm
Other engines offered: 250/327, RPO 583 300/327, RPO 396 340/327

PERFORMANCE

Acceleration -
0-30 mph: 2.4 secs.   0-70 mph: 7.3 secs.
0-40 mph: 3.8 secs.   0-80 mph: 9.2 secs.
0-50 mph: 4.9 secs.   0-90 mph: 11.6 secs.
0-60 mph: 5.9 secs.   0-100 mph: 14.6 secs.
Standing quarter mile: 14.9 secs.
Speed at end: 102.5 mph
Top speed: 132 mph
Braking -
30-0 mph: 34 ft.
60-0 mph: 167 ft.

'60 CORVETTE...more than ever,

the pure definition of a sports car!

Here is the latest edition of America's only sports car. Because, like its forerunners, it is unique in concept and performance, its designers are required to solve only one problem: How much pure driving pleasure can be engineered into a road machine? What does this single-mindedness produce? ■ You'll have to drive a Corvette to find out. Small, inky words just can't tell you the exultant feel of a Corvette in javelin-swift motion. The deep assurance of its road-holding. The meaning of dead-true steering. The solid, soft, absolutely flat way a Corvette slices around a curve. ■ As you may have sensed, we are almighty proud of the Corvette. Because it is a car built to uncompromising standards of road behavior—and because it has been polished, honed and perfected year by year with this one end in view. Down below we outline some of 1960's technical accomplishments. But you don't have to study these to know what Corvette stands for. All you have to do for that is slide behind the wheel, flip the switch—and wait for that first wonderful moment of astonishment!

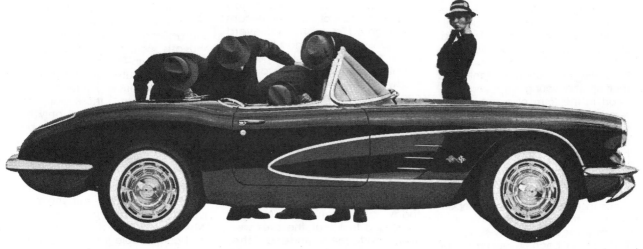

There are some really remarkable results hidden under modest-sounding specification changes in the 1960 Corvette. For example . . . **Suspension:** A stabilizer bar has been added at the rear . . . and rear spring rebound travel has been increased one inch. Result: every Corvette now has a more supple "boulevard" ride . . . but *every* Corvette will corner flatter, stick better and definitely outhandle *any* Corvette offered before, even those with the 1959 heavy-duty suspension option. **Engines:** The two Fuel Injection versions* now come with aluminum alloy cylinder heads—and they don't use inserted valve seats or guides. This is a major breakthrough in design and metallurgy:

durability of the valve seats is better than cast iron, heat transfer is far faster. Cylinder head and breathing refinements add 25 more horsepower; compression ratio is now 11 to 1. For '60 there's a weight-paring aluminum bell housing for all manual shift models; on the F.I. competition engine this, plus a new all-aluminum cross-flow radiator and the aluminum heads, shaves 80 pounds of weight. **Brakes:** Advances in the optional sintered-metallic brakes enable them to cope with the most severe heavy-duty service while giving a perfectly docile brake for street use. **Summary:** The 1960 achievement in suspension puts Corvette in a class occupied by virtually no other sports car, com-

bining the softness of "touring" springs with the absolute stability of full competition suspension. The range of five engines, from the 230-h.p. standard V8 to the 315-h.p. edition, the three transmissions, from standard 3-speed to extra-cost Powerglide or 4-speed manual shift, give drivers an opportunity to suit their desires perfectly. In all, Corvette today stands as the supreme road car, America's outstanding triumph in the international field of sports car design. . . . Chevrolet Division of General Motors, Detroit 2, Michigan.

*Optional at extra cost.

FIRST V-8 YEARS

THE COMING OF AGE OF THE PLASTIC SPEEDSTER.

BY JAY STORER

Romantic nostalgia can grip automotive fanciers firmly enough to prompt them to savor and collect vehicles that in their prime time weren't worth the gasoline used to turn them over. Viewed in the proper blindsight, even the most forgettable Crosley station wagon or Edsel 4-door can be the object of someone's passionate study and restoration. However, it is our humble belief that if Chevrolet hadn't introduced their new V-8 engine to the Corvette in 1955, the car would have died quietly right there and then, leaving later corporate GM historians with nothing more to crow about, in terms of a company sports car, than the almost-as-ill-fated Corvair of another decade.

The early Fifties were the perfect automotive years to have brought out an American sports car, or at least an American car of sporty size and styling. The British and European manufacturers had had this market to themselves in America, and the enthusiasm of the Fifties (now that the second of two wars in a row had ended) manifested itself in the young and young-at-heart in the form of a growing interest in automobiles as more than mere appliances. While many stayed with the strictly American hot rods and custom cars, a growing contingent chose to endure leaky tops, uncomfortable interiors and balky, small-displacement engines in order to have the imported cars that went like stink on a country road. The gray-suiters in Detroit had become aware of this alarming trend, and intended to counter with American sports cars of their own that would rate high in handling and performance without the comfort sacrifices they knew most of "their people" would never tolerate. Along the way, they reasoned, some further luster and sales appeal could be gleaned for their overall corporate car lines, too.

Chevrolet's entry hit the market first, although so far from the intended bull's-eye that sales stayed dismally low for the first two years. Harley Earl and the others at Chevrolet had the best of intentions with their Corvette program, but the internal workings of a huge corporation full of bean-counters

and the necessarily crash development program for this wholly new machine resulted in a vehicle that not only didn't meet with overwhelming public approval but fell short of their own expectations. The 6-cylinder Corvettes of '53-'55 satisfied neither the sports car aficionados who were looking for an American version of a European car nor the bulk of other Americans who wanted a sporty boulevard car. Despite the modifications made to the venerable Chevrolet Stovebolt six, the Corvette did not supply blistering performance, except when compared to some of the really underpowered imported cars. When analyzed in comparison to sports cars of similar displacement, the Powerglide-equipped plastic cars were sluggish; even some very unsporty American sedans had better acceleration.

We can look back on those cars today, and even drive restored ones, and feel that the sixes were lively performers (indeed, they

could out-accelerate all but the best V-8 American cars), but the Corvette six was also one of the most expensive American cars you could buy. While it could mop up most import sports cars in a straight line, it did so only with the help of an engine that was bigger, not more developed.

The Corvette was destined to be a V-8 automobile, but it wasn't only performance that was a detriment to those early cars. Sports car purists also found fault with the brakes, steering and transmission. While the brakes may have been adequate for normal driving, they were assuredly not designed for competing in sports car rallies or races, and although Chevrolet described the 16:1 Corvette steering as "quick," the almost four turns lock-to-lock hardly elicited praise from those used to Jaguars, MG's or Austin-Healeys. And nothing about "America's first production sports car" could have offended the growing ranks of sports car enthusiasts more than equipping the Corvette with—horror of horrors—a wishy-washy automatic transmission! Sometimes derisively referred to as the "Powerslide," those early cast iron automatics offered only two speeds at a time when some buyers looked at imported vehicles as fun to drive solely because of their close-ratio 4-speeds.

The obverse of this coin was that the Corvette didn't suit the more typical American consumer either. While the automatic transmission and comfortable interior made the

Corvette the ideal "personal" car for the ladies, it was priced in the limousine category, and the pre-liberation women didn't appreciate the drafts and water leaks, the balky convertible top or the lack of roll-up windows. So unsuccessful were the first Corvettes that as late as January 1955, a surplus of 1076 cars remained at the factory, representing 27% of all the cars built up until that time. There was serious talk at Chevrolet of dropping the idea entirely, but the Corvette was Harley Earl's pet project and he had elicited enough support elsewhere in the company to keep the dream of a American production sports car alive.

Meanwhile, Bob Morrison at the Molded Fiber Glass Body Company (MFG) in Ashtabula had to slow down molding of the parts for the world's first production car with a plastic body. His brand-new plant was the largest, such facility in the world, and he had built it specifically to handle the Chevrolet contract. So to keep his plant occupied during the slowdown that resulted from the Corvette surplus, Chevrolet had him build some fiberglass body parts for a special truck model they were offering, the Cameo pickup. The tailgate, rear quarter-panels and spare-tire carrier were all made of FRP (fiberglass-reinforced plastic) from MFG until production resumed on the sports car.

SAME SKIN, NEW GUTS

When the 1955 Corvettes finally emerged from St. Louis, they were disappointing clones of the previous two years. Although they looked exactly the same externally, under the hood was a different story. For the first time, two Corvettes were offered: a 6-cylinder model and a new V-8 model. The latter was to revolutionize the Corvette.

Chevrolet hadn't had a V-8 engine since the ill-fated 1917 V-8, which had been cobbled together from two of their 4-cylinder engines. The untouched sales record with the mass of buyers was based on the sturdy 6-cylinder engine known as the "Stovebolt," introduced in 1929. While this engine was reliable and economical, it was no fireball, and despite excellent styling, Chevrolet had never been a name associated with youth, performance or excitement. How times have changed! That little 265-cu.-in. V-8 introduced in the 1955 Chevrolet line-up made engineering history, saved the Corvette

2

3

4

5

1. Everything was new in the Chevrolet line for 1955. The passenger cars had completely new bodies, new suspension and drivelines, and for the first time, a V-8 engine, which the Corvette shared.

2. The introduction of this engine to the outwardly unchanged '55 Corvette had the result of virtually wiping out the 6-cylinder Corvette, as only a few were ordered in that last year it was offered for the sports cars. At 195 hp, this was the forerunner of many lightweight revvers to come. The cable from the generator drives tach.

3. One of the few external differences for '55 was the gold "V" in the side trim that signified this was a V-8.

4. Chevrolet engineers had to make a lot of changes, mostly minor, to fit the new 265-cu.-in. V-8 into what had been a 6-cylinder car. One of the changes of their "engine swap" was to make this depression in the right frame rail to clear the V-8 fuel pump.

5. The tweaked front end of this '55 is mute testimony to the fact that the new 265 was all the impetus some owners needed to jump into racing. Success was limited by weight distribution and braking, but road-racing was one of the reasons so few survive today.

FIRST V-8 YEARS

from certain discontinuance and forever changed Chevrolet's image as solely a producer of "inexpensive family cars."

Certainly the Chevrolet engineers knew they had to come up with a good engine for their genuine V-8; they didn't realize until later just how well they had done their homework. The car buyers of the Fifties were V-8-conscious in those halcyon days of 30¢-a-gallon gasoline, and the Detroit horsepower race flared unhindered by the long arm of Uncle Sam's restrictions. Chevrolet knew that if they jumped into the V-8 foray as they really had to, it had better be with an engine worthy of the Chevrolet name. They wanted to build an engine that was light in weight, a good performer and cheap to produce. That 1955 engine was the first production engine to use techniques that are still considered de rigeur in the industry even today. Chevrolet has produced some 32 million small-block V-8's since then, based on the same design, but in 1955 it seemed revolutionary. Using fewer casting cores, the block was built with cylinder walls and water jackets much thinner than the norm even at sister GM divisions. This was done in an effort to make the engine smaller as well as lighter, because less material would be required to build one, making them cheaper to produce than other V-8's. Other design factors that made the Chevrolet V-8 what it was (and still is today) included: an intake manifold that served as the lifter valley cover (instead of the separate part used on Cad/Olds/Buick V-8's and even the new Ford overhead engine introduced in 1954); a low deck height on the block; lightweight valve gear; and a small crankshaft with the shortest stroke in the industry.

What has made the small-block Chevrolet the most popular engine of all time is that the very same factors that made it cheap to produce made it a scorcher in stock form and even more adaptable to performance purposes when modified. The short stroke, short connecting rods and lightweight valvetrain made it a revvin' fool, and the combination intake manifold/valley cover had high enough porting to give the intake charge a pretty direct shot at the free-breathing heads. The new wedge-shaped combustion chambers responded well to increases in compression (from hot rodders as well as the factory engineers). Also, the tubular pushrods and stamped-steel rocker arms combined with the low-friction nature of the small crankshaft to allow the 265 to rev to 6000 rpm with solid lifters at a time when other V-8's were lucky to break 5000 rpm. Although it's been said many times before, that little 265, from which every Chevrolet small-block since then has been derived, made more horsepower than it had any right to. Overnight it redirected the always lucrative youth/performance/racing market over to the Chevrolet camp. Up until that time, the Ford flathead V-8 had had the sporty image of speed all to itself for over 20 years.

Although Ed Cole is often referred to as the father of the Chevrolet small-block V-8, the actual project at Chevrolet was started under E.H. Kelley. As early as the end of 1953, one of the Motorama show cars had been equipped with one of the early 265 V-8's for testing, because those who really wanted the Corvette project to survive knew this new engine would be perfect for the sports car. The very first prototype engine had displaced only 231 cu. ins., a displacement actually slightly smaller than the six it was to replace. When Ed Cole took over as Chevrolet's chief engineer, this was en-

larged to 265 cu. ins. and the valvetrain and combustion chambers were modified. At 531 lbs. stripped, the V-8 weighed 41 lbs. less than the old 6-cylinder, which didn't hurt the Corvette's weight distribution at all. In road tests, the V-8 not only out-performed the six in every category, but it miraculously delivered better fuel economy as well, to the tune of several mpg, which was further testament to the low-friction efficiency of the new engine. That it was a sales point is evident in the fact that of the 700 Corvettes built for '55, only about 1% were delivered with the Blue Flame six.

Back in March of 1954, when the 1955 model was being considered, a number of changes besides the V-8 engine were proposed to update the two-year-old car. Pictures of the styling mock-up show the addition of a hood scoop, an egg-crate grille replacing the now-classic chromed teeth, four chromed vents on the sides of the front fenders and a different headlight treatment. None of these changes made their way into the production '55's, in part because of the emphasis placed on the V-8 Corvette development and in part because of the slow sales that had created the unfortunate surplus of the previous year's cars. Incidentally, that prototype 1955, which had a factory code of "SO-2151" for Styling Order, is still around today, a one-of-a-kind "proposal" car.

While the addition of the V-8 engine finally gave the Corvette the muscle it needed to make some attempts at competition with the established imported sports cars, there was still a resistance from the

> Some lucky dealers were treated to a special driveway presentation in San Francisco to bring them the new '56 Corvette. Sufficiently impressed, the dealers went home and sold some 3467 of them with the new body, new power and comfort options.

rank-and-file of enthusiasts and the magazine road-test writers, who generally wrote from a purist's newpoint at that time. The interior, as unchanged as the exterior, was still considered cramped and uncomfortable by the bulk of the buying public, and the annoying water leaks and drafts were still present. The factory still didn't supply a hardtop for the Corvette, and the convertible top wasn't the easiest to operate. The aftermarket people responded right away to consumer

1. Still very reminiscent of the first Motorama car's dash, the '56's dash was enlivened by the first appearance of the tri-spoke "racing" wheel with the holes that became a trademark for the Corvette.

2. Also new to the '56 interior was the "waffle-pattern" vinyl upholstery on seats, door panels and kick panels.

3. Operation of the '56 optional power top was initiated by pressing the top compartment release button (1) which opened the lid. When the dash switch was pushed in, an electric motor made the hydraulic cylinder lift the lid all the way and then the soft-top. When the top was all the way up, the lid was closed by the hydraulic unit and the driver could release the straps, allowing the rear of the top to come down and be attached by the rear bow latches to the decklid.

complaints, supplying non-factory fiberglass hardtops like the Plasticon unit. The aftermarket couldn't do much about the transmission selection, though, for the Powerglide was still the basic Corvette transmission. A 3-speed standard transmission finally became available late in the short model run, but only a few dozen cars are believed to have been delivered this way. The other major drawback was the braking, at least from the standpoint of enthusiasts who expected more than passenger-car performance. The brakes were okay for normal driving, but not for diving into a corner in a road race, which the new V-8 was tempting more and more Corvette owners to do. At least the Corvette didn't have to worry about competition from America's other two-seater, the new Ford Thunderbird. This was a handsome car which also had a new V-8 engine, but with its steel body it was heavier than the Corvette. As was noted by Chevrolet fans and even the Corvette advertising agency, the Thunderbird was more of a "scaled-down convertible" than a sports car. Even more of a boulevard car than the early Corvette, the Thunderbird appealed more to the public, but represented no threat for the attention of racing enthusiasts.

Although the 6-cylinder Corvettes had crisp performance and the new V-8 265 cu. ins. added even more for the '55 model, it remained for the new 1956 Corvette to first establish a real reputation for the marque. No matter how big or powerful the engine, sports car purists were going to scoff at any Corvette that came with an automatic transmission. It wasn't until the '56 model came out that the 3-speed manual transmission was really available in quantity.

With the first styling changes of any kind since the car's introduction three years before, the '56 'Vette came out typically late: Jan. 11, 1956. The last model to be styled at the GM headquarters before the styling people moved north of Detroit to the GM Tech Center, the '56 Corvette retained the basic shape of the original Motorama car, but with cleaner headlight and taillight treatments and new side sculpturing. The scooped-out portion of the front fenders that extended into the doors was an idea that had been on the La-Salle II show car GM had used in their 1955 Motorama show. Two air scoops were added to the tops of the front fenders, borrowed from

FIRST V-8 YEARS

another GM Motorama car, the original Corvette prototype. But unlike the original's, the air scoops on the '56 were nonfunctional. The existing cowl vent remained as the source of interior ventilation. The rear fenders were shaped to the general curve of the deck, with streamlined taillights mounted flush in the fender peaks. Perhaps influenced by the talked-about Mercedes 300SL introduced two years before, Chevy stylists added two ridges down the sides of the '56 hood and pushed the front fenders out at the front, where standard headlight buckets could be used instead of the screened-over depressions. To carry the fender line even further forward, the original plan was designed to have the external headlight rings in body color for a "frenched" look. However, paint kept flaking off the pot-metal rings, so the bulk of production cars had conventional chromed rings. The front and rear wheel openings were cut back on the trailing edges to give the car a look of forward motion, and the windshield glass area was increased for more visibility. Complaints of poor visibility from the previous models were further silenced by reshaping the side window openings in the folding top. The profile of the soft top was also refined. The tops on the previous cars had had such a bulge in the center that the cars took on a whole different character with the top up. For '56, the center of the top was lowered to take the bulge out of the middle. Answering still another consumer demand for the Corvette, this attractively restyled new model was the first to offer a factory hardtop, very much like that seen on the '54 Motorama Corvette hardtop model.

The exhaust problems that had plagued owners of the earlier cars were also taken care of on the '56. In fact, in one of his first assignments, Duntov airflow-tested the Corvette to find out why the exhaust fumes stained the rear of the car and why owners complained of fumes when the heater was on. The vent windows were sucking the exhaust in at speed, and Duntov recommended the exhaust outlets be moved to the tip of the rear fenders for '55, but this feature didn't arrive until the new body was introduced for the '56 year, in which the exhaust exited through the bumperettes.

Chevrolet had spent the first three years of the Corvette's life in a wait-and-see approach, checking the consumer reaction and making a few changes here and there, but nothing major. The 1956 model represented a real turning point in the car's history, because changes were made in every aspect of the car in an effort to make the car more salable and more capable of bringing good publicity to the rest of the Chevrolet line. If these changes hadn't resulted in something GM could be proud of, then the whole project might have died an ignominious death, overshadowed and shamed by overwhelmingly greater sales of the other company's "cut-down convertible."

The new top shape and the availability of the plastic hardtop answered some complaints, but the sometimes-uncomfortable interior came in for its share of changes, too. Roll-up windows finally appeared, and even power window mechanisms were optional. Other changes on the doors included integral armrests inside, outside handles and locks required by the roll-up windows, and new hinges similar to the passenger-car type, which allow easier entry and exit by allowing the door to swing

out more. The dash remained basically unchanged except for knurled Bel Air knobs and the first appearance of the now-famous drilled, tri-spoke Corvette steering wheel. The Powerglide shifter was relocated further forward and housed in a boot/ashtray combination on the tunnel. Although the bucket seats remained in the same general form, the passenger seat was now adjustable like the driver's seat and new "waffle" pattern vinyl was used on the seat insert's as well as the doors, kick panels and hardtop headliner.

With the influence and enthusiasm of Duntov upon them, Chevrolet engineers didn't rest on their mechanical laurels either. Both the '56 chassis and the drivetrain were considerably improved over the previous year. In the case of the chassis, improvements were really a matter of fine-tuning rather than substitution of new parts. In interviews in later years, Duntov would reflect on the early Corvette chassis as "a patch-up job, a good start, but we were constantly making little fixes." Thanks to his observations of the car's handling, cornering was improved with only minor adjustments. The caster was increased slightly by shimming the front crossmember, the same was done for understeer by shimming the central control arm, and the shackle angle of the rear springs was decreased by new hangers. New brake linings that the early slalom competitors had screamed for became reality, to reduce fade and wear longer. A new rear axle was employed, too. No longer a one-of-a-kind unit, the Corvette got the same good Hotchkiss-drive rear end that the passenger cars were now using (passenger cars went to the open drive in 1955, two years after the Corvette). Instead of having a separate rear inspection cover, the cover was welded to the housing for extra

strength, and a stronger third-member casting was used with bigger bearings all around.

One of the reasons they needed better handling and a beefier rear end for the '56 Corvette was the increased horsepower of the refined 265 engine. Another was the real availability of the stick-shift transmission, which transferred the engine power more directly than the Powerglide, and which, it must be assumed, encouraged Corvette owners to ask for a little more in handling. The mid-Fifties began a decade of spirited freedom for engine designers in Detroit and hot rodders working at home. Smog had begun to rear its ugly head, but the government hadn't yet begun to wave it in the faces of the engineers, and the oil companies were merrily producing higher-octane gasolines that allowed the Motor City people to raise their compression ratios every year almost religiously.

In the case of the still young 265, the compression was raised from its 1955 introductory level of 8:1 to 9.25:1, which helped the engine in single 4-bbl. form achieve 210 hp. New and exciting on the still-short option list that year was the 2x4 or twin 4-bbl. Carter carburetion, which upped the sports car's horsepower to 225 @ 5200 rpm, healthy enough in anyone's book at that time.

Actually, in the first few months

3

4

5

1. Borrowing styling thoughts from both the Mercedes 300SL and in-house GM show car Lasalle II, the '56 was the first restyling since the original 1953 Motorama car.

2. The small-block V-8's potential for extra power was tapped in '56 with the 225-hp twin 4-bbl. option. In conjunction with the new "Duntov" cam, power was boosted to 240 hp.

3. Though Thunderbird sales had forced Chevrolet to improve on the Corvette's interior comfort, performance changes to the '56 kept its reputation as the only American sports car intact.

4. Among the three Vettes brought to Daytona Beach in early 1956 was the "Duntov-modified" car, which was in fact E56S001001, or the first car off the line, since the record attempts came right after the introduction of the car. Shown here with John Fitch at the wheel, this car set a 150-mph record when Duntov drove it.

5. Driving a standard version, Betty Skelton is here given the checkered flag at Daytona Beach by 1956 NASCAR flagman Frank Swain as she sets a new record at 137 mph.

6. Surrounded here by the Mercedes 300SL gull-wing coupes—the cars to beat—is No. 106, campaigned by Petersen photographer Bob D'Olivo and Hot Rod magazine editor "Racer" Brown. The Venetian Red '56, driven by Bill Pollack and Dr. Dick Thompson, was a frequent visitor to the winner's circle and took the SCCA class "C" Production championship in 1956.

6

FIRST V-8 YEARS

1. Shown here in May 1956 being driven by Max Goldman at Cumberland, MD, the SR-1 Corvette was one of the factory's earliest "semi-sponsored" racers.

2. The SR-2 Corvette, driven here by Dick Thompson at Elkhart Lake in '56, was owned by Jerry Earl, son of GM's Styling boss Harley Earl. Special body sat on chassis identical to those used on the Sebring cars for 1956.

3. One of the major aesthetic problems of the earlier cars had been the top, so the '56's featured a redesigned soft-top without the bulge. The rear view was cleaned up by shaving down the rear fenders and moving the license "out of the closet" and below the deck.

4. Externally, the '57 Corvette was no different from the previous year, but under the skin were a host of new mechanical features, not the least of which is alluded to by the chrome emblem in the fender insert here.

5. Aviatrix/stunt driver Betty Skelton posed with '57 version of the car she won fame with at Daytona Beach.

6. When Motor Trend magazine road testers took the injected '57 to the old San Gabriel drag strip, they scrubbed more than a few miles off of those rear wide whitewalls. Performance of the injected engine was remarkable.

7. The 1 hp per cu. in. of the new 283 (enlarged 265) with injection was a milestone for American production cars. Basic f.i. design incorporates an air meter (A), a fuel meter (B) and a plenum chamber (C) or "doghouse." Through the air cleaner, air enters and goes through the meter (B) that is connected by vacuum lines to the fuel meter. The airflow past the 3-in. venturi signals the fuel meter how much fuel the engine can use.

8. Externally, the '57 shared the '56 body, but even that was different on the inside, where metal first appeared for reinforcing the 'glass body. One of the areas '57's featured the metal reinforcements was inside the doors.

after introduction, the dual 4-bbl. setup was in the category of a "necessary option" (at $160). In order to get one of those early '56's, you also had to order the following extra-cost options: parking brake alarm ($5), courtesy lights ($8), windshield washer ($11), and the hydraulic folding top (power) mechanism ($100). By early April, however, a car could be ordered without these options.

The engine was improved in other ways, too. The original 265 V-8 had not been equipped with an oil filter. This oversight was corrected, and the radio interference shielding was vastly improved. Where the '55 Corvette V-8 had a chromed "pressure cooker" sitting over the distributor and braided wire coverings over the individual plug wires, the '56 engine had the chromed sheetmetal housing over the distributor, coil and wires that have become a familiar sight on Corvette engines ever since. To go along with the power-increasing smaller combustion chambers that had upped the compression, new exhaust manifolds were utilized that had more generous interior passages and a central outlet.

These were the first of what later became famous as the "ram's horn" exhaust manifolds, one of the most free-flowing of stock Detroit designs. Another first for this engine was the use of aluminum components, both for looks and for saving weight. The twin 4-bbl. option was mounted on an aluminum manifold that saved some 21 lbs., and the finned-cast-aluminum valve covers with the Corvette name in raised letters really made this engine look like more than just a warmed-over passenger-car 265. Then and now, those neat valve covers can give a standard Chevrolet V-8 a psychological boost worth at least 20 hp. Along with the chromed ignition shield, extra carburetion options, dual-point ignition and the free-flowing headers, the covers first created the public's image of the "Corvette Engine" that has been sustained by a host of hot small-block and big-block engines since.

The new power, new look and improved chassis finally gave Corvette buyers a serious chance in competition events. Through weight-saving up front and other changes, the car's weight distribu-

1

2

3

4

tion had improved to 52% front and 48% rear. While not in the Ferrari category, this was capable of respectable road-race performance in the hands of a competent driver who knew the car's tendency to drift the rear in corners.

Duntov, himself a former racing driver for European teams, knew the car was ready to demonstrate its potential without making Chevrolet look foolish, so the new 1956 model was the first to see any serious competitive effort by the factory. Shortly after the car's introduction at the Waldorf Motorama, three Corvettes were brought to Daytona Beach for the annual speed week in this Florida resort. Chevrolet's idea was to at least set a few records to give the boys at Cambell-Ewald something to tout. Driven by Duntov himself, road-racer John Fitch and aviatrix/racer Betty Skelton, the cars made a creditable showing against the well-prepped Ford Thunderbirds. Chevrolet lost on the standing-mile tests, but won the high-speed honors at 145 mph for production cars.

Duntov, who had been doing aerodynamic and other at-speed tests of a mule car at the GM Proving Ground in Mesa, Ariz., had brought a slightly hotter version to set his own mark. Duntov developed his famous Duntov camshaft for the occasion, with faster ramps and more duration than the standard Corvette bump-stick. With compression upped to 10.3:1, Duntov managed 150 mph, using snow tires for traction on the wide, flat beach. This first "Duntov cam" became homologated as a genuine option (though installed on few production engines) which helped the dual 4-bbl. engine achieve a 240-hp rating. The Duntov cam has been a mainstay of high-performance small-block Chevrolet and Corvette engines ever since, but in 1956 this $175 option (which could only be ordered with the $160 dual 4-bbl. option) was aimed mainly at the racing crowd. On factory option lists, this 449 option was recommended "for racing purposes only."

Daytona, it turned out, wasn't the only Florida city where Duntov's camshaft and other tricks were to be utilized for the greater glory of the Chevrolet name. In March, John Fitch brought a team and four white-with-blue-stripes Corvettes to Sebring to prepare for the 12-hour annual endurance race. As the team made modifications to the cars to suit them for road racing, the bean-counters back in Detroit were busy making up new part numbers so the modifications could be cataloged as "stock optional."

The 240-hp engines really were pretty much stock except for some minor porting, but the chassis featured stiffer springs and shocks, 37-gal. fuel tanks special Cerametallic brake linings and finned drums, Hy-Tork (limited-slip) differentials and Halibrand magnesium wheels. A fifth car was entered with an engine slightly more modified, enlarged to 307 cu. ins. to fit it into the 5-liter Class B, and equipped with a German ZF 4-speed transmission, something the Corvette really needed for racing.

While the Sebring results were nothing to rave over, a real point had been made. Two of the cars did not finish, and the two that did (9th and 15th) were limping at the end of their race, but the tea-bagger railbirds who had come to see Ferraris and Maseratis and Jags controlled by the likes of Hawthorne, Moss, Fangio and Taruffi

5

6

7

8

FIRST V-8 YEARS

had seen the handwriting on the wall. The Corvette was truly an American sports car to be reckoned with after such a showing in the first real try at competition and among the finest men and machines, too. The Corvette was to go a long way in future races of all kinds, keeping the nameplate high on the desirability list of young and old. It was never an embarrassment to the corporation. Road & Track magazine tested a new '56. Noting that it fit into Class C Production in SCCA sports car rules, they predicted it would "liven up proceedings in this category considerably." The remark was prophetic, coming when it did, because later the fiberglass machine did win the 1956 SCCA Class C championship with Dr. Dick Thompson at the controls. Chevrolet and Campbell-Ewald could justifiably and proudly refer to their baby as the real McCoy.

1957, AN ENGINEERING ZENITH

The word "classic" is as overused today in reference to automobiles as "antique" and "special interest," but if the description can fit any of the early V-8 Corvettes, it describes the '57 model. Although shrouded in a shell identical to the previously new-for-1956 model, the '57 Corvette will always be remembered for its major engineering achievement: It was the first American production car with fuel injection. The prestigious Mercedes-Benz 300SL, with which the Corvette had been dicing in road races, had introduced fuel injection in late 1954, but this (the Chevrolet unit) was a remarkable American achievement nonetheless. The automotive enthusiast magazines had been pipe-dreaming about fuel injection for passenger cars for several years, speculating as to who would come out with the first workable street system; when Chevrolet, of all marques, took the engineering lead, the press outdid itself in whipping up the public's enthusiasm about this new form of induction.

It must be remembered that until this time, the only common fuel injection unit in this country was the racing type built by Stuart Hilborn and others. These were all of the constant-flow type with the metering device governed only by the position of the throttle linkage. Although they served the needs of an all-out racing engine admirably well, they didn't make a smooth

transition between idle and full throttle and they exibited poor low-speed drivability. Such problems seemed to eliminate constant-flow injection as a production-car possibility.

The German Bosch system used by the 300SL's, on the other hand, featured a "timed" fuel injection system. Instead of having constant flow, fuel was injected to the cylinders only at the right time and in carefully metered amounts. This resulted in a very precise-running engine with flexible performance and instant throttle response at all speeds, but the cams, plunger rods, valves and other hardware necessary for this system made it prohibitively expensive to produce for the American market. This was why knowledgeable observers of the Detroit scene were anxious to see how General Motors would combine the best characteristics of both types and sell it for a reasonable cost.

The f.i. fans weren't disappointed. When the new Corvette was announced in January, 1957, not only was this bold advance offered in several engine versions for the only car in the world with a fiberglass body, but it was to be considered available on the standard bread-and-butter Chevrolets sedans as well! Through the combined efforts of John Dolza of the GM Engineering staff, E.A. Kehoe and Donald Stoltman of the Rochester Products Division (which actually produced the units) and Duntov, the new f.i. became an instant success after years of research.

What made the Rochester unit different from both the Hilborn and Mercedes types was the method by which it sensed the engine's fuel requirements. A metering diaphragm was hooked to both sides of a large venturi to sense the pressure differential as airflow fed the f.i. plenum chamber. The diaphragm could control the amount of fuel going to the nozzles and not depend on engine rpm or

throttle position for proper signals.

The result was a practical fuel injection system that was superior to the dual 4-bbl. option for power, didn't starve out on acceleration or hard cornering (a real problem with the WCFB Carter carbs) and offered instantaneous throttle response in almost every gear. All this from a system that engineer John Dolza had envisioned as a way to reduce air pollution and improve fuel economy and starting ability over conventional carburetion! Mr. Dolza may have been right, but he was ahead of his time by about a decade. The most important aspect of fuel injection to the average car nut of 1957 was that it went like blazes! The members of the automotive press almost stumbled over themselves to be the first to report the smoothness and outstanding first-gear 0-60 times.

Fuel injection was the most spectacular of several mechanical improvements for the 1957 Corvette. Through an increase in bore size of ⅛-in., the 265-cu.-in. V-8 that had served so admirably was enlarged to 283 cu. ins., a displacement that Chevrolet would retain for five more years in the sports car and 10 years in their pasenger-car line. The new bore size made the lightweight small-block Chevrolet V-8 even more over-square, one of the features that made it such a performer. A staggering total of five separate engines were available in the Corvette for '57, ranging in horsepower from the base 220 to the top fuel-injected version of 283 hp, the magic number of one horsepower per cubic inch in a production engine. The base 220 engine and three of the optional engines had a slight increase in compression ratio, to 9.5:1, while the 283-283 had a decidedly premium-fuel ratio of 10.5:1. The next step in performance from the base engine was the twin 4-bbl. version with hydraulic lifters at 245 hp ($140). Then came the hottest carbureted version at 270 hp with twin fours and the hot valvetrain

158

($170). This latter engine was "recommended for high rpm operation."

There were actually three f.i. engines. The "base f.i." engine at 250 hp featured the mild valvetrain and a $450 price tag, while the 283-hp version with the special Duntov valvetrain and 10.5:1 compression was available for the same price but "not adapted to ordinary pleasure driving" and available only with standard-shift transmissions. A rare '57 option was R.P.O. 579E, which was listed at the same 283 hp, but the option price of $675 bought the top f.i. motor with a special cold-air intake system and a mechanically driven tach mounted on the steering column. This is probably a case of an option listed more for racing homologation than for sales appeal to the consumer.

To the base price of $3176.32, other neat options could be added besides the engines. For the first time, a 4-speed transmission ($188.30) with full synchronization was available (only after May 1, 1957). This is what the Corvette really had needed for road racing. Some road testers claimed it was worth a full second in upper-speed acceleration testing. For a paltry $45, you could complement the 4-speed with a Positraction (limited-slip) rear differential with your choice of 3.70:1 (standard), 4.11:1 or 4.56:1 gearing, but the "Posi" was not available with the Powerglide automatic.

A truly "homologation-type" option that seemed to naturally go with the above two options for those with a racing bent was R.P.O. 684, the heavy-duty brakes and suspension. What came with this most-expensive '57 option ($725) were stiffer springs front and rear, larger shocks with stiffer valving, heavier front sway bar, quicker steering and better brakes. The quicker steering, from 21:1 to 16:1, was arrived at with an adapter plate bolted between the center pivot and the tie rods. The super brakes included "ceramic-metallic" linings, finned brake drums and vented backing plates with air scoops. Interestingly, the air ducts from the front of the car started just behind the grille, where cold air was picked up, and continued all the way back through the rock-

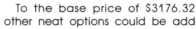

3

4

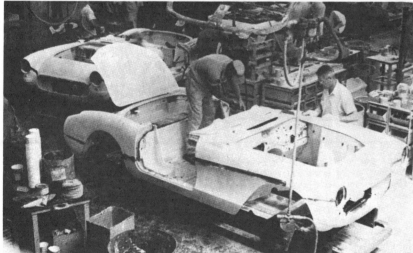

5

6

7

1. Upside down here, you can see how the cowl area was braced with metal for 1957, too. Note just behind the headlight openings how the body seams are backed up.

2. The floorpans were reinforced at the rocker panels with sheetmetal.

3. Like a grown-up version of one of those "3-in-1" plastic model kits is this assemblage of 1957 body parts.

4. Taking a peek at how the Corvette was assembled from the Ashtabula-made pieces, here we find a well-protected employee preparing the bonding surfaces of the parts by sandblasting.

5. Dark lines around the bodies here on the 1957 assembly line in Flint are the seams where bonding agent has been used to "glue" the panels.

6. When the bodies are completely assembled, the glued seams are ground down and the entire body is sprayed with several coats of primer.

7. After the final primer and sanding, the bodies are painted and rubbed out, then the windshield, interior and other parts are added. Hoods are then raised so drivelines can be installed.

FIRST V-8 YEARS

er panels to the rear brakes. This option was also "not suggested for ordinary pleasure driving," and could only be ordered with stickshift, Positraction rear axle and either the 270-hp or 283-hp engines.

The amount of racing-oriented options available for 1957 indicated GM's willingness to offer a "factory race car" if it would help the overall corporate image, as Duntov kept assuring them it would. That what they were offering was a good package to boot was proven that year in street races, drag races, road races and endurance races, with the Chevrolet passenger cars equipped with some of the Corvette options like f.i. and Positraction doing equally well for the marque in their own types of racing. The Corvette team at Sebring finished 12th, 15th and 16th, again against the cream of the crop, and the SCCA B Production championship (up from Class C) was once again taken by Dick Thompson in a Corvette.

These racing successes and "hot" options were what the ad men and PR types had to work with for 1957, since the body and interior were essentially unchanged. But this year that brought the Corvette name such fame as legends are born of also brought an end to overt factory participation in racing. While Zora had made his points with the brass

and the Corvette name was assured of continuance with the best production year ever at 6339, 1957 was also the year the Automobile Manufacturers Association got the major Detroit people to sign an anti-racing pact. With fuel injection (Chevrolet and Corvette) and superchargers (Ford and Thunderbird options) being offered, the AMA thought the Detroit horsepower race had gone far enough. Perhaps it had at that, for who knows what incredible options would have been available if the AMA ban hadn't forced the factory hipo programs to assume a low profile from then on?

In summing up the early V-8 years of the Corvette, the Campbell-Ewald ad men weren't far off in their early 1957 advertising for the Corvette that was headlined "Toward an American Classic . . . the 1957 Corvette With Fuel Injection!" Yes, in later years the Corvette offered more horsepower and bigger engines, but the car's personality was changed, too. The price kept growing, as did the

comfort and convenience option list, and the car grew heavier by the year. It's our opinion that no other Corvette hits as close to the mark of "classic" by being ahead of its contemporaries than the fuel-injected '57. Period. Some of the prose of that 1957 ad no longer sounds purple from our present vantage point: "This is another major step in the creation of a proud new kind of car for America: a genuine sports car, as certified by its record in competition. But a unique sports car in its combination of moderate price, luxurious equipment and low-cost maintenance with fiery performance, polo-pony responsiveness and granite stability on curves.

"It is our intention to make of the Corvette a classic car, one of those rare and happy milestones in automotive design. We take pleasure in inviting you to drive the 1957 version—and see just how close we have come to the target . . . ." Our only regret is that we can't turn back the clock to take advantage of that offer. 🦀

1

Ed Cole, a GM vice president at the time, and the General Manager of Chevrolet Motor Division, had seen "his" Corvettes race at Sebring in 1956. As well as the modified production cars did, it was plain that such machines could never dominate sports car racing; they were too big, they were too heavy, and because reliance was placed on proprietary Corvette parts in many cases, they could never maintain a comfortable edge over the winning sports cars of the time; namely, Jaguar and Ferrari. Zora Arkus-Duntov knew this too, and he knew further that the imported machinery was hardly the type that could be bought from a showroom. These pure race cars were the results of extensive factory effort to enhance the marque through race-winning performances. The sales of everyday Jags and other makes went up in proportion to how the all-out racing versions finished in the big, much-publicized races, so Ed Cole decided that the Corvette needed such a stimulus.

With the help of Duntov and styling chief Harley Earl, Cole would get his

race car, and get it in time for the '57 Sebring event even if it meant expending one-and-a-half million dollars in the quest—which it did.

The project was coded XP-64 and it didn't matter how much physical resemblance there was between it and the production Corvette, just as it didn't matter how many production parts went into it, the basic 283-cu.-in. V-8 powerplant being the only exception. Thus it was that the Corvette SS, as it was later officially titled, began its genesis in Chevrolet's Engineering Center under the personal direction of Duntov.

As noted, the heart of the SS was the 283 V-8, but it mounted some unusual features—aluminum cylinder heads and water pump, and a magnesium oil pan. On top went a special version of the Rochester fuel injector with seperate plenum chambers and two venturis, the inlets facing forward and to which air was rammed via a duct on the grille. This initial powerplant developed a little over 300 hp at 6400 rpm, could wind several hundred r's over this, and tipped the scales at only 450 lbs.

The chassis reflected the genius that is GM's, and utilized a tubular space frame which, when completed, weighed 180 lbs. Styling of the SS was handled by Clare MacKichan, but fiberglass would not be the medium with which he would work. With weight-saving of prime importance, sheet magnesium was chosen, and the body came together quickly after final design had been "frozen."

At the outset of the project, and with Duntov knowing full well the folly of going big-time racing with a single machine, five SS Corvettes were projected. But corporate powers higher up the ladder than even Cole put the axe to this plan, and in the end just the one finished car was produced. Under the excuse of needing certain mockup chassis pieces for laboratory evaluation, however, Duntov was able to get enough parts to build a second SS chassis with drivetrain. This was bodied with "quick-and-dirty" fiberglass panels, looking only superficially like the real SS, and it was generally cobbled together with bits and pieces scrounged

1. In acceleration, handling, clean looks and engineering milestones, the '57 Corvette established itself as a latter-day classic among American cars. Even the '57 AMA racing ban didn't stop the development ball that this car got going. As the later cars got heavier, few could accelerate like the '57 until the 327 in 1962.

2. "We don't mess around" might have been Duntov's words in the race-buff's vernacular. When Chevrolet officially goes racing, it's a no-holds barred proposition. Here Duntov inspects some of the SS components, built from blueprints drawn in the car's assembly area.

3. A virtual 24-hours-per-day proposition, the SS was rushed from its beginning in late '56 to its Sebring race in March, 1957. Duntov is shown conferring with a draftsman while the chassis goes together in the background.

4. The over-150-mph racing potential of the SS depended largely upon its brakes, and there's no denying that four of these would halt almost anything. Yet, the brakes were the car's nemises through the failure of a mercury-actuated switch intended to isolate the rear brakes from the front ones under panic-stop situations.

5. Adding to Duntov's woes was GM's insistence that any car they built had to be visually perfect. More time was spent detailing the body than on chassis/drivetrain studies, partly leading to downfall of the SS.

6. Over-attention to detail—"Oops, I found a speck of dust!"—made late the arrival of the SS at Sebring.

from here and there. In the end, Duntov had what was termed his "mule car," one on which some of the SS innovations could be tried out on the track before being built into the SS itself. This chassis would later play an important role in the development of the '63 production Sting Ray, but for the time being Duntov managed to coax 150 mph out of the mule and felt confident that the even lighter, real SS could do better.

The Corvette SS made its debut in pre-race practice at Sebring in March, under the capable direction of Italian driver Piero Taruffi who had been chosen as co-driver by team manager John Fitch. The car was from outward appearances ready to race, yet it was in truth not finished to anywhere near Zora's satisfaction. Even the mule car, upon which more development and practice time had been spent than on the SS, suffered from braking and other problems, yet Taruffi bravely took it for its first trial scant hours before the race. The car proved terrible; the magnesium body did not provide the heat insulation that the fiberglass body on the mule did,

and an experimental braking system, which had "worked" on the drawing boards but not in actuality, kept the car from being pressed too hard. Even so, Fitch, who was slated as the first driver in the 12-hour event, started bravely off in the unproved car, but his troubles began almost immediately. Severe vibration brought him into the pits to have a suspect tire changed, then a few laps later the coil wire came loose and he coasted to a stop with a dead engine. After a hurry-up fix Taruffi took the car back into the fray, but the suspension felt strange to him and he retired the car on its 23rd lap, just a little over an hour after the start of the race.

Ed Cole was understandably disappointed, as was Duntov and the various engineering and styling staffs that had worked so hard to bring off a miracle. Yet the powers at Chevrolet were nevertheless impressed with the car's eventual potential, and the order came for two more SS cars to be built and a three-car team would make a grand assault on the most prestigious race of them all; the 24 hours of LeMans.

The next development was as sudden as it was unexpected, the big Automobile Manufacturers' Association absolute ban on racing by its members. As the AMA pointed the way, so did Chevrolet obediently follow, and even before the AMA's edict felt a date stamp, GM's President Harlow Curtice ordered each of his division's racing efforts to stop—and this meant the immediate scrapping of all plans, race car parts, special race-oriented laboratories and assembly areas. Everything was canned except, in Chevrolet's case, the SS race car itself (which would go on the show car tour) and the chassis of Zora's mule car which was eventually consigned to GM's new Styling Chief, Bill Mitchell. Duntov did manage to spend additional engineering and development time on the SS, with the excuse that the SS made a good testbed for various components that might someday find their way into production Corvettes, and in late 1958 managed to turn the Phoenix Proving Grounds' 5-mile banked track at over 183 mph.

DEVELOPMENT CONTINUES

This model year brought the greatest changes yet in the Corvette, changes perhaps not visually relevant to the more nearly pure-sports heritage of the preceding model. It marked the second body overhaul in the car's five years of existence. Styling at that point in time was directed toward the bulbous and over-bearing—remember the entire General Motors car line-up for that period?—and with Corvette's cosmetics now handled openly by Chevrolet's central styling staff, it was natural that the-then desirable big-car look was passed to the plastic speedster.

1958

Product lead-time in Detroit is slow and tedious, with an average of three years required to bring drawing board sketches to reality. It was in late 1955, then, that hurry-up work began on developing the '58's, and conflicts arose between certain factions within those hallowed walls at GM. It became the goal of the advertising and marketing people to stimulate Corvette sales by designing a car that would appeal to a larger segment of the car-buying market than the mere sports car set represented. They hoped, too, that a flashier Corvette would help draw foot traffic into the showrooms where many might move over to the standard Chevrolet lines once they were in the doors.

At this point, GM was at odds with federal and state headlamp regulations which mandated the use of but two sealed beam lights of a minimum/maximum circumference and meeting certain requirements as to brilliancy, length of reach, and so forth. Design doodlers had been toying with the use of four headlights of smaller-than-standard size grouped as two pairs. Perseverance by GM relaxed some of the regulations and allowed the stylists to fit quad headlights to the car lines, and the Corvette was among the other unfortunate recipients of this bold, bug-eyed treatment.

Cars of all kinds and within all price ranges were growing in terms of physical size in those years; up-sized might be an appropriate

SOLDIERING ALONG WITH EVER-INCREASED PERFORMANCE, CHASSIS DEVELOPMENTS, STYLING, PRODUCTION TOTALS... AND PRICES.

BY SPENCE MURRAY

term to coin, just as down-sized is now. The Corvette grew in virtually every dimension; it grew more than nine inches of total length, most of it concentrated in front-end overhang on the still-retained 102-in.

wheelbase. Width blossomed similarly, over two inches In bulk, the Corvette made it beyond the 3000-lb. mark for the first time by virtue of the over-200 lbs. added to a similarly equipped '57 model.

Whatever is to be said about the general appearance of the '58 Corvette model year, it should be remembered that the stylists did, in fact, labor hard and long to satisfy both the heavy demands of the so-called bean counters, and those of a more sports car persuasion who wanted very much for the new car to retain a strong front end semblance of its former self. The challenge was admirably met, the pop-eyes of the quad headlights notwithstanding, but some unfortunate gimcrackery crept into the mix, much of it appearing almost as late-hour afterthoughts.

UP FRONT

The at-the-time desirable look of big-car bulk, and which necessitated the weight increase, was helped by the substantial bumpers which were bracketed directly to the frame front and rear. Two heavy ribs were incorporated in the hood—a carryover but serving no apparent purpose other than the possibility of stiffening the front-hinged panel to prevent oil-canning or surface flutter at speed. They did, however, serve to break up the hood expanse and give both the driver and his passenger

1958

a sight-line down the road ahead. Possibly for the same reason (eliminating oil-canning) no fewer than 18 ridges were impressed across the rear half of the hood between the ribs, obviously intended to emulate business-looking louvers.

The new Corvette grille managed to retain an appearance generally similar to the now-famed toothy design of the earlier models, but the individual teeth were decreased in number from the 13 of all earlier cars to nine, each of which was more massive in keeping with the theme of the big-car image and they were set within a heavy and chromed surround. Instead of a single grille opening, though, there were three; two smaller grilles were set beneath the pairs of headlights. Early consideration was given to making the small, outer openings functional in terms of brake air-ducting and added engine compartment cooling. Cost-conscious planners eventually considered such a system unnecessary for normal-use cars, largely because of the increased production costs such an installation would require. On special order, however, the '58 could be opted for with RPO 684 if it included either the 270 or the 290 engine; ducts lead through the grille cut-outs to assist in cooling the rear brakes. But on most cars, the outer grilles became just more gimcrackery.

Things were similarly handled at the rear; visual bulk came via bold twin chrome strips flowing somewhat uselessly down the trunk lid, and physically heavier, more massive bumperettes were used, styled in keeping with the ones forward

and incorporating fish-mouthed exhaust outlets in place of the more business-like tubular style.

The new car retained the depression that extended rearward from the front wheel cutouts to a point midway in the doors, but this year the foremost part was panelled to both add a touch of smartness and to emulate the similar but

longer shroudings carried by Duntov's toy, the Corvette SS.

INSIDE

If the general look of bulkiness was what the product planners at GM wanted for the Corvette, at least the driving-oriented engineers and designers within this Chevrolet

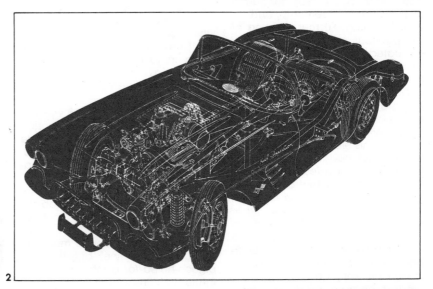

1. New and bold for 1958, the face of Corvette changed to emulate the desireable (then) "big-car" look. GM Photographic further enhanced its image with this widely publicized wide-angle view. Unnoticed was that standard outside driver's mirror missing on this prototype model.

2. Whatever purists may have felt about the bug-eyed front end and overall bulbous styling, the Corvette was more of a sports car underneath than ever. Buyers chose between five engines; 230-, 245-, 270-, 250-and 290-hp versions of the time-proven 283 V-8. An accompanying chart shows their sales popularity.

3. Superfluous were the 18 simulated hood louvers which, aided by the quad headlights and chrome-dripping grille, gave the car an overall look of size out of proportion to its physical measurements. This is the prototype again, without the exterior mirror.

1958 CORVETTE ENGINE POPULARITY

HORSEPOWER RATING	CAMSHAFT	FUEL SYSTEM	UNITS PRODUCED	% of TOTAL
230	Regular	Single 4bbl.	4243	46.28%
245	Regular	Dual 4bbl.	2436	26.57%
270	Hi-Lift	Dual 4bbl.	979	10.67%
250	Regular	Fuel Injected	504	5.50%
290	Hi-Lift	Fuel Injected	1007	10.98%

DEVELOPMENT CONTINUES

sub-division had more of their own way with the freshly conceived interior. Totally new was the dashboard—in concept, in gauge and switch placement, and in overall styling. Further, seating of the previous model was carefully evaluated and, mostly due to Duntov's insistence, new bucket seats were supplied. In fact, about the only carryovers to the new car from the old were the steering wheel and a few assorted knobs.

Zora Arkus-Duntov, perhaps a little out of his element in the field of styling, had had at least enough experience in professional racing machines to know that a tachometer should be in a driver's field of vision—not centered in the dash, small, and mounted low-down where the eye would have to search hard for it. This had been one of Zora's initial complaints about the early cars, but this was his first chance to do anything about it. He pushed to have the tach mounted where it could be easily seen by racers and pseudo-racers alike, and the earliest interior styling mockups reveal the bold instrument steering column-mounted.

Above and ahead of the 6000

rpm tach, stilt with its curious rev accumulator, was a huge 160-mph speedometer. Mounted in pods beneath the speedo, and paired for visibility to either side of the tach, were the four all-important gauges. The new cockpit, still without a conventional glovebox, had a deep recess in the dash ahead of the passenger and across which was mounted a vinyl-covered and convenient grab rail. Overall, the '58's interior retained its lean and lithe look to a large extent, more so than the exterior which GM found fit to herald in its Corvette literature as ''imparting smartness'' and having been ''revitalized in looks.''

An innovation on the '58 was the under-dash console, an extension of the lower floor-mounted console between the tunnel and the instrument panel. It held the clock, radio, heater and defroster controls, and set the style for years to come. Early in planning, some debate was made over whether to offer the '58 as a coupe only, or at least to add a fixed-top coupe model to the convertible line, but this was pigeon-holed for a more propitious future time. Instead, the '58 was offered as before; with the automatic soft top and removable hardtop.

DOWN UNDER

If the outer wrappings of the '58 were met with some eyebrow rais-

ing by hard core sports car devotees (although the corporate money men were later vindicated by the soaring sales that this model enjoyed), there were a few other raised eyebrows but of another kind at what lay under that skin. While the basic suspension and chassis layout was much the same as before, albeit with some minor modifications to the tips of the frame to receive the bumper bracketry and newly designed rear springs to help road adhesion as much as ride, there was a stouter optional heart than ever. It was capable of beating out a stimulating 290 hp at 6200 rpm—now better than a horse-per-inch from the time-proved 283 V-8. This top-of-the-list RPO 579D included f.i. with redesigned injector nozzles. With it came a special mechani-

1. Very early doodles by Styling began to show up some of the '58's later configuration. One sketch shows the quad headlight treatment; while the other indicates a try toward the tri-grille motif.

2. The retouch artist gave this photo the rear reflex buttons beneath the taillights, but they didn't appear on production cars until some 200 to 300 cars had been built. Decklid chrome strips were intended to match the ''bulk'' of the front end.

3. Only the drilled-spoke steering wheel and a few knobs were carried over from '57. Large tachometer was centrally mounted and was backed by a huge 160 mph speedo. Under-dash console mounted clock, radio, heater and defroster controls. ''Chicken bar'' gave the passenger a secure grip.

4. Car at left carries the now-rare RPO 684—the famed ''brake kit.'' Air was fed via complex ducting to the rear brakes from the side grilles.

5. Front brakes were cooled by this neoprene shield which came with the competition brake option, but it came in the car's trunk and you (or your dealer) had to install it.

cally driven 8000 rpm tachometer as a warning to the also-rans. The healthiest carbureted engine carried Duntov's famous cam and two 4-bbl. carbs. Dubbed the RPO 469C, it produced a satisfying 270 hp at 6000 rpm. Under the fakishly louvered hood was mounted a new Harrison radiator, of what was termed cellular construction in place of the earlier tube-on-center type.

At the opposite end of the performance scale was a new entrant; a docile, about-town 230-hp version of the 283. Apparently it was aimed at the boulevard-car buyer who enjoyed the snobbishness that the Corvette gave but without an ability to jar the senses too hard when the right foot went down. In deference to all those enthusiasts who felt a big-engined Corvette was the only thing in life, the grocery-getter managed to appeal to a wider stripe of the car-buying public and undoubtedly help Chevrolet close out the '58 model year with Corvette sales substantially higher than any year previous. When the results were tallied, and although the magic 10,000-unit figure had not been achieved, close to 9200 Corvettes found homes, a rousing 2800—roughly 30%—more than the 1957 record year.

On the performance side of the coin, little harm was reflected in the new Corvette's overall performance by the added bulk and excess weight. Sports car buff/advertising executive Jim Jeffords showed the pack at Sebring the '58's heels in a car ably prepared by Nickey Chevrolet of Chicago under the hand of Ronnie Kaplan. When the checkered flag fell, Jeffords was the SCCA B Production champion.

Out West, Bill Thomas was building his racing versions with outstanding engine and suspension

work and his cars showed right well by themselves during the annual tour of the road circuits. A first place in the GT class was garnered by Dick Doane, a Chevrolet dealer operating without factory help, and Jim Rathmann, who, in addition to their class victory, took 12th overall at Sebring.

Although the Corvette was a scant five years removed from the production of Job One, it had advanced virtually centuries ahead of the first 150 sluggish-horsepower, 6-cylinder engine and the only transmission available, the Powerglide. The term Corvette now elevated the hopes and spirits of America's sports car lovers, but what had been done in these early years was but an inkling of what the Corvette's future held.

1959

It was perhaps through embarassment over the superfluous gee-gaw that the '58 Corvettes had sported that some of the gimcrackery disappeared for 1959. Thankfully ash-canned were the phoney hood louvers, all 18 of them, as well as the overly bold decklid strips. The wheel covers were redesigned for the first time in three years—with an eye to improved brake cooling via peripheral slots—and the interior which had been so markedly improved the previous year was even further refined.

The chassis got a looking-at, too. What had been needed ever since horsepower began going up in 1957 was a means of controlling wheel hop on hard acceleration. Stomping a pre-'59 Vette from a dead stop passed enough torque through the driveline that the rear axle assembly wrapped up against the springs. The springs in turn overcame the torque and wrapped

down again, only to roll up once more as the torque continued. This led to wheel chatter and slippage, not conducive to the accelerative capabilities of the car. Duntov saw to it that this was overcome. Radius rods were extended rearward from brackets at the top of the frame side members to the rear axle housing. The rods could pivot at the front and allow the rear end to ride up and down as required, but they cancelled housing twist. The springs were freed of the influence of torque and in this one fell swoop, the Corvette's most serious chassis shortcoming disappeared.

Braking effectiveness was raised, at least in option form, to halt the go-ability that any of the five versions of the 283 V-8 were capable of producing. Sintered metallic brake linings were offered on production cars for the first time and which improved the anti-fade characteristics under severe operating conditions—read racing. Not really helping performance, but saving many a 4-speed transmission from inadvertent disintegration was a T-handled shifter with a reverse gear lockout.

While the previous model's seating had been improved, it was helped even more for '59. Possible sliding-about by both passenger and driver was reduced by form-fitting bucket seats that gave improved lateral support. The door handles were pushed forward to a more convenient location and the passenger's "chicken bar" was padded instead of being little more than vinyl-wrapped. Instrument lenses were made convex to help eliminate distortion and glare of the instruments they protected, and sun visors became optional equipment.

There was now a sizeable legion of Corvette followers—23,600 cars had been built by the end of the

DEVELOPMENT CONTINUES

'58 model run—and many of them were fiercely loyal to the marque. Since the car was coming of age, and since early-year cars were piling up the miles and becoming in need of replacement, Chevy had itself a healthy regular market. Add to this the people who had wanted a Corvette but couldn't see their way clear until now—not to mention the go-fast enthusiasts who were finding the Corvette the fastest of all American cars in showroom-stock condition—and it became clear to the sales people that the Vette would have an especially good year and St. Louis was forewarned accordingly. In the end, nearly 9700 units were produced—still shy of the 10,000 mark but this gap was rapidly closing.

THE MITCHELL INFLUENCE

During this period Duntov was up to more than just adjustment and refinement of the innovations embodied in "his" production Corvettes. A bare chassis, a back-up to the Corvette SS race car that Zora himself had piloted to a Daytona lap speed in excess of 150 mph and which later turned the Phoenix Proving Ground's 5-mile banked track at over 183 mph, had come home to roost when the decree against GM's racing involvements was handed down. Upon this imposing platform was to be mounted not only one of the slickest-looking sports/racing cars ever devised, it would become a harbinger of future Corvette styling. Bill Mitchell personally saw to not only his own acquisition of the earlier racing testbed, but also to some close styling overseeing of designs laid down by Larry Shinoda. The resulting Sting Ray, for that

was its name, under the guidance of the racing doctor, Dick Thompson, began its racing career in early 1959. To on-lookers the spectacular design of the car was matched only by its excellent performance, but few of the track-siders correctly guessed that under its knife-edged skin rolled the two-year-old SS chassis or that the car was in any way connected with Chevrolet. Its nameplate identified it only as a Sting Ray—whatever that was.

John Fitch later took his turn behind the Sting Ray's wheel, but Thompson did most of the racing chores—always with Mitchell as the entrant of record. The car contained inherent problems, chiefly with the experimental braking system that had plagued the SS, but it racked up a good accounting of itself through two seasons. It was finally "trailered" after the '60 outings. Because it was Mitchell's own car, it remained his after its retirement. The body was refurbished, Sting Ray entered the show car circuit. Mitchell was, after all, head of the Styling Section now that Harley Earl had retired, and it was easy for him to get GM's pros to dress up his personal machines.

When the show series was over, the Sting Ray was again re-done, this time with the intent of making it fit for the street. It got not only a license plate bracket, but a windscreen for the passenger. It also got Corvette emblems and the crossed-flag symbols.

In place of the several 283's that had powered, first, the SS then the Sting Ray versions, Mitchell had a whopping big 427-cu.-in. V-8 inserted, topped with Weber carburetors which lurked under a Plexiglass hood cover. Its racing color had been silver, its show color red, but Mitchell had it painted silver once again and so it remains today in Mitchell's garage.

Few of the race fans lucky enough to see the Sting Ray in action correctly predicted that the car's unique shape would ever be emulated by a production auto-

mobile, but Mitchell was GM's styling boss and his pet, the Corvette, was the best place he could think of to try out some of his ideas which may have been somewhat stifled under the direction of ex-boss Harley Earl—Corvette's founding father.

1960

If the cosmetic, external differences between the '58 and '59 Corvettes were small, the changes between '59 and '60 were certainly miniscule. But if you stooped to look underneath or popped the hood on the new car, '60's alterations would be immediately apparent. These were largely of Duntov's doing and brought the developments based on the original chassis about as far as they could progress without total refinement—and which Duntov was now about. Improved handling, roadability, performance and driver comfort/convenience had all come under Zora's microscope while the '60 was in the developmental stages.

For openers, while the rear-end assembly had been vastly upgraded by the addition of radius rods to prevent wheel hop for the previous year, '60 found it fitted with an anti-roll or stabilizer bar. This allowed the discontinuing of the extremely stiff, optional rear springs which even avid racers found a trifle too stout for them. The similar stabilizer bar up front was increased in cross-section, reducing the tendency to heel over on hard cornering. Duntov had long been privy to the fact that the effect of increased horsepower could be gained in another way—weight reduction. He insisted on, and got from Engineering, an aluminum flywheel/clutch housing on the manual-transmission-equipped models. This pared 18 lbs. off the car which by now was beginning to take on a little more bulk each year. The Harrison Division of General Motors had done its homework, too, and had readied for produc-

tion its long-experimental aluminum radiator. Where it was ordered as an option, it also trimmed off excess weight, but equally important it helped solve earlier model cooling problems. Cooling was further abetted by a redesigned fan shroud, the fan was positioned two inches nearer the radiator, and optionally available was a five-bladed unit with a temperature-sensitive viscous drive.

The 283 received Zora's genius as well; top-of-the-line output went up to 315 hp, thanks in part to 11:1 compression and a larger f.i. plenum chamber. A radical step in the interests of weight reduction was taken by the introduction of aluminum cylinder heads. It turned out, however, that they were difficult to produce in quantity and with the earliest versions gaining a bad reputation (undetected casting flaws caused no end of customer grief in service), they were quietly discontinued as production-line parts.

If you wanted to do a little serious racing with the '60, you would have ordered RPO 687, a package of options which included a fast-steering adaptor, finned brake drums in combination with the sintered linings, and a steel multi-blade fan in each brake drum to reduce temperatures when the going (or, rather, the stopping) got rough.

Corvette-spotters will be quick to point out that the steering column-mounted tachometer dial now read to 7000 rpm regardless of the **4**

engine installed, and that the rev-counter was gone for good. The sun visors which had been an option the previous year were now standard equipment. The seats, seemingly ever the center of Duntov's nit-picking attention, were once again refined and one sat a little deeper in them.

From the sales standpoint, the Corvette continued its upward march. At last the 10,000-unit figure was topped, by 261 cars, and the total was about equally divided between the soft top and hardtop. Earlier in the Vette's life, statisticians had deduced, and so stated, that low production of the car meant it was economically sensible to use a fiberglass body. Beyond a certain point, however, steel was the economical way to go, all things considered. That cross-over point was said to be 10,000 units. That level was now surpassed, and while outside observers began predicting that all Corvettes would soon be wrapped in sheetmetal, Chevrolet had discovered that fi-

berglass had a certain buyer appeal and that the cars, as far as the forseeable future was concerned, would continue to be manufactured using this material.

1961

The Corvette's largest single body part was redesigned for the '61's, the announcement coming out on the public release date of Oct. 4, 1960. It may not have been immediately apparent upon viewing the car, but seated in one it was quite noticeable. The underbody, as long as the engineers revamped it to accommodate the new rear-end styling, had a narrower driveshaft/transmission tunnel. This translated to an increase of several inches for the driver's and passenger's footroom, a welcome addition to creature comfort. More obvious at a glance was the ducktail-like body design at the rear and a new, sleeker-looking trunklid. Taillights disappeared from atop the fenders and went in circular pairs, down to the rear body panel where they would stay, in shape and number, to the present time. Wraparound bumperettes flanked a chrome-trimmed license tag insert. Part of Mitchell's scheme for the upcoming production Sting Rays was thus produced, following the styling

1. Severe road test by Motor Trend magazine's 1958 staff resulted in front tire marks on rear brake cooling duct which lead back from front grille, up and over front wheels, and back through the rocker panels.

2. Air duct through rocker panel exited at front of rear wheelhouse to "blow" air at rear brake scoops.

3. Air flow was "caught" by scoops on rear backing plates. System seems overly complex and makes one wonder why the factory handled the option in this way. Simpler and probably more effective was the "backyard" addition of external scoops on quarter panels, as seen on the professionally prepared Sebring race cars.

4. The 283 V-8 was raised to a high of 290 hp with RPO 579D, the Rochester fuel injection with improved injector nozzles and a larger plenum chamber. A total of 1007 were sold for '58.

5. Fast-steering adaptor quickened ratio to 16.3:1 (left) from the standard 21:1 ratio (right).

6. Regular production rear suspension (left) was adequate for street driving, but sports buffs and race types went for the heavier-duty suspension (right) with 5-leaf springs, heavy shocks.

5

6

DEVELOPMENT CONTINUES

themes established by his personal Sting Ray race car.

Still stuck, however, with the basic front-end parameters, the syling people were hard-pressed to make many alterations here. But they did away with the toothy grin that Corvettes had worn since their inception and substituted in the grille opening a simple, expanded metal panel. It somewhat lessened the bulky look that had been introduced on the '58's, and cleaned up considerably the overall styling which, replete with its new tail end, was now once again lithe-looking.

The powerteams remained about as before; the base was the 230-hp 283 with single 4-bbl. and 9.5:1 compression. Up a notch was the 245-hp engine with dual 4-bbls., but again at 9.5:1 compression. These two utilized hydraulic lifters. In the 270-hp version, with dual 4-bbls., mechanical lifters were used but compression remained the same as the lesser engines. The least oomph you could get with fuel injection was 275 hp, with hydraulic lifters, but its more potent brother delivered 315 hp with mechanical lifters, both f.i.'s coming with 11:1 compression.

GEARBOXES

Transmissions from the past continued along for this year's ride—with one huge exception. Basic equipment was the 3-speed manual, with a close-ratio 4-speed as an option. Still on the option list was the Powerglide which the pussyfooters enjoyed, but coupled only with the lesser 230- and 245-hp engines.

While gearbox choices and their ratios remained from the previous year, enthusiasts were overjoyed to find that the 4-speed manual box was cast from aluminum to reduce weight by some 15 lbs. The aluminum radiator was standardized across the board, a further concession to pound-paring as well as to cooling. This use of aluminum, incidentally—radiator, transmission and bellhousing (in those models so-optioned)—knocked off a sizeable 43 lbs.

Long-legged drivers, cramped for space in the former cars, discovered that a much-needed inch of increased legroom was available by moving the seat tracks rearward

to an alternate set of bolt holes in the new underbody. And all drivers, whether leggy or not, appreciated the improved water- and draft-sealing between the headers of both types of tops and the windshield frame.

These moves meant much to performance-oriented buyers, for the tally at the model year's end showed that very nearly 11,000 Corvettes had been moved out of St. Louis. Of these, the buyers opted equally between the soft and the hardtop, just as the bean counters

had predicted and which had been holding true for several years.

1962

There were big things just ahead in the Corvette's future, and announcement of the '62's brought some of these to light. Sales of cars the past few years had always matched production quotas, meaning that if more Vettes were manufactured, sales could well be increased. As it was, though, the St. Louis facility was pushed to its

3

4

5

1. Effectiveness of Positraction is illustrated by two '58's accelerating with right wheels in dirt. Note that the Posi-equipped car below has the tail reflex buttons, the other one doesn't.

2. Bizarre-looking, perhaps, but it was Bill Mitchell's personal car that he designed just before taking over Styling. It was based on a '58 production Corvette, but presaged the coming Sting Ray ducktail. Termed the XP-700, it featured a tightly nipped-in front end and a transparent bubble top. Elimination of rocker panel allowed side-pipe installation.

3. Cockpit refinement was part of the game's name for 1959; redesigned bucket seats, more-forward door knobs, improved armrests, heavier assist-bar padding with a package shelf underneath.

4. Elimination of the phoney hood louvers helped clean up the '59's appearance. The ash can received the bold decklid chrome strips.

5. What's a Sting Ray? For all the trackside-watchers knew, it was a way-out, one-of-a-kind, Chevy-powered race car. Most frequent driver was Dr. Dick Thompson. The entrant of record during the car's '59 and '60 seasons was Bill Mitchell. Few knew there was GM involvement in the project, or that the car was the SS, rebodied.

6. Stark but neat cockpit layout shows GM builder's infinite attention to the smallest detail. This is how Mitchell's streetable ex-race car appears today.

limit and, short of plant enlargement which would have cost enormous amounts of money but which GM was not willing to invest at that time in the Corvette, the only way to manufacture more units was to add a second full shift. Morrison's Ashtabula body component factory had solved many of its earlier problems and though the Corvette was now comprised of more and larger individual fiberglass parts than the

6

early cars, parts-production could easily keep pace with the demands set by St. Louis. A night shift was scheduled in to work almost as soon as '62's began rolling from the line and, as a result, the production pace picked up by nearly

50% over the previous record year.

The Corvette as a Chevrolet marque had been in general service so long now, and was thankfully enjoying such a good history of body durability, that there was no longer any car-buyer's qualms over the "strange" material. Enough agency personnel had been properly schooled in Corvette maintenance and repair, including body patching, that almost any general Chevrolet dealership in the nation would tune or otherwise service the car as easily as they could a Corvair or Chevy II. (Almost; the author found himself suddenly sans a water pump in mid-Oklahoma in 1964 while driving a '63 cross-country. The small but multi-GM Division product dealership effected repairs, but the service personnel admitted they had never seen a Corvette in the flesh, much less worked on one!)

DEVELOPMENT CONTINUES

THE ENGINE PICTURE

Many a hot rodder had by now bored, stroked, milled, supercharged and otherwise reworked the Corvette's 283, or at least had substituted big-inch Cad, Olds, or even a Ford V-8 into it. These guys were finding out what Duntov had known all along, that the Corvette could stand all the super horsepower that could be crammed in without driveline failure. Transmissions, drivelines, axles—all the components that receive stresses under

1. The cockpit needed little seeing-to for '60, but Duntov ordered better lateral support built into the seats.

2. Styling stood pat for 1960, but performance and roadability got some upgrading, thanks primarily to Duntov. With the racing ban in effect, Zora could turn all his thoughts to bettering the production cars.

3. GM Photographic faithfully shot everything that Styling did toward the upcoming year's car, and just as faithfully the retouch artist would produce what the motoring press got, at least in part, at the annual long lead previews. This was '60's offering.

4. Long-needed, and much-appreciated when it bowed for '60, was the rear anti-roll or stabilizer bar. At the same time, the front stabilizer was increased in diameter and handling was instantly improved.

5. New for '60 was RPO 687, ceramic metallic brakes with a 24-blade cooling fan. This option also included the popular fast-steering adaptor.

6. Duntov knew that weight-saving was as good as horsepower-adding, and ordered aluminum used where possible. In the 315-hp f.i. version, this meant cylinder heads, but these were quickly discontinued when service problems arose. Bellhousing is also aluminum.

7. Official GM photograph of the aluminum Duntov heads introduced for '60 but just as quickly discontinued due to casting flaws undetected until cars so-equipped reached their buyers. Weight-saving was a hefty 50-plus lbs. Compression was 11:1. Chevrolet had worked to perfect a new aluminum alloy and while this early application saw failure, it presaged the much-later Vega aluminum 4-cyl.

full acceleration and braking could take everything that even the 315-hp f.i. could dish out, and more. But, big-engine powerplants in the hands of a cross-section of American drivers must contain a large dose of reliability. All those hot-rodded 283's, while fast and furious at the drag strips or out on road courses, were likely close to the ragged edge in terms of operational longevity. Boring meant thinner cylinder walls. Stroking brought with it increased piston travel and at greater revs. Higher horsepower equated higher operating temperatures, and so forth. To properly engineer a V-8 of greater internal displacement meant adding weight through larger and heavier castings. The bulk of this necessary poundage would fall smack dab on the front wheels to upset the almost-marginal fore-and-aft weight distribution of the car overall. Duntov knew his next-generation Corvette would solve such a problem for behind the scenes in GM's styling and engineering departments great things were under development. But whatever misgivings Duntov may have had about engine reliability through an increase in the 283's cylinder bore of 1/8-inch (to 4 ins.), and a piston stroke 1/4-inch longer (to 3-1/4 ins.) were overcome and the 327-cu. in. V-8 became the Corvette's engine across the board.

Such decisions were above Dun-

tov's station at GM. Ed Cole had been moved up the corporate stairwell from the Chevrolet Division and in his place now resided Semon "Bunkie" Knudsen. He'd been shifted over from the Pontiac Division where, largely through his inordinate interest in pure racing and high performance in general, he had succeeded in moving the ho-hum Pontiac up several notches on the sales charts. Fears for reliability be damned, the 327 was what Knudsen in particular and Corvette buyers in general wanted, and the 327 was what they got.

A full recount of Motor Trend Magazine's August issue road test of a '62 "fuelie" puts into proper perspective the effect this rousing model had on sports/racing writers at the time.

(As writt   by enthusiastic MT tech Ed., Jim Wright) "America's only true production sports car is still going strong after eight years on the market and shows no signs of letting up. True, every year one hears the rumor that the factory is going to drop the beast because they don't make a profit on them. But don't you believe it—the profit on this one is measured in prestige, and Chevrolet loves it. In fact, as long as Chevy continues to build it

4

5

6

strictly from the prestige angle, it'll probably remain a great car—built on a straight dollar-profit basis they'd probably ruin it.

"Exterior changes are minor this year: the grille is painted black, a wide piece of chrome trim covers the rocker panel, and the three horizontal bars in the cove have been replaced with a multi-bar grille configuration. The only real change for '62 is in the engine compartment.

"The old 283-incher has been bored ⅛-inch and stroked ¼-inch to give 327 cubic inches. This is the only engine size available for the Vette, but it comes in various stages of tune.

"The basic engine uses a single four-barrel, 10.5-to-1 compression ratio, and a mild cam with hydraulic lifters to put out 250 hp. The addition of a larger four-barrel (RPO 583) ups this figure to 300 hp. RPO 396 consists of the large four-barrel, a wilder cam with mechanical lifters and relieved dome pistons, giving a compression ratio of 11.25 to 1. This one is rated at 340 hp.

"The real bear of the line is known as RPO 582 and uses the RPO 396 goodies plus fuel injection to pump out 360 horses at 6000 rpm! This represents 1.1 hp per cubic inch, which is not bad at all— Ferrari 250 GT's put out only two-tenths more horsepower per cubic inch, and they cost almost four times as much.

"A wide variety of power trains is available, and with a little thought, a prospective owner can order just

about any combination to meet any condition imaginable.

"The three-speed manual transmission is the standard offering with any engine option. The Warner four-speed box is available with either the 2.54 or close-ratio 2.20 low gear, but the factory recommends the 2.54 version with the 250- and 300-hp models. Powerglide can also be had with both of these models.

"The standard rear axle for Powerglide and three-speed models is 3.36. The four-speed with 2.54 low also uses the 3.36 ratio, but the 3.08 axle is optional. Close-ratio boxes take a 3.70 axle. Positraction axle ratios are the same for all models, with the exception of the 340- and 360-hp close-ratio combos. With these two, the choice is expanded to include ratios of 3.08, 3.55, 3.70, 4.11 and 4.56.

"The Motor Trend test car was equipped with the 360-hp engine, close-ratio transmission and 3.70 Positraction rear axle. This car also happened to be the work horse of the local Chevrolet zone office and had over 5000 miles logged on it by everybody from their janitor to such visiting firemen as Astronaut Allan B. Shepard, who had it just before MT. We didn't get a chance to ask him how the car compared to his space capsule, but we'll bet the Vette had a better e.t. for the first quarter-mile.

"The car felt and sounded healthy when we picked it up, so we didn't do anything to it in the way of tuning. While our times

7

DEVELOPMENT CONTINUES

aren't the best you've seen, they are at least the most honest. With the usual load—full gas tank, instrumentation and two up—we racked up 0-to-30, 0-to-45 and 0-to-60 mph in 2.4, 3.9 and 5.9 seconds. Through the quarter-mile trap our fifth-wheel-connected electric speedo recorded a top time of 102.5 mph with a 14.9 e.t.

"This goes to show that the stock 6.70 x 15 boots aren't the answer for traction. No amount of experimenting off the line could keep the tires from smoking, clear to second gear. Several 'top-end runs produced an honest 132 mph long before the end of the Riverside straight.

"The stock brakes worked well, but after the high-speed runs they needed a ten-minute break because they were all through. After the binders had their rest we were able to run the regular braking tests, and these were carried off with no apparent fade, grab or swerve. Stopping distances from 30 and 60 mph were 34 and 167 feet.

"If you can stand a little squealing and don't mind the heavier pedal pressures, RPO 686 gives more stopping power with sintered iron brake linings. For all-out competition, choose RPO 687. This option includes sintered iron linings with special cooling provisions at each wheel, also heavy-duty shocks and fast steering adaptor.

"We had the car long enough to put over 1000 miles on the odometer, and one trip to the high desert exposed the car to temperatures that ranged from a low of 35° to a high of 93°, and the Rochester fuel injection unit worked perfectly. It was very responsive at any rpm in any gear. Even when idling along at 1500 rpm in fourth cog, the throttle can be floored and the car will take off strongly without missing a beat. In fact, around town we seldom used any gears except first and fourth. The characteristic "lope" of a hot engine isn't felt until the mill is lugged down below 1000 rpm in either first or second. We never had to use any gear but fourth to pass anything on the highway above 50 mph. This is like second, or passing gear, in most other cars.

FUEL MILEAGE

"Fuel consumption wasn't too bad. Overall average, for 1000 miles of all types of driving, was 13.8 mpg. This included a low 9.8-mpg figure recorded during acceleration tests and a high 16.4 mpg for open road (65-90 mph) cruising.

"The stock suspension feels just about right—a trifle on the hard side, but we, personally, wouldn't want it any softer. We had it up on our favorite mountain road and found we had no trouble negotiating the curves 20 to 25 mph faster than we've been taking them in sedans. The 'Vette is rock-steady and dead-flat in the corners.

"Understeer is slight, with the front end pushing only on the tightest corners. At high speeds through sweeping turns the feeling is definitely towards understeer. If the rear end starts to come around, one has to apply corrective steering wheel lock and throttle lightly because the Positraction axle has a tendency to grab a bite and send the car in whichever way the wheels happen to be pointing.

"At high speeds (100 to 130 mph) the ride is completely smooth, and the Corvette displays a directional stability and solid road feel that can be matched only by a few high-priced Grand Tourers from Europe.

"The interior is unchanged from last year. The vinyl-covered bucket seats are contoured in the right places and give excellent support to the back and upper legs. There is enough fore-and-aft adjustment to satisfy just about any size driver.

"The steering wheel is a beautiful thing, with its three drilled, engine-turned spokes, but its location leaves much to be desired. It is mounted in a vertical position and most drivers will find it too close. It also leaves very little room between the driver's lap and the bottom of the rim. This and the miserably mounted throttle pedal (it kept falling off) are the only real beefs we have with this otherwise completely satisfying car. All-around visibility is good with the

soft top in place, and better with the hardtop.

"The trunk offers a surprising amount of usable space and should be big enough for two people for a weekend. The engine compartment is crowded and it is pure hell to change the plugs, but carburetion and ignition components are in the open.

"This is an exciting high-performance automobile with real hair on its chest—the type of car that only the true enthusiasts will appreciate."

Duntov's early-on fears about reliability of the poked and stroked 283 block, to 327 cu. ins., did nothing whatsoever to deter Corvette buyers from swamping agencies with orders. When all was said and done, and with thanks to the second shift at St. Louis, no less than 14,531 new Corvettes were parked in garages all over America.

The body introduced in '58 had worn well during its five seasons, despite its somewhat gargantuan styling for the introductory year. In fact, even in this era of over-embellishment in terms of gimcrackery and superfluousness, the stylists had managed to keep cool heads about the Corvette and even cleaned up things as the five years had progressed. But now the body had run its course, as had the underpinnings which were basically unchanged from the 102-in. wheelbase platform for the '53 but with some tweaking here and there by Zora. Facility engineers and workmen poured into the St. Louis plant to set the stage for the biggest changeover in Corvette's history.

The Sting Ray was ordered launched!